D0227195

SUNK ON THE SUNRISE COAST

400 SOLE BAY SHIPWRECKS

PETER HANCOCK

The
History
Press

Peter Hancock has also written:

Sailing Out of Silence: 30,000 miles in a Small Boat
 (Airlife Publishing, 1995)

*Sailing Into Sunshine: 5,000 miles Through the Caribbean and the Gulf of
 Mexico* (Airlife Publishing, 1997)

Sailing Home: Honduras Towards England in a Small Boat
 (Thomas Reed Publications, 2001)

and is associate editor of Nigel Calder's *Cruising Guide to the Northwest
 Caribbean* (1991)

Front cover image: The Dutch fireship *Vrede* attacking HMS *Royal James*
during the Battle of Sole Bay, 1672, pictured by William van der Velde
the Younger. (Netherlands Maritime Museum, Amsterdam)

Back cover image: Beached and possibly benighted (Ernie Childs)

First published 2008

Reprinted 2009

The History Press Ltd
The Mill, Brimscombe Port
Stroud, Gloucestershire, GL5 2QG
www.thehistorypress.co.uk

© Peter Hancock, 2008

The right of Peter Hancock to be identified as the Author
of this work has been asserted in accordance with the
Copyrights, Designs and Patents Act 1988.

All rights reserved. No part of this book may be reprinted
or reproduced or utilised in any form or by any electronic,
mechanical or other means, now known or hereafter invented,
including photocopying and recording, or in any information
storage or retrieval system, without the permission in writing
from the Publishers.

British Library Cataloguing in Publication Data.
A catalogue record for this book is available from the British Library.

ISBN 978 0 7524 4747 6

Typesetting and origination by
The History Press Ltd.
Printed in Malta

Sunk on the Sunrise Coast

400 Sole Bay Shipwrecks

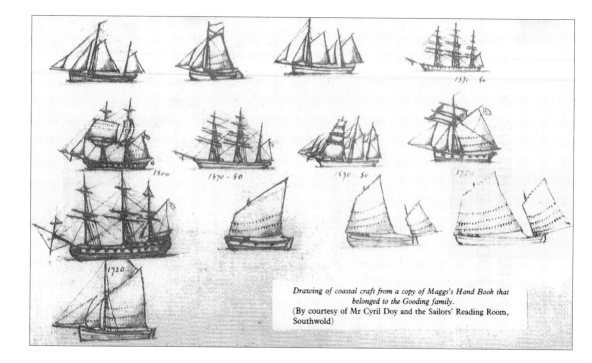

Drawing of coastal craft from a copy of Maggs's Hand Book that belonged to the Gooding family.
(By courtesy of Mr Cyril Doy and the Sailors' Reading Room, Southwold)

CONTENTS

Dedication   6
Acknowledgements   7
List of Illustrations   9
Notice to the Incoming Mariner   12

1   The Watcher on the Cliff   26
2   The Shore and the Shoals   41
3   Pilotage and the *Fairy*   60
4   Ships and Cargoes   70
5   The Lifeboats   90
6   Why the Wrecks?   115
7   'The People' and their Captains   132
8   Chronology of Sole Bay Shipwrecks   149

Appendix 1 The Storm that Sank the *Fairy*   176
Appendix 2 Beaufort's Wonderful Wind Scale   177
Appendix 3 The *Alfred Corry*   180
Appendix 4 Prim Deal: *Lyking the Sea Lyfe withal* ...   182

Bibliography   186
Index of Vessels   188

For reasons that will become obvious to whoever reads it, this book is dedicated to the men and women of the Southwold lifeboat.

John Huggins	Lifeboat Operations Manager
Jonathan Adnams	Deputy Launching Authority
Peter Shore	Deputy Launching Authority
Colin Fraser	Launch Crew
Dr John Stammers	Lifeboat Medical Advisor
Marcus Gladwell	Senior Helm
Alan Scoggins	Helm
Cath Fox	Helm
Simon Callaghan	Helm
Dirk Bougard	Helm
Charlie Townsley	Crew
Vicky Gladwell	Crew
Steven Lee	Crew
Julian Heal	Crew Mechanic
Sam Doy	Crew
Harry Cooper	Crew
Simon Clack	Crew
Jochem Voogt	Crew
Pete Norval	Crew
Marcos Allen	Crew

ACKNOWLEDGEMENTS

I'd like to think that this book is all my own work but of course it never has been. Many others have contributed, often unknowingly, to its making. Foremost are the diarist James Maggs and his editor, Alan Bottomley, whose commentary inspired the genesis of the book and forms its backbone.

A wider but no less deep obligation is to the many other writers whose diligent researches have illuminated the Sunrise Coast with a clarity that was beyond me.

Thanks, in particular, to John Blatchly at the Suffolk Records Society for allowing me to quote from Maggs's diaries; to Richard and Bridget Larn, whose compendious *Shipwreck Index* supplied many facts and figures; to meteorologist Alan Watts for his analysis of a notorious storm; to Ernest Cooper for his history of Southwold's nineteenth-century lifeboats; to Sir Richard Dales for material on the *Idun*; and to Nicolette Jones for her revealing biography of Samuel Plimsoll. Rowland Parker's *Men of Dunwich* gave me essential information about Southwold's nearby rival, and Rachel Lawrence's *Southwold River* fleshed out my skeletal knowledge of the Blyth Navigation. From the published work of Peter Earle, Eric Newby, Lord Walter Runciman, Sir James Bisset and my early mentor, Ronald Hope, I drew substantial evidence of the hostile conditions endured by seamen in the days of sail. For each and every word, I thank them very much.

Thanks, too, to the staff of the Suffolk Record Office in Lowestoft, the National Archives at Kew, Lloyd's Register of Shipping, the Archives of the University of Glasgow and the National Maritime Museum in Greenwich, where Brian Thynne, Gillian Hutchinson and Gudrun Muller piloted me through unknown waters. Closer to home, Charlotte Clark and Jenny Twomey at the Southwold Library, David Lee and Cynthia Wade at the Southwold Museum, John Winter and Douglas Pope at the Southwold Sailors' Reading Room, James Steward at Great Yarmouth Museums, Stuart Bacon at Suffolk Underwater Studies in Orford, John Saunders and Morgan Caines at the Dunwich Museum and David A. Male of the Harwich Society have all answered my persistent requests with enviable promptness and calm.

As always during the past twelve years, Joan Goldsmith has cheerfully laid aside her mountainous workload to marshal the manuscript into logical order and readable form.

By no means least, I thank William Stannard, Marcus Gladwell and Jonathan Adnams for allowing me to tape record their experiences of working the waters of Sole Bay and combating its tides and winds. Their words have been set down faithfully and, I hope, accurately, just as they were spoken. However, it is impossible to claim similar authenticity when rendering the discourse of the dead, and so I hereby acknowledge that the Georgian and Victorian conversations in these pages are products of the imagination, though I believe they carry within them more than a grain or two of truth.

The illustrations could not have been assembled without the generosity of the artists, photographers and copyright holders named in the captions. I am particularly indebted to Alan Hale and Richard Wells for their photographic expertise; to Ernie Childs, John Robbins, Wendy Coleman and Rupert Cooper for allowing me to reproduce their paintings; to Dennis Ball for the many pictures from the *Alfred Corry* Museum; to Robert Malster for images from his priceless archive; to Jamie Thompson for photos collected by his father, Arthur 'Pimple' Thompson; and to Keith and Joy Deal for sharing their mementos of Prim. Bart Lahr at the Netherlands Maritime Museum in Amsterdam has been especially helpful in obtaining the fiery image that appears on the cover.

Head-wags from Karen, Sarah, Esther and Lucy Hancock have despatched a number of wayward paragraphs to the dustbin, and Rory MacFarlane has practised corrective wizardry on my computer. I can therefore assert with confidence that the remaining errors are entirely my own. While every effort has been made to contact copyright owners, not all have been successful. I apologise to anyone who has been overlooked or otherwise offended, and ask that they contact me via the publisher.

LIST OF ILLUSTRATIONS

CHARTS & MAPS   *Page no.*

C1 South-east England, East Anglia
& the Sunrise Coast   13
C2 Sole Bay, AD 850   14
C3 Sole Bay, 1575   15
C4 Dunwich to Lowestoft, 1693,
   puts Red Sand five miles east of
   Kessingland   16
C5 Orford Ness to Southwold,
1693   16
C6 Cromer to North Foreland,
1693, showing Red Sand to seaward
of Pakefield   17
C7 Suffolk coast, 1752–85, placing
Red Sand near Easton   18
C8 Sole Bay (North section), 1824   19
C9 Sole Bay (South section), 1824   19
C10 Sunrise Coast, 1842   20
C11 Wreck chart of Southwold
   foreshore, 3 November 1855   21
C12 Wreck chart of the British Isles,
   1868   22
C13 Wreck chart of the Sunrise
Coast, 1868   23
C14 Covehithe Channel, 1910   24
C15 Southwold harbour chart, 1923   25

MONOCHROME PICTURES

Kilcock Cliff, Southwold, and the
   southern shore of Sole Bay   13

Chapter 1

James Maggs in old age   28
Steam packet on the Orwell, 1829   29
The Lord Nelson Inn, Southwold   30
A pilot and his six-oared gig   30
The Ship Inn, Dunwich   32
Southwold beach yawl in the 1890s   32
Lugger *Three Sisters*   32

Baden Powell of Southwold   34
Georgiana of Lowestoft   34
Shemo Palmer   35
Fitz Hurr   35
Airing sails on Southwold beach   35
Workshop of boatbuilder James
Critten   36
Beachmen at cribbage   37
Tarring the haul-off warp   37
A hard-earned catch of sprats   38
Gutting herring outside Southwold
fish market   38
Paddle steamer *Eiderstedt*, wrecked
at Covehithe, 1872   39
A nameless wooden wreck, Sole
Bay beach   40

Chapter 2

Southwold harbour before the 1908
   improvements   42
Walberswick punt and the Kissing
   Bridge   42
Blackshore, Southwold, after the
storm surge of 1 February 1953   43
Entering harbour against the ebb,
   1822   43
River Blyth entrance, 1890, with
   extensive shoaling   45
Punt leaving harbour at Low Water   45
Dredging Southwold harbour, 1907   46
Pile-driving at the harbour entrance
Amelia, the first vessel to lie at the
new harbour wall, 1907   46
Collier ketch opposite Dunwich
   creek   47
Southwold railway   50
The branch line to the harbour   50
Halesworth basin, the head of the
Blyth navigation   50

The Victorian Southwold pier and
  bathing machines   51
Paddle steamer of the Belle Line,
1910   54
Zulu skirting the North Hale   55
Cliff damage at Southwold, 1905   56

Chapter 3
The Black Mill, Southwold   62
All Saints church, Dunwich   62
East Barnard buoy   65
Compass rose, 1910   65

Chapter 4
Medieval depiction of Dunwich
cog, showing its side rudder   73
Modern replicas - cog and Viking
  longboat   75
Thirteenth-century galley   74
Fifteenth-century fishing boat   74
Tudor cargo vessel   74
Seventeenth-century herring buss   74
Dutch *fluyt*, seventeenth century   75
Revenue cutter, 1750   75
Brig *Berbice* of Southwold, built
1816   77
Barge *Marjorie* on the Thames   78
Barge *Harwich* navigating the harbour
  bar   78
Paddle tug *Pendennis*   78
Sole Bay beach punt of the 1890s   78
Bowler-hatted skipper and his
spratter   82
Schooner at Walberswick quay   82
Zulus invade Blackshore   82
Billyboy anchored on the Blyth, about
1900   84
SS *Abercraig* entering harbour, 1908   84
Torpedo boat *119* at Southwold,
1909   84
HMS *Solebay*, 1946   86
Belgian refugees enter Southwold,
1914   86
Martin Luther on the riverbank, 1965   86
MV *Ordinence*, a coaster of the 1950s   86
Sailing drifter warping alongside, aided
  by a steam capstan   88

Southwold quayside about 1910, and
  200 barrels   88
Sole Bay Inn   89

Chapter 5
Dunwich lifeboat *Lily Bird*   91
Harbourmaster Upcraft crossing the
  bar   92
Schooner *Voorwaartz*, stranded at
  Minsmere sluice   93
Voorwaartz crew   94
Wreck of the brigantine *Isabellas* at
  Covehithe, Christmas 1884   94
Trinity pilot Griffiths   95
Pilot Magub   95
Bittern, the second beach yawl of that
  name   97
Harriett II capsizes, drowning three
  passengers   97
Breakers on the inshore shoal,
  Southwold   97
Surf lifeboat *Rescue* and Coxswain
  Sam May   98
Harriett II goes to aid the *Princess
  Alice*   98
Lifeboat launch using setts   99
Launch using haul-off warp   99
Alfred Corry launches to aid the
Nina   100
Crew of the *Corry* on exercise   100
Deck layout of *Alfred Corry*   100
Corry beating across the inshore
  shoal   101
Corry surfing towards the beach   102
Crew of *Joseph et Yvonne* prepare to
  use a breeches buoy   104
Coastguard life-saving equipment   105
Dunwich lifeboat *John Keble*, 1873   106
James Leath setting out from Pakefield
  beach   107
Lifeboat *Bolton*   108
Motor-sailing lifeboat *Mary Scott*   109
Mary Scott towing *Damaris*, 1932   110
A yacht is assisted by the lifeboat   110
ILB *Solebay*, 1982   110
ILB *Quiver* and its crews, 1998   112
Quiver at speed   112

ILB *Leslie Tranmer* 113
Spirit of Lowestoft 113

Chapter 6
SS *Hawk*, wrecked 1862 116
Barque *Nordhavet*, wrecked off
Gun Hill, 1887 117
Idun, stranded below Kilcock Cliff,
1912 118
Idun, seen from Long Island Cliff 118
Crew of *Idun* 118
Stranded in a fog 119
Chelmsford at Astoria, Oregon,
1894 120
SS *Magdapur*, sunk off Thorpe Ness,
1939 120
Last moments of the *Magdapur* 122
Barge stranded on Southwold bar 123
Kilcock Cliff lookout in the early
1900s 126
Wildflower, 1952 126
Salvaging *Wildflower*'s figurehead 128
Beachmen beneath the outligger of a
yawl 129
Three boats in rough water on the
bar 130
Delphis pilots a Dutchman to safety 130

Chapter 7
Steamer in a sinking state alongside
harbour wall 133
Zulu at the harbour wall 133
Harvest Gleaner, sunk 1940 136
Sailing drifter shooting its nets 137
Hauling nets 140
Mending the nets 140
Torn sails and broken cross-trees on
the storm-damaged *Decima* 142
Princess Augusta, driven ashore at
Southwold, 1838 144
'… a ruminating beast, an insatiable,
indefatigable lip.' 145

Appendix 3
Plan of *Alfred Corry* 180
John Cragie 181

Sam May 181
Charles Jarvis 181

Appendix 4
Clipper *Mount Stewart* 182
Crew of the *Chelmsford*, 1894 183
Able Seaman Deal, aged
twenty-one 183
Seaman's discharge certificate, 1895 184
George VI landing at Southwold,
1938 184
Two ancient mariners in festive
attire 185
Prim Deal in his eighties 185

COLOUR PLATES

1 The Harbour Inn
2 The House in the Clouds
3 The lookout at Long Island Cliff
4 Viking coastal trader
5 Barge *Marjorie*
6 Lifeboat *Lily Bird*
7 Beached, and laying anchors
8 *Wildflower* figurehead
9 Southwold Sailors' Reading Room
10 Barge *Martin Luther*
11 California Sands
12 Southwold from the North pier
13 Landing the night's herring
14 *Richard L. Wood*
15 Armless figurehead
16 Kilcock Cliff
17 Southwold lighthouse lantern
18 Wreck of the *James & Eleanor*
19 Smack *Excelsior*
20 *Martina Maria*
21 Figurehead from *William IV*
22 *Corry* leaving harbour, 1911
23 Launching the surf lifeboat
24 High Water Springs at Southwold
seafront
25 The Hale
26 Figurehead and two chastened
longshoremen
27 *Nordhavet* trailboard

Notice to the Incoming Mariner

According to one insurer, the North Sea is more dangerous than most, and he may be right. On two calamitous days in the eighteenth century, no fewer than 250 vessels were sunk or cast ashore on the fifty-three-mile stretch between Cromer and Thorpe Nesss – five wrecks in every mile – with the Sunrise Coast in the thick of them.

The coast I write about is a fifteen-mile strip of Suffolk extending southward from Lowestoft to a low headland seven miles past the smaller town of Southwold, where its sometimes shifty beaches are flanked on their western side by whispering reedbeds, wind-blown dunes and crumbling cliffs. Though it is well liked by visiting birdwatchers and artists, a stranger coming on to the coast from the sea when the wind is blowing strongly from behind him is likely to feel twinges of unease, especially if his insurance is only Third Party, as he is borne towards the off-lying shoals.

Sole Bay is the southern length of the Sunrise Coast, with a territorial boundary which matches the port of Southwold – in former times called Sowowlde, Swole or Sole – as set out in an Exchequer document of 1738, where the port is '… declared to extend from Cove Hithe … along the shore to the promontory or point commonly called or known by the name Thorp[e] Ness …'

The seaward boundary of the bay is the horizon visible to me – and, I hope, the interested reader – when we are looking out from Kilcock Cliff in Southwold, where our height of eye above Mean Sea Level will be 12.5m and the horizon will be seven and a half nautical miles (14km) distant. Here, on a clear day – of which there will be many – our northern horizon will lie three miles north of Benacre Ness (the lowly successor to the vanished Covehithe Ness), and we will be gazing over the shallows covering the whole of the Barnard and much of the Newcome sands. Our view to the south will take in the Dunwich and Sizewell banks and terminate at Thorpe Ness.

'Wrecks', insists the Admiralty, with masterly cunning, must include grounded or sunken vessels that have later been salvaged and given new lives. Happier though their histories may be, few such vessels will be listed in the shipwreck chronology, where they will only find a place if they have a unique historical interest characterised in 1829 by the packet boat *Suffolk*, which became the first steamship to enter Southwold and may later have continued its voyage, though my informant does not record that it ever put to sea again. With these few exceptions, 'wrecks' in these pages mean vessels that sank in Sole Bay or were abandoned or broken up on its shore.

Above: Southwold and the southern length of Sole Bay, with Kilcock Cliff in the foreground and Sizewell power station on the horizon. The piers at the entrance to the River Blyth are just to the right of the power station, half-smothered by surf. (*Alfred Corry* Museum)

Right: C1 South-east England and East Anglia. The Sunrise Coast extends from Lowestoft to Thorpe Ness.

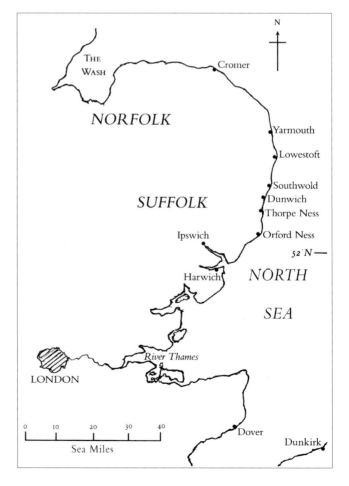

They range in size from a 5m dugout from the reign of Ethelwulf to the 8,000-ton cargo liner *Magdapur*, launched in 1921 and sunk by an underwater explosion in the Second World War with the loss of six lives. The listings are just a fraction of the vessels lost in Sole Bay since men hewed boats out of tree trunks or cobbled them from skins. There is little here from the age of the Saxons and Vikings, no tally to mark the rise and fall of medieval Dunwich, nothing much on record until the mid-eighteenth century. Even so, this incomplete chronology has enough in it to fill a furlong of novels. All the ingredients are here: bloodstains on moonlit beaches, damsels in distress, global swindles, daring rescues, and calamities brought about by strong wind, strong drink and uncharted currents in the human mind.

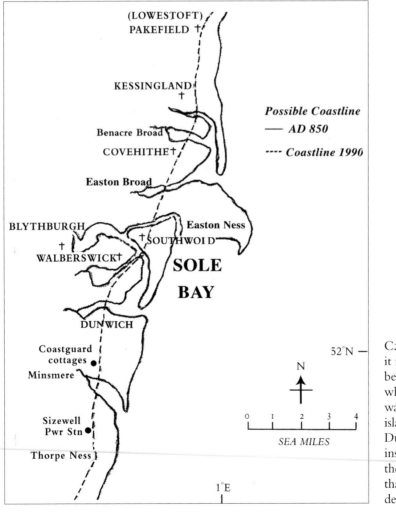

C2 Sole Bay as it might have been in AD 850, when Southwold was possibly an island and Saxon Dunwich was insulated from the storm surges that eventually destroyed it.

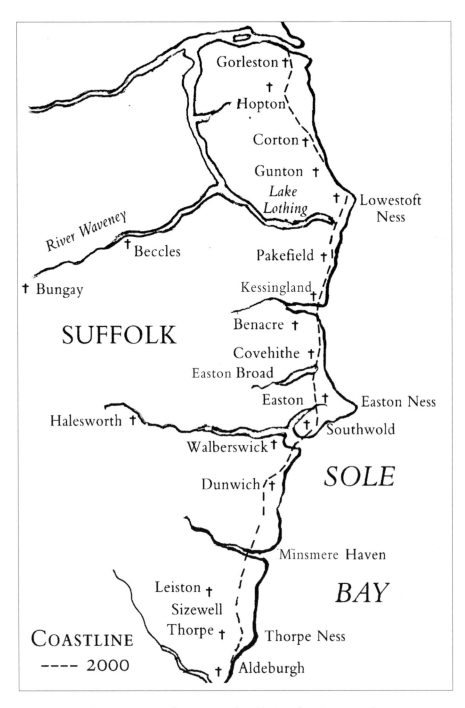

C3 Sole Bay in 1575, from a map by Christopher Saxton, when Easton Ness was the most easterly headland of the British Isles. Together with the churches at Easton and Dunwich, the ness was later pared away by the sea, so that Sole Bay then extended northwards to Covehithe and Benacre.

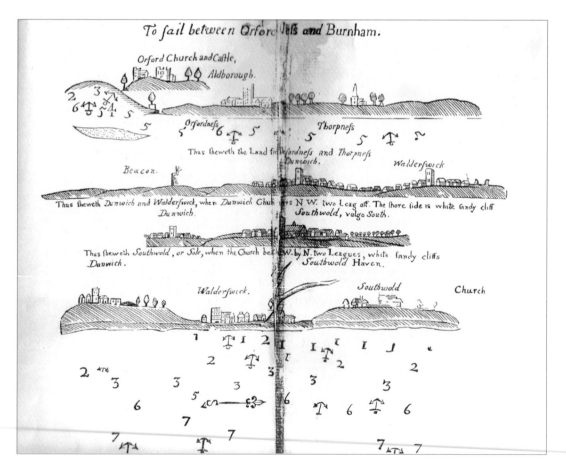

C4 Dunwich to Lowestoft, 1693, positions the Red Sand five miles due east of Kessingland church (but see C6 and C7).

C5 Orford Ness to Southwold, 1693.

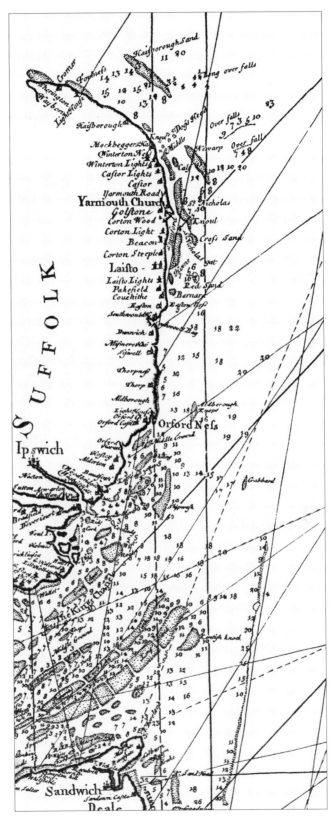

C6 Cromer to North Foreland, 1693, drawn by Captain Collins, places the Red Sand to seaward of Pakefield (but see C7).

THE SUFFOLK COAST
(From the 1785 edition of the English Pilot of 1752).

C7 This chart of the Suffolk coast in 1752 puts the Red Sand near Easton.
(Ernest R. Cooper)

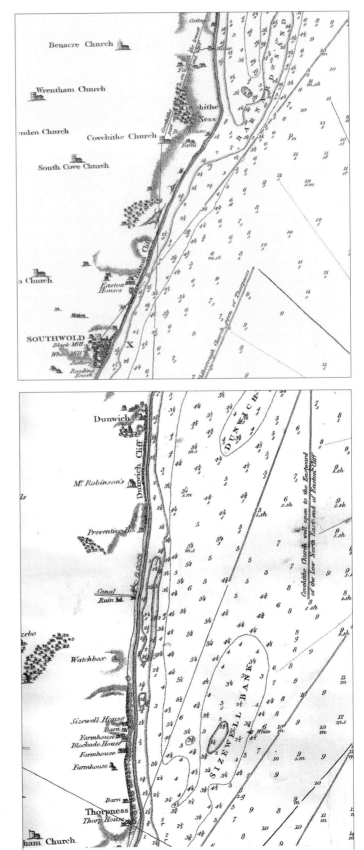

C8 Sole Bay, 1824 (north section), as surveyed by Master George Thomas RN and Midshipmen Lord and Cudlip. The Barnard Sand had not yet been buoyed. (UK Hydrographic Office)

C9 Sole Bay, 1824 (south section). The lines of bearing of conspicuous landmarks were essential aids for avoiding the Sizewell and Dunwich banks. (UK Hydrographic Office)

C10 The Sunrise Coast in 1842, as charted by Captain William Hewett RN and the officers and men of HMS *Fairy*. (National Maritime Museum)

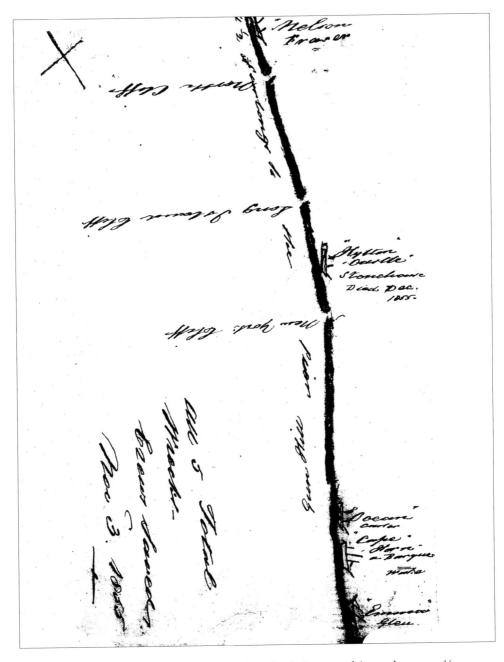

C11 Southwold beach, 3 November 1855, when five brigs were driven ashore on 4½ furlongs (905m) of Southwold seafront. 'Crews saved,' wrote Maggs after mapping their wrecks. (Southwold Museum)

Note: The text on the image reads as follows:
At North cliff: *Nelson*, Captain Fraser
Between Long Island & New York cliffs: *Hylton Castle*, Captain Stonehouse (died Dec. 1855)
Between New York cliff & North harbour pier: *Ocean*, Captain Curtis(?); *Cape Horn*, Captain Wake; *Emma*, Captain Glen.

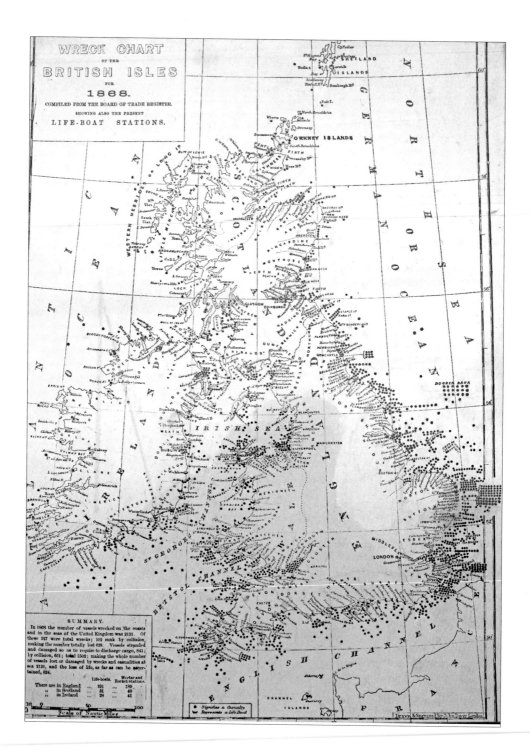

C13 Shipping casualties on the Sunrise Coast in 1868 were so numerous that they have burst the frame of the chart. During the nineteenth century, Sole Bay accumulated eleven wrecks for every mile of its length. (Colin Fraser/Alan Hale)

Opposite: C12 Wreck chart of the British Isles, 1868. (Colin Fraser/ Alan Hale)

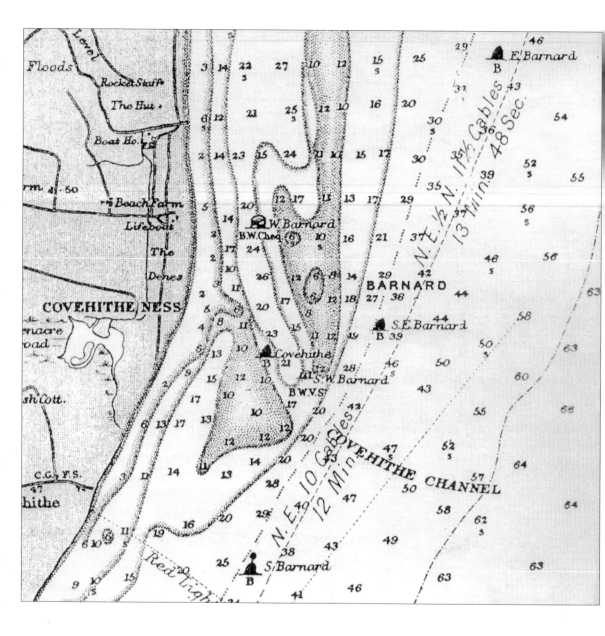

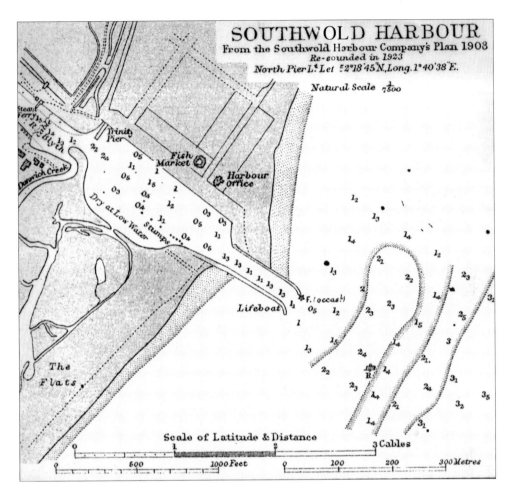

C15 Southwold harbour, 1923. Unlike during many other years in its history, here the harbour approach has a minimum depth of 1 fathom (1.8m), with similar soundings at the new harbour wall. The hooked piers were straightened when the wooden structures were re-built in concrete in the late 1930s. A haul-off hawser was attached to the red buoy moored 200m off the piers. (UK Hydrographic Office)

Opposite: C14 Covehithe Channel and its approaches, 1910, by Captain Close. (Soundings are in feet)

The Watcher on the Cliff

I imagine that he left his wife spooning cough linctus into their youngest and stumped into the Swan with half a yard of camphorated flannelette flapping from his greatcoat pocket, complaining to Ellis that his head felt it was filled with liquid cement. Harbourmaster Ellis would have buttonholed him about the need to hire a mechanical dredge. The Blackshore gang had dug out 10 yards between yesterday's tides, but by morning the channel had been overtopped with so much sand that carts were being hauled across the bar without even wetting the horses' pasterns.

'We're caught between wind and water,' growled Ellis, 'with too bally much of the first and too demn'd little of the other.' Ellis was a bustling naval officer with connections to London Society but was presently mired in a dispute with the Clerk to the Commissioners about grazing rights. It was discreet, lowly born Maggs who had the Clerk's ear.

'Only two bottoms across the bar the whole week,' fretted Ellis. 'They'd anchored under Orford and beat up during a lull. They scraped in because they was drawing shallow.'

'I doubt that elsewhere's doing any bedder,' croaked Maggs, exhaling consolation through his flannelette. 'Lowesdofd's booked no more than five arrivals – and two of dose pud in through stress of weather.'

'Tell Gooding I could keep the channel open if I had that dredge from Leiston and twenty navvies.'

''Tis my belief I shan't be saying overmuch to anyone till I've bidden farewell to this liddle burden in me lungs … Led us sid near the fire an' look into the brighter side of dings … Where did I pud the *Journal*?'

'Dings', in the *Ipswich Journal* of Saturday 25 March 1843, had few bright sides. True, Mrs Clark was begging to inform the ladies of Yoxford that she had an entrancing array of spring bonnets in stock, and Sir J.F. Herschel had discovered an enormous comet, but the prospect of enjoying these novelties was dimmed by the disturbing news that the kingdom of Greece had declared itself stony broke. Even J.S. Henslow, ardently requesting his readers to send samples of gypsum to Hitcham, allowed that Suffolk's '… unmacadamized roads and tardigrade carriers' horses …' would seriously delay their arrival, in which case the carriers might have been tempted to couple their mares with a stallion stabled at Shadingfield, where thoroughbreds could be served at five guineas a go and half-breeds at two, with an additional 2s 6d payable to the person who assisted the coupling. It was unlikely that the stallion's activities would have been overseen by the headmaster of Ipswich Free Grammar School, who, on an annual salary of £115 6s 8d was instructing his charges on the historic inertia of the wooden horse of Troy. Nor would viewing equine copulation have been in the curriculum followed by young ladies in Stowmarket, where a Mr Curtis was imparting a thoroughly Christian education with unremitting attention to mental culture.

Mrs Clark's metropolitan customers could have reduced their road mileage by travelling most of the way to Yoxford by sea. Captain Rackham in the *Orwell* packet left Nicholson's wharf at Lower Thames Street every Monday and Thursday and steamed ninety-four nautical miles to Ipswich, where passengers could board an Old Blue stagecoach that would deliver them safely to Yoxford, but only if the coachman was a better driver than the one who'd departed this life on the high road to London when he'd overturned another Old Blue and injured thirteen people, ten of whom had been flung off the roof.

They were not the only human beings to have suffered pain in Suffolk in March 1843. A brush-maker had been murdered at Ipswich. William Britton, Thomas Strowger and Freeman Smith had been sent to jail by Sir Charles Blois for trespassing on his Cockfield Hall estate and would be kept to hard labour for two calendar months. John Hewes, twenty-two, had been sentenced to seven years' transportation for the theft of three pairs of shoes, and for stealing eleven biscuits, James Carruthers, aged twelve years, had been tethered to a post and whipped.

Biscuits would not have been easy to come by for the lower classes. Wheat was selling at 56s a quarter at a time when the wage of a farm labourer was 7s a week, which may explain why John Edward Freak, twenty-eight, dubbed 'ANOTHER SCOTCH MANIAC', had tried to break into Buckingham Palace, where Queen Victoria, twenty-three, might fill his sporran with Highland shortcake, a bounty unlikely to be shared with the inmates of the Wangford Union workhouse in Suffolk, where the main meal of the day comprised a platter of mangolds, buttressed by fourteen Imperial ounces (400g) of boiled dough.

Suspecting he'd caught Maggs's cold, the clerk to the Southwold Harbour Commisioners blew grimly into a handkerchief, wrote 'Meeting of 1st April 1843', and read out:

'Arrivals and Departures.
1st–17th March: In: 9. Out: 14. Pilotage Precepts: 23.
18th–31st March: In: 2. Out: *Nil.* Pilotage Precepts: 1.
Channel blocked since 26th *ult.* Request disbursement of £4 10s 0d to hire further labour to clear it. F. W. Ellis.'

Opposite: With Blue Peter flying at the foremast head, a paddle-steam packet of the Ipswich Steam Navigation Co. is about to depart the Orwell for London. Passengers are embarking via the companion ladder while their baggage is swung aboard from a derrick on the foremast. The black-and-white chequered sheerstrake suggests the vessel is armed with cannon as a defence against privateers. The powerful barquentine rig will supplement the steam power to ensure James Maggs makes the fastest possible passage. (E. W. White, 1829)

Left: James Maggs in old age, with his dog Leo.

'Pray allow him the money, Mr Gooding' said the Commissioners, 'though, heh-heh! puff-puff! our noble firebrand can't expect to clear the channel till the wind hauls.'

Forty hours later the north wind at last fell away by 20 knots and the town's ancient weather vanes swung by slow degrees to the south-west. Ellis despatched his knockers-up at three in the morning, with the message that waggoners were to report to his office at four-thirty and lumpers to their foremen at five. Boys from the beach village below the cliffs pattered through alleyways, tapping on doors and windows. They were overtaken by silent figures with lanterns who bobbed down the cliff paths to haul their pilot yawls nearer the breaking seas.

In a slate-grey dawn a listless youth in the Kilcock watch house focused the company's spyglass, monitored by a crusty shareholder with a burbling pipe. 'Doan't yew be lookin' so much eastuds,' growled the elder. 'They'll be comin' up two fists ter seaward o' the ness. Jus' yew rub the curd from yer eyes and point th' glass nearer th' eye o' the wind.'

Maggs popped another of Hamond's Miraculous Cold Cure Pills between his chapped lips, pulled a nightcap over his ears and mused on the revenues the changed wind would bring to the town. His journal of the twelve months to April 1843 had made dismal reading. Far too many ledgers had been seeing too much red ink. No one had yet put an end to their miseries by lifting a razor to their throats but he feared that some might be on the brink. Sarah Bardwell and Butcher Reeve had been forced to sell up their shops, Palmer, Botham, Cleaveland and Everrett had been distressed for their rents and poor Neech taken forty

miles to Ipswich and imprisoned for debt. What with Patrick Stead getting fewer shillings a quarter for his malt and Alfred Crisp going to America, it was plain that even the better-off merchant families were feeling the pinch.

The fisherfolk and mariners, Lord help them, were suffering cruelly. George Palmer had been lost overboard at Jarrow from the *Active*; *John & Elizabeth* and *Permanent* had been wrecked on coasts nearer home. And those were just the natural disasters – run-of-the-mill casualties, so to speak. Add the mortal injuries the beachmen were inflicting on each other and it was small wonder the Bishop of Norwich had hurried down to Southwold in his coach and four. 'Understandeth thou what thou readest?' the bishop had thundered, at which the congregation in St Edmund's had looked fittingly blank. 'Utterly *tabula rasa*,' was how the High Steward had put it. The sermon and a bazaar had raised £381 for bettering the education of the town's children, but it had come a lot too late in life to improve the intellect of James Martin. Gunner Martin hadn't greatly understood the Standing Instructions for the Loading and Firing of Artillery, with the result that his head had been blown off his shoulders by an untimely boom from a Gun Hill cannon. Only eight days later Abraham Girling had been killed in a brawl at the Long Island watch house during a squabble about pilotage. Studying their hollow-cheeked widows at the gravesides, Maggs had known that the pittance he'd be paying out from the Sailor's Friend Society would be the only income keeping them from the workhouse.

His feelings on these matters have to be read between the lines. His diary simply says that the deaths prompted the Revd Birch to quote the fourth chapter of James as a reminder that his listeners must occupy their remaining time on

Above: A Trinity pilot and his gig. On a September afternoon in 1838, Maggs and six imprudent amateur oarsmen ventured nine miles offshore in the gig *Princess Victoria* to clamber aboard passing vessels and speak with their skippers, returning home safely at ten in the evening, 'to the surprise of many'. (Peter Jenkins)

Left: The Lord Nelson pub, a biscuit-toss from the Long Island lookout, was one of eight inns in the town during the nineteenth century.

Earth's surface to preparing themselves for the Day of Judgement awaiting above the clouds.

The only bright interlude in the general drama of pain had been January's lunar rainbow, which had brought people onto the cliff-tops to gaze at the glimmering marvel with admiration and hope. The church party had pondered the apparition for days, Widow Honeydew telling the town pump that the rainbow had appeared so close to the Epiphany that it must signify Southwold was the chosen site for the Second Coming. No doubt about it, Jesus would walk upon the waters of Sole Bay, the virtuous would go to Heaven and purveyors of Demon Drink dispatched to the Other Place, a verdict which had provoked the taproom of the *Lord Nelson* to clatter their cannikins and declare that Ma Honeydew couldn't tell a hawk from a harnser. In the opinion of those present, the only apparition that mattered was the sight of landlord Thomas Penny coming forth with a second flagon of ale, for the regular doing of which he should be sanctified twice daily till the Honeydew cows came home.

Their lightness of heart lasted no longer than two weeks at most, the celestial promise of betterment speedily cancelled out by more disasters and deaths. The *Liberty* and *Commerce* had gone down with the loss of Messhach and Edward Lilly. Then the bailiffs had taken every last timepiece from Jo King's workshop to settle a longstanding debt, which had goaded Ma Honeydew into informing the market place that the passage of time by sinful toss-pots in the *Nelson* would be regulated henceforth by none other than a grim figure with a scythe.

Maggs would have sided with neither faction. He was before everything a man who kept his opinions to himself. The only prediction he might admit to was that a south-west wind coming after six days of gale-force northers would bring instant improvement to the town's tills. Before the day was over, pilots would be in demand and baskets of spring herring would be landed. If the wind held fair for just three days, sundry debts would be settled and one or two ledgers might even be brought into balance.

True to his nature and training, the diarist rubbed oil of camphor into his flannelette, fixed a clerical furrow to his brow and limped his way to Kilcock Cliff. Wearing his workaday hat of Auctioneer and Valuer, James Maggs was about to take stock of Sole Bay.

To his entire satisfaction, in the space of a morning the whole bay was filled with ships.

Maggs watched the pilot yawls racing seaward through the dying swells and started counting. By the light from an oil lamp, he later wrote in a clear, neat hand: 'A fleet of fro[m] seven to eight hundred sail of vessels appeared between the two Nesses!!'

Pent up for days by strong headwinds, liberated at last by the wind-shift, most of the fleet would have been collier brigs scurrying home to the Northumbrian coal staithes. Home-trade vessels in the 1840s averaged 80 tons and carried four crew; foreign-going merchantmen averaged 200 tons and carried ten. 750 ships, each with an average crew of seven, meant that at a time when the bricks and mortar of Southwold were housing 2,500 people, the wooden walls crossing Sole Bay were sheltering 5,000. If Maggs's figures were right, twice as many eyes could have been gazing at Southwold from Sole Bay than gazing at Sole Bay from the town. As an opening for an epic, Hollywood could not have done it better.

Such a spectacular spread of sail may seem incredible. These days, the greatest number of vessels we can see from Kilcock cliff at any one time will be during a regatta, if a fleet of Old Gaffers sailing north from Essex happens to cross course with a squadron of yachts racing south from Lowestoft – but the number of mainsails in the bay will still be fewer than sixty. There are good reasons, though, for thinking his figures are true. Only a few years before he wrote them the *Yarmouth Mercury* had reported up to 3,000 vessels under sail between Yarmouth and Lowestoft during five hours of a single day, their sails '... so close and uninterrupted that the sea could not be discerned beyond them'. A second reason for believing him is that his livelihood depended on the accurate recording of facts.

Coroner, Census Enumerator, Overseer of the Poor and disposer of their distrained possessions, the Maggs of the diary is a hard-headed recorder of what's what. Whether writing of the deaths of his wife and children, suicides, public executions, the bankruptcies of neighbours and their subsequent transportation

The Ship Inn, Dunwich, where Maggs drank 'refreshment' and went home happy.

This yawl at Southwold in 1890 is probably the *Bittern* or *Victoria*. (Robert Malster)

The Sole Bay lugger *Three Sisters*, built at Thorpe Ness in 1896 and restored a century later by Robert Malster. (Mike Stammers)

to the dreaded Bulcamp workhouse – or, if their minds should give way, the Melton madhouse – he tried to set down all that happened on the shores of Sole Bay without betraying a hint of his feelings about the events. Here are 285 vessels named and 132 shipwrecks noted, with the writer's emotions never ever getting their say. Then, on that April day in 1843 the impassive recorder of death and destruction suddenly plumps down a couple of exclamation marks to express his astonishment at the sight of so many lively looking ships. But was it only astonishment he was feeling? Deeper emotions may have been coming out too: pride in Britannia's maritime supremacy perhaps, and – less upliftingly – a notion that he was witnessing not only the passage of a remarkably large number of sailing ships but also the passing of the Age of Sail itself.

Though not cut out to earn a living as a sailor, 'Limping Jem' Maggs liked to go boating. On a September afternoon in 1838 he and six friends had ventured nine miles offshore in a lightly built gig to clamber aboard three passing ships and enjoy the rough good fellowship of their crews. Climbing rope ladders could not have been easy for crippled Jem, and his deformity would probably have meant he was always steering the gig rather than rowing it, but an unusually revealing bout of notemaking after the escapade shows just how much he enjoyed himself. He writes of the amateur mariners concluding their 'imprudent' jaunt by running the gig on to Dunwich beach and taking 'refreshment' with landlord Joe Dix in The Ship Inn before returning happily home to their anxious families at ten in the evening – 'to the surprise of many'.

Messing about in boats may have given him a deal of innocent weekend pleasure, but when it came to conveying himself to the largest, richest city in the largest, richest empire in the world, the fine-weather boater turned his back on wind power and put his money on steam.

By the age of forty-six Maggs had travelled to London three times, each time by stage-coach from Yoxford or Halesworth to Ipswich, then onward for the greater part of his journey by steamer. Though he'd not set foot in the National Gallery during his most recent visit, he would no doubt have heard talk of Turner's newly hung painting of the fighting *Téméraire* being dragged off to the breaker's yard by a diminutive tug. The subject must have touched a nerve. Maggs enjoyed watching ships working the wind and relished the occasional excursion to rub shoulders with their skippers, but he got a good part of his income by selling their wrecks and carting their destitute families off to the workhouse.

He was no stranger to death and debt. Born lame in 1797 as the youngest of twelve children, he had lost his father when he was two years old. Six of his own twelve offspring had died in early childhood and his three remaining sons were to die in their teens or twenties. During his ninety-three-year lifetime the population of the little town was afflicted more than once by national epidemics of scarlet fever, cholera and smallpox. Compared with other places, Southwold got off lightly, and Maggs gives the fatalities only the briefest mention: '1825, Small Pox: – raging here … Only five deaths' is a typical entry, and the numerous obituaries of the

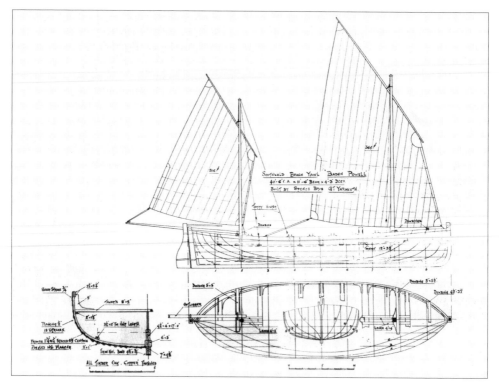

Named after the defender of Mafeking and subsequent founder of the Boy Scouts, the 40ft 6in (12.3m) beach yawl *Baden Powell* was built by Spence Bros at Great Yarmouth sometime between 1900 and 1903 and did her last recorded service in 1930. (Sailors' Reading Room/Alan Hale)

The fine-lined hull and vast sail area of the Lowestoft-registered *Georgiana* typifies the pilot yawls employed on the Sunrise Coast. (Peter Jenkins)

Between 1895 and 1912 eight men of the Palmer family were awarded medals for courageous service in the lifeboats. Here, Edward 'Shemo' Palmer in his canvas hat and guernsey portrays their workaday lives as longshore fishermen. (*Alfred Corry* Museum)

Sporting his distinctive tam o' shanter, beachman 'Fitz' Hurr is possibly the Henry H. Hurr listed as bowman of the Southwold lifeboat in 1896. Six other Hurrs were among the seventy-eight longshoremen deemed worthy to serve. (*Alfred Corry* Museum)

The longshoremen air their sails in an endless campaign against mildew and rot. In 1851, forty-five fishing boats plied from Southwold alone, crewed by 172 men and boys, providing regular shoreside employment for 118 coopers, packers and labourers. (Robert Malster)

breadwinners who died at sea are equally brief. The drownings from the *Liberty* and *Commerce* were just four among scores of local seamen who perished in the North Sea. Among them, Robert Crickmore and Francis Stannard had been lost in the *Alert*; two men had died in 1821 when a Walberswick fishing boat had capsized in a squall, and the Sterry children had lost their father and brothers in 1837 when *Lady Nelson* sank off Margate. George Palmer's drowning at Jarrow in 1842 was to be followed by the loss of his kinsmen, Edward, from the pilot yawl *Jubilee* and the death of a second Edward, crushed by a falling mast. The death roll seemed endless. Though Maggs records the tragedies without comment he was not unmoved by them, organising a town collection in 1838 for the twelve widowed mothers and thirty-two children made fatherless by the loss of the fifteen crew of the *Peace*.

The people who worked – and even dwelt – on the beaches of the Sunrise Coast have always sung the harsher tunes. As far back as 1384 the Black Friars of Dunwich, 'whose mansion-house is in peril by excursion of the sea', were beseeching a landowner to give them a plot of higher ground beyond the reach of the encroaching waves. Two hundred years later the cash-strapped burghers were imploring Queen Elizabeth to lend them £62 18s 4d to repair their once-profitable harbour that had been closed 'by Diverse Rayges of Wyndes'. And the eighteenth-century lyric 'Who'll buy herrings / Fresh and sound? / Who'll buy herrings / By the pound?' echoes the worries in the minds of the few Sole Bay longshoremen who still get their living from a fishing net.

James Critten, on the right, built yawls, gigs and punts for Southwold beachmen. (Pimple Thompson)

Reeking of cut-plug tobacco and cough drops, the elders play cribbage. (Peter Jenkins)

The starboard oculus of the lifeboat inspects the labours of its two coxswains and a tam-o'-shantered bowman as they give the haul-off warp a coating of tar. (*Alfred Corry* Museum)

A hard-earned catch of sprats. The sou'wester worn by the member of the Upcraft family on the left was waterproofed by the application of linseed oil, as too was the smock of his companion. (Robert Malster)

The Scotsmen were followed by troops of nimble-fingered wives and daughters, seen here gutting herring outside the Southwold fish market. (*Alfred Corry* Museum)

Bound for Tonning in Germany with a cargo of coal, the paddle steamer *Eiderstedt* was wrecked at Covehithe in 1872, where its iron hull withstood the elements for at least ten years. Here, longshoremen are gleaning salvage from the bow section. (*Alfred Corry* Museum)

Maggs never wrote of Sole Bay as anything other than a risky and often perilous workplace in which he and others on the beaches stood to make – or lose – any number of hard-earned shillings. Even in the better times, the wolf was never far from most doors in the town. A grandly buttoned Master Mariner might easily go from riches to rags between one moon and the next. John Bokenham, up there on the crest of the wave when he was made Trinity Pilot in February 1840 and looking to earn a princely £400 a year if he lived long enough, was doing time in a debtors' prison by the autumn.

In the hours when they're not working on it – and sometimes under it – the surviving longshoremen on the clifftop will always be looking at the sea through different eyes. Pass the time of a summer's day outside the Sailors' Reading Room and some will tell you of a gyre in Walberswick Bight where the tidal current runs north while the rest of the water in the bay is moving south; others will point out a crinkled patch of sea between Dunwich and Sizewell that's called Hell's Kitchen; a diver who has charted 106 wrecks in the bay will speak of places outside the Walberswick gyre where the sea can be moving in one direction on the surface and in a completely opposite direction underneath, of the current reversing so strongly that it flips him upside down, of descending through metres of clear water and suddenly finding he's swimming in what looks like vermicelli soup.

The Sole Bay communities were not the worst sufferers. In 1836 a Parliamentary Committee reported that the four years of 1832–5 had seen the thousand-strong fleet at Newcastle on Tyne lose no fewer than 26 per cent of its ships and 682 crewmen. For many years afterwards the losses continued at even higher rates, so that by the close of the nineteenth century anyone with a head for statistics could reason that no other workforce in the western world was suffering a higher death rate than the sailors in the North Sea trading and fishing fleets. But it wasn't only

Timber from this nameless wreck would have been used in the building of many a house and barn on the Sunrise Coast. (*Alfred Corry* Museum)

the sea that was killing them – their employers were doing it too. Many of the lovely looking vessels Southwold's summer visitors were admiring from the clifftops were found, on closer examination, to be leaky, lousy, overladen, jerry-built, worm-eaten wooden boxes that all too often turned out to be the sailors' coffins.

Their passing-bells tolled throughout the land, summoning a flurry of Parliamentary orations intended to reduce the appalling loss of life by shipwreck. The nation's compassion for 'Poor Jack' and his fatherless family was stoked by a brace of popular writers who teased open enough purses in the thirty years before 1858 to finance a nationwide fleet of sixty-six lifeboats.

Many of the mariners clinging to the wreckage bore names that could indeed have been thought up by Dickens: Captains Fungelius of Friborg, Ezekiel Yennis, Jo King, Fidgett, Mutch, Mullett and Mapplebeck rise spluttering from their waterlogged hulks and take up lodgings in your head. And then there are the mysteries. Why did an emissary from His Prussian Majesty Frederick William III to the opulent Court of St James wish to venture up a 'lousie creek' like the River Blyth to muddy his Hessian jackboots in the unpaved streets of a poverty-stricken backwater like Southwold? What became of the gold watch and fifty golden guineas, plundered from his corpse by rascally old Will Skelton and ne'er-do-well Midshipman Skinner of the Easton signal house, after the Prussian galley had overturned on Southwold bar?

Perhaps we shall never know. But, picking through their scattered bones, the reader may feel that he is touching on an epic.

2

THE SHORE AND THE SHOALS

A thousand ages in Thy sight,
Are like an evening gone.
– Isaac Watts, 1714

Nine thousand years ago Sole Bay had no sea.

Three hundred summers had to pass before sufficient ice had melted to furnish northern Europe with a brawling infant ocean on which the tribes who roamed its shores could launch their earliest seagoing craft and endure their first truly maritime shipwrecks. These could not have been witnessed by a watcher on Kilcock Hill (which wasn't yet a cliff), because the sea was still twenty-six miles away and did not come close enough to be seen by the Iron Age ploughman on the hill until a thousand years before Christ walked upon the shore of Galilee.

And the water kept coming. 'The coast, up and down, for miles, has been, for more centuries than I presume to count, gnawed away by the sea … which moves for ever, like a ruminating beast, an insatiable, indefatigable lip,' wrote Henry James after staying awhile in Dunwich in 1897.

Some parts had been devoured more rapidly than others. Christopher Saxton's map of 1575 (C3, page 15), shows Easton Ness, then the most easterly point of Britain, lying more than two miles seaward of the present cliffs, which suggests that Easton's green and pleasant acres, once containing a populous town with a church dedicated to the patron saint of pawnbrokers, have been tumbling into the sea at an average rate of 10m a year over the past four centuries. On the other hand, the southernmost littoral of Sole Bay seems to have lost little. Hodgkinson's map of 1783 depicts a coastline between Sizewell and Thorpe Ness which fits Imray's 1990 chart quite neatly, a coincidence that may owe more to the shortcomings of eighteenth-century mapmaking than to any let-up by the sea. Even so, it is difficult to believe that our Whitehall mandarins would have allowed a nuclear power station to be built only 100m from Sizewell beach if they had thought the sea would ever undercut its foundations and muck up their CBEs.

The earliest wreck to have been found in the bay is a 5m dugout, trawled up in 1998 off Dunwich. 'It was encased in peat and came from Covehithe,' said Stuart

THE RIVER BLYTH AND CREEK, WALBERSWICK.

Southwold harbour before the improvements of 1908. Two bridges on the far bank span Salt Creek and to the right of them is Trinity Pier, often the place for transhipping coal. The last vessel to heave coal here was the SS *River Trent* in 1939. The path in the foreground leads to the Kissing Bridge across Dunwich creek. (*Alfred Corry* Museum)

A Walberswick punt lies downstream of the Kissing Bridge. (Robert Malster)

Bacon, the director of Suffolk Underwater Studies, at his small but impressive museum at Orford, on a leaden November day which his conversation greatly lightened. Pickled in rotted vegetation, prised from its resting place and rolled five miles south by boisterous tides, the seemingly indestructible dugout has been dated to about AD 850. Driven by paddles and perhaps assisted now and then by a primitive sail, it could have seen service under Alfred the Great.

The area contains three small lakes or broads at Covehithe, Benacre and Easton. Covehithe and Benacre are fed by anonymous rivulets and Easton broad is fed by a larger stream called the Wren. It seems the broads are the shrunken remains of navigable tidal rivers and lagoons, for near the village of Frostenden, a mile and a half from Easton Bavents and the sea, the Wren skirts a mound which overlooks the

A storm surge in the early hours of 1 February 1953 drove the water in Sole Bay 11ft (3.35m) above its normal level. At the predicted time of low water the bottom bar of the Harbour Inn (centre) was still flooded, while the barge *Martin Luther* (centre right) and, off-photo right, the schooner yacht *Wildflower* had floated from their mud berths. The still-receding floodwater is gushing seaward through breaks in the Walberswick dyke. Such inundations will be commonplace by 2060, declare our soothsayers in their temples of science. (Pimple Thompson)

Entering harbour against the ebb, 1822. (Pimple Thompson)

site of what is thought to have been a Roman port. 'As a boy, I heard tell of boats that used to go upstream past Potters Bridge to Cove Bottom,' recollects seventy-seven-year-old Charlie Martin of Reydon, 'but they were said to be just small ones, not the seagoing sort.' Together with the Hundred River flowing south of Kessingland beach, the broads would have formed a communal estuary three miles

Rather a lot more sand than water. The River Blyth entrance in 1890, with a boomie barge in the offing. (Keith Deal)

long. Here, shielded from North Sea storms by wide banks like the one which still shelters the River Ore, and another which once protected Dunwich, the owner of the Covehithe dugout would have gathered oysters to supply King Alfred's keels.

Other hints of Covehithe's maritime history came to light in the 1980s with the finding of a side-rudder on Easton beach and the trawling-up of a second rudder 1.4 miles north-east of Covehithe church. Gillian Hutchinson at the National Maritime Museum believes they were probably made in the eleventh century and came from similar types of vessels. However, electronic surveys extending one and a half miles from the coast have not found any wrecks from the period, so although their remains may still be somewhere in Sole Bay they could also lie far away from it.

More ancient wreckage was found in 1991 when a longboat and its steering oar were discovered 90m west of Mights Bridge in Buss Creek, which had been a shipbuilding site and a base for a large herring fishery in Saxon times. Thought to have been built between AD 890 and 1155, the boat is 11.5m long, with planking overlapped at the edges in the clinker system practised by the native shipwrights three hundred years before the Viking invasions in the eighth and ninth centuries.

Though in ancient times it would probably have emerged more directly into the sea, nowadays Buss Creek is a blind alley leading off the River Blyth, with no direct way out to Sole Bay because its eastern end has been blocked by sand and shingle. At some time before AD 1000 until 1328 the river turned hard right at Walberswick to flow two and a half miles south before escaping into the sea at the up-and-coming port of Dunwich, populated in 1086 by 428 families, including twenty-four recent arrivals from mainland Europe in the wake of William the Conqueror.

A punt leaving harbour at Low Water Springs. The black speck just discernible to seaward of the bar is a buoy with a haul-off warp attached to it. (*Alfred Corry* Museum)

Defying continual assaults by the sea, the Dunwich people strove to develop their maritime trade. Throughout the thirteenth century their 30- to 60-ton single- or twin-masted hulls carried cargoes to and from Prussia in the east to Spain in the south, exporting sackfuls of wool to Flanders, bags of corn and dried herring to any port or usable beach between the Elbe and Brest. Their ships were often in demand by the reigning monarch, most notably King John, who hired thirty for an expedition to Ireland, thirty more to carry his army to Poitou and ten to convey his sister to her wedding with the Holy Roman Emperor. The Dunwich ships came home laden with wine and salt from Gascony, cloth from Antwerp, alum from Spain and wax and bowstaves from Prussia. The town became a major shipbuilding port, launching large fifty-six-oar galleys equipped with 'masts, booms, yards, straps, sprits, hair-cloth, pikes and ropes' for the sum of £41 4s 1d, as listed by Rowland Parker in his *Men of Dunwich*. In the beady eyes of the medieval tax-collector, Dunwich was a boom town, accounted in 1218 as being half as rich again as Yarmouth and more than three times wealthier than Ipswich, with a harbour two miles long by half a mile wide, giving anchorage for a hundred ships. 'There was no port to equal it between Lynn and London, and few better in the whole kingdom,' wrote Parker.

But the town's prosperity was built on sand. When, in 1328, the harbour entrance was blocked by north-east gales, the Blyth responded by forcing a new passage two miles nearer to Walberswick. This northward shift of the river mouth was the beginning of the end for Dunwich. Six years later the 428 families living there at the time of the Norman conquest had dwindled to 150, and when the new passage was itself blocked in the early years of the fifteenth century, Dunwich

A dredger attempting to deepen the channel. The unyielding combination of London clay and Cambridge crag tore off several of its buckets. (*Alfred Corry* Museum)

The pile driver is strengthening the North pier during the harbour works in 1907. The sand was sometimes only a couple of feet below the level of the pier walkway. (*Alfred Corry* Museum)

THE FIRST BOAT AT THE SOUTHWOLD HARBOUR QUAY WALL JUNE 13th 1907

In June 1907 the *Amelia* of Lowestoft became the first boat to berth at Southwold's newly built harbour wall, though much dredging still needed to be done. (Robert Malster)

A collier ketch lies opposite Dunwich creek. 'She's got a cod's head and a mackerel tail,' remarked Billy Stannard. (*Alfred Corry* Museum)

gradually silted up. Two years after Good Queen Bess came to the throne her muscular subjects in Walberswick and Southwold dug out another channel near to where it now runs, giving the Blyth a straighter fall into the sea. Their energetic spadework led the Admiralty to establish a court in Southwold, which meant in effect that the once lively port of Dunwich was as good as dead, its demise confirmed by Daniel Defoe in 1724 when he reported that the town's remaining merchants were having to load their cargoes at Walberswick.

Knowing that thousands of ships must have anchored in its harbour, docked at its wharves or been winched up its slipways, the reader who has stayed the course this far may now expect to be rewarded with a number of more-or-less impregnable assertions about the many Saxon and medieval wrecks found at Dunwich. After all, he may reason, not without justification, if Southwold has the remains of only a single longboat and Covehithe has given us one solitary dugout, the much larger port of Dunwich must have yielded dozens. I am sorry to have to disappoint him, but it hasn't. *Men of Dunwich* contains only six 'wreck' references in its 265 pages. All six are deeply relevant to the history of Dunwich, and some – including a decree of 1275 that, 'If a man, woman, child, *dog or cat* escaped alive' from it, a wreck was not technically 'wreck' – are sharply arresting, but only one entry actually gives details, and even then only the cargo and its owner are named; the ship itself is scarcely mentioned:

A certain ship of Prussia with a cargo of flax, bowstaves and barrels of wax of Osmund Ferro was cast by a storm upon the soil of the king at Dunwich, between the present port of Dunwich and the former one called Old Haven.

That was written in 1375, 300 years after the last Saxon king ruled England, a time when ship records would have been even sparser.

The main reason for not finding ancient wrecks at Dunwich is that the sea not only gnawed away the protective banks but also hurled large amounts of sand and shingle westward, burying the silted harbour and its abandoned ships. So, just as Covehithe only gave up its dugout when the sea had dug far enough inland to break open its grave, Dunwich will begin to do the same only when the sea immerses the visiting four-wheel drives to the level of their bull bars.

More wrecks could probably be discovered at the nature reserve at Minsmere, two miles to the south, where a tidal estuary would have been accessible to Roman, Saxon and Viking seafarers until it was blocked by the débris carried down from Dunwich. Though Saxton closes the river mouth on his map of 1575, he still labels Minsmere as a haven, probably meaning only that its nearby cliffs would give the mariner useful shelter in westerly gales. (But Greenville Collins in 1693 shows the haven as an estuary extending a mile or so farther south-eastward than Dunwich, which suggests the North Sea can open harbours as well as shut them.)

However – and more importantly – Saxton's map (C3, p 15), makes plain that till the last quarter of the sixteenth century the then quite deeply indented coast of Sole Bay offered seamen 30 per cent more protection than it now does. Today, a vessel anchored one mile south-east of St Edmund's church at Southwold is vulnerable to all winds between North through East to SSW, whereas an Elizabethan sea-captain who anchored in the same spot would have been sheltered by Easton Ness, which bore ENE from him and lay more than one mile further seaward.

To offer the reader a picture of what the Sunrise Coast looked like in the seventeenth and eighteenth centuries, I must lay Christopher Saxton to one side and open the works of Collins and Hodgkinson. The charts in Collins's *Coasting Pilot* (C4–6, pp 16–17), were not begun until Elizabeth I had been dead for seventy-eight years, and so I am not at all sure that any drawings done in 1693 would have been recognisable by Her Majesty's eager English Admirals who chased the Armada eastwards up the Channel and northward past the Sunrise Coast. I am pretty sure, however, that if Alfred's oyster-loving captains could have seen the sketches they would have looked more than a little dismayed, for the saltwater shellfish beds at Benacre, Covehithe and Easton have been sealed up and their offlying protection swept away. Worse navigational news was to follow. A glance at Hodgkinson's map of 1783 would reveal a seascape so altered that the narrator of the tenth-century epic *Beowulf* is likely to have uttered a horrified 'Hwæt?!' before stomping off to spread quantities of gloom among his oysterless companions on the mead bench. The navigator's dismay would have been well founded, for Alfred's Dunwich is no longer a haven, Collins having lately awarded the title to the formerly less significant port of Southwold, which is now sporting as tall a church as Dunwich as well as having a larger-scale chart attached to its name. Worst of all, by 1783 the bold but welcoming face of Easton Ness has been reduced to a nose-less horror. For Beowulf, approaching the Sunrise Coast in the eighteenth century would have been as joyful as encountering his monstrous enemy Grendel on a dark night in a swamp.

Collins made his Sole Bay sketches two leagues (six miles) from the land, perched in the prime lookout position, where the topsail yard crossed the foremast, 10m above the deck. From here he could see, on the first hilltop south of Minsmere, a beacon as tall as Walberswick church. There'd been five beacons between Minsmere and Southwold in the thirteenth century, but by 1693 Collins was showing only one. Primarily intended to be lit as warning signals of piratical raids, they were also valuable aids to navigation, maintained by the Corporation of Trinity House of Deptford Strand. Established by Henry VIII in 1514 for the advancement of navigation and the licensing of pilots, the corporation's powers were enlarged in 1565 to include the setting up of beacons. Anyone cutting down the beacons or other navigation marks such as conspicuous trees was liable to a whopping fine. If the culprit happened to be a common sailor, the fine was the equivalent of nine years' wages, which must have made Jack Tar feel quite a lot less jolly.

Between AD 1000 and 1700 the population of England and Wales grew from just under a million to 5.5 million, which suggests that Collins would have spied many more buildings on the coast than would the Saxons because – owing to the eating habits of up to ten million sheep in the kingdom – they would have been hidden by fewer trees. Utility always being more marketable than fidelity, Collins ignores the less important navigational features of the landscape and exaggerates others. Thus, Walberswick is given a four-storeyed church tower and fourteen bold houses but no trees. In fact, between Thorpe Ness and Easton he shows only fifteen: three near Thorpe church and twelve representing Woods End near Easton Bavents. Though crude and out-dated, the sketches are still relevant, something I found out while inspecting the coast in my 5.5m lugger *Pippin* on a November day in 2004. With eyes only 1m above the sea instead of at the lordly elevation achieved by Collins up his foremast, I could afford to be only two miles offshore rather than six when I backed the foresail, hove-to and got out a compass on a chilly bright morning on which a wintergreen sea was tipped fawn at its tops and the land was standing up boldly in the west. Collins had sketched when a church in Dunwich bore NW, two leagues distant. Well, Dunwich had lost its last remaining tower in 1919 and the north magnetic pole had wandered thirty degrees eastward in the interim, but a church tower was still visible at Walberswick. I took a bearing of the tower, another of the cottages in Sizewell Gap, corrected them for magnetic variation and plotted the result on my 1990 chart. The position was half a mile north of the bearing Collins gave for Dunwich church, so I let draw the foresail, sailed a few hundred metres south and sharpened a 4B pencil.

Three centuries of storms had been digging away at Suffolk since Collins sketched it but surprising amounts of territory were still left. Comparing my drawing with his, I could match up most of the rises and dips on the landward horizons to the north-west and south-west. More excitingly, however, the coast immediately to the

Freight train on the Harbour Branch in 1924.

From 1914 till its closure in 1929, a 3ft-gauge railway carried cargoes to and from Southwold harbour to Halesworth, nine miles inland, where they were transhipped to mainline wagons. (*Alfred Corry* Museum)

The rails in the left foreground extended back to the terminus in Blyth Road, one mile distant, and the right-hand branch served nearby Blackshore quay. (*Alfred Corry* Museum)

The head of the Blyth navigation at Halesworth, five locks upriver. Between 1759 and the 1850s, black-sailed wherries discharged coal cargoes here and loaded malted barley. (Robert Malster)

Viewed from the Grand Hotel, the bathing machines await the trippers. Many were owned by Sam May, the lifeboat coxswain. (Robert Malster)

west was unchanged in its most significant seaward aspect. There, the south-facing edge of Minsmere cliff still ran down towards the reed bed at exactly the same angle for me as it had done in 1693 for Collins. And, sharpened against a grey eminence in the background, it pointed unmistakably to Minsmere Haven.

Although the bay's far south-western coastline has altered since Collins, the erosion there has been less radical, and at its northern end the process in recent decades has reversed. A sailing club established at Kessingland in the early 1960s had to shut down its clubhouse fifteen years later because the beach had grown 300m eastward, and in 2005 the Lowestoft Cruising Club cancelled a race to the East Barnard buoy because an inshore channel, which in 1910 had had a least depth of 20ft, was reported to have shoaled at its northern end to only 6ft. However, these addings-on have been very limited and local; the general process continues to be relentless subtraction, taking away in the eighteenth century a hamlet named Southmere, Searow or Sero that lay between Covehithe and Benacre, a further forty acres (16 hectares) of farmland from Covehithe during the last quarter of the nineteenth century, followed by three concrete blockhouses and nineteen arable acres (7.7 hectares) between 1961–84. Costly though they must have been to landowners, these more recent losses seem minor when compared with the fifteen square miles (3,885 hectares) eroded during the preceding 700 years. Looking at this diminishing loss-rate, the reader may be tempted to think the North Sea is losing its muscle. Such a thought would be mistaken. The sea is labouring just as energetically these days as it ever did – and possibly more so. Global warming and the continuing rise in sea levels argue that storm surges and tidal streams have become stronger. Though it has been famously written that hurricanes hardly happen in Hampshire, a severe storm savaged Sunderland in 1840 and another, the Fastnet Gale, punched a hole in my 26ft (7.9m) *Kylie* when it spilled into the North Sea in August 1979. The sea hasn't weakened its attacks on the land, it's just that for the past 250 years some of its earth-moving endeavours in Sole Bay have been frustrated by a couple of man-made extrusions called The Piers.

The earliest piers were built between 1749–52 to stabilise the river mouth, which had the habit of changing shape and direction according to the prevailing wind. Their construction induced George II to grant Southwold a royal charter incorporating the Free British Fishery and led to the growth of a sixty-seven-strong fleet of herring boats in Buss Creek. Though it did nothing to check the erosion of Southwold cliffs and was itself often mashed up by gales, the first North pier marked the beginning of Man's most substantial attempt to prevent the choking of Sole Bay's last remaining port. Difficulties were great and disappointments frequent. The sandbank at the entrance did much to kill off the Free British Fishery only twenty-two years after it was founded, and during the first quarter of the nineteenth century the entrance had to be dug out thirteen times in as many years. In 1833 and 1839 Lieutenant Ellis had employed steam dredgers to reduce the shoals, but, as we have learned already, four years later Maggs was noting that the entrance was again so firmly blocked that horse-drawn carts were using the sandbank as a short cut to Walberswick. Attempting to cross it in 1852, the laden schooner *Spring* stuck fast and was speedily wrecked by a force nine gale. Shallower local boats like the 32-ton *Halesworth Trader*, built 1799 at Southwold (and not to be confused with a 95-ton vessel of the same name that was lost in 1812 off Scotland), which had a draft of only 4ft, would have crossed the bar at high water in favourable weather with no trouble. However, the resourceful harbourmaster was able to keep the port usable by deeper-draft ships by off-loading their cargo into lighters, receiving and dispatching between 1831–41 a yearly average of 425 vessels containing cargoes such as timber from the Baltic ports, coals from Newcastle and cattle cake from London, and carrying outward cargoes of fish, corn, peas, beans, cheese and many, many bushels of malt. The malt came downriver in Norfolk keels and black-sailed wherries from Patrick Stead's maltings in Halesworth via the Blyth Navigation, which had opened in 1759 following the building of brick locks at Halesworth and Wenhaston, more locks with faggots at Mells, Blyford and Bulcamp, as well as the widening of the river below Blythburgh.

Reasoning that sail was about to be overtaken by rail, in 1852 Stead sold his shares in the maltings and the Blyth Navigation to Truman's the brewers. It was a timely move. By 1884, road transport improvements and a growing railway network were bruising the river traffic so heavily that the Navigation directors were obliged to throw in the towel. Their action did not however signal the end. The 120-ton *Woodland Lass*, owned by Edward Chapman of Southwold, later sailed up the Navigation with a cargo of timber, and for a few short years in the early twentieth century the wherry *Star* carried cargoes as far as Blythburgh, though by 1911 even *Star* had given up. The Wenhaston lock, still functioning in the early twentieth century, was blown to small pieces by His Majesty's energetic sappers during the Second World War to hinder a German invasion that never happened.

The Navigation was the scene of a scandalous incident in more recent years. Filled with piccalillied beef sandwiches and a barmy desire to sail my red-sailed lugger into a glorious red sunset, in 2005 I got as far as Bulcamp before losing my wind in the reeds and becoming disgracefully stuck. 'Coo! Looks like yew's all of a-huh an' swangways,' cackled a local resident.

In spite of its upriver mudflats and the sandbank clogging the harbour entrance, nineteenth-century Southwold was the home port of some surprisingly deep-drafted ships. Published in 1842, Maggs's *Hand Book of the Port and Shipping of Southwold* ('Price 2s 6d ... convenient for the Pocket or Pocket-Book') lists all the vessels belonging to the town during the years 1782–1842. Of the thirty-nine in service at the time of publication, thirty-one were in the coasting trade, five were pilot cutters, two were foreign-going and one, the shallow-draft *Halesworth Trader*, was employed on the river. Coasters like *Active*, *Albion*, *Brother's Friend*, *Gleaner*, *Louisa Elizabeth*, *Perseverance* and *Victoria* drew 10ft (3.08m) of water and measured between 68 and 95 tons, measurements exceeded only by the 130-ton, foreign-going *Pegasus*, which drew 11ft (3.38m). Thirty-seven (24 per cent) of the vessels listed were subsequently wrecked: five in Sole Bay, twenty-eight in other British waters and four in foreign seas. One was the 107-ton *Greyhound*. Commanded by Rowland Twaddell and carrying a crew of eight, the *Greyhound* was 'Lost on Goree island' in 1832. Maggs probably meant Goeree in Holland, but he may just possibly have been referring to the former slave-trading station off the coast of French West Africa (now Senegal), for it would not have been unknown for vessels the size of *Greyhound* to venture so far afield from Sole Bay. Ten years before Maggs compiled his handbook, the Southwold brig *Berbice* was carrying cargoes from Mediterranean Europe and North Africa. He records the smaller, 73-ton *Dispatch* voyaging to foreign parts beyond home-trade limits, and notes the 123-ton *Rose & June* had been wrecked on the Spanish coast in 1814.

Fifty-six vessels were sold to other ports, thirteen broken up, and nine were either captured by the French or Dutch or confiscated by the government for non-payment of debts.

A century after Lieutenant Ellis's dredging operations, the wooden North pier at the harbour entrance was replaced in the late 1930s by a concrete bastion which was bolstered in 1990s by several hundred tons of Norwegian rocks at its head. In 2006 a further 16,500 tons of granite was deposited on the much-depleted beach above the Penny Pier, the pleasure pier one mile north of the North pier, and 270 cu.m of Guyanan greenheart timber was bolted together beneath Southwold cliffs to form what is hoped will be a long-lasting series of sixteen groynes. By late summer of the same year, 114,000 tonnes of sand and shingle had been piped on to the denuded beaches on which children were once again building castles out of sand or gleefully burying their fathers. Extensive though they seem, the defences are just for the

Belle Line steamers ran a daily summer service to the town's Penny Pier from Thames St wharf in London. The 743-ton *Southwold Belle* could carry 900 passengers, and the fare in 1900 was 9s. (Mike Stammers)

protection of Southwold town. What keeps the greater length of Sole Bay in its present sequence of gently curving beaches are the North and South piers forming the harbour entrance. If the piers go, the sea will seal up the river mouth and the only harbour of refuge between Lowestoft and Harwich will vanish from the chart.

Today the River Blyth runs out between a curiously matched couple of Laurel-and-Hardy structures which churn out an entertaining variety of whirls and eddies that can be contemplated, with much benefit, for hours. The not-so-pleasant news is the prediction that sea levels will rise between 3.5 and 6mm a year during the present millennium. Anyone hoping to enjoy the performance in 2999 will need to be wearing flippers.

James Maggs began his diary in 1818 and went on till 1876, a period that encompassed a ten-fold expansion of British shipping and the burgeoning of the Admiralty Hydrographic Department, which had produced its first chart in 1801. By the mid-1830s the department had published 2,000 charts, including sheet 102, which depicted the Suffolk coast between Orford Ness and Lowestoft, as surveyed by Master George Thomas RN in 1824, when Maggs was twenty-seven. Supplemented by Captain Close's semi-official but entirely reliable fisherman's chart published in 1910, Thomas gives us a detailed picture of Sole Bay as it used to be during the heyday of sail and the worst period for shipwrecks (C14, p.24.)

Besides the eye-catching churches, what other landmarks might an early nineteenth-century captain be looking for when Thorpe Ness comes abeam and he's nagging an able seaman at the wheel to steer 'Nor'east a quarter east, with nuthin' ter larbud' along the Sunrise Coast on his way to, say, Whitby? Scanning the land from south to north, he would see a spindly semaphore station one and a half miles south-west of Thorpe Ness, its signals readable through his spyglass for up to four miles. 'Wunnerful hinventions, them summerfores,' he might remark to the mate as a light-hearted precursor to giving him the job of navigating the vessel as far as the Stanford Channel. 'D'you know what? I b'lieve they can send messages from London ter Deal an' back in under two minutes! Just think of it!

The breakers on the starboard beam of this zulu mark the seaward breadth of the dangerous shoal immediately north of the piers. Variously called 'The Hale', 'North Hale' or 'Sand Hale', it is being given a wide berth by the canny Scotsman at the helm. (Southwold Museum)

You could be sendin' kisses to your missis at a better rate o' knots than a pigeon what's hinflicted with the 'ow's-yer-fathers!'

'Nor'east a quarter east, was it?' replies the tight-lipped (and rather uppity) mate, who has heard the story twenty times before because he happens to be the captain's youngest brother.

'An' nothin' ter larboard, mind!' snarls the captain, before going below for his afternoon cocoa.

When distance made its signals unreadable, the semaphore was still a distinctive landmark. Less conspicuous – but more closely familiar to Sole Bay fishermen than to cocoa-swilling skippers who were hasting home to Whitby – were twenty-three isolated or closely huddled buildings overlooking the sea: a cluster of farmhouses at Sizewell Gap (where lived John Merrells, friend of Jem Maggs and 'much and deservedly respected by all who knew him'); a blockade house at Sizewell, a watchbox one mile north of it, and the Preventive Service lookout on Minsmere cliff that testified to the centuries-old and widely feared threats from French privateers as well as the more locally known – and secretly appreciated – activities of native smugglers; three barns and farmhouses between Dunwich and Walberswick; a farm and boathouse at Covehithe, and, at intervals along the coast, a thin scattering of windmills. Though none had been shown on the Collins chart, by 1824 Sole Bay had acquired eight, including the White Mill and the Black Mill, which stood on Southwold Common. The Black Mill was built in 1798 by a Mr Dawson, who sold it to Peregrine Edwards in 1806 for £745. Edwards, a very all there sort of person, sold it in 1842 for £2,900 to someone who evidently wasn't, because three years later Maggs noted that the poor man was selling off the mill for less than half of what he'd paid for it.

Close's chart of 1910 covers only the northern half of Sole Bay and is drawn to scale 40 per cent smaller than that used by Thomas in 1824. On it we can nevertheless see that the passage of eighty-six years had brought many changes. According to Close, by 1910 Southwold had lost its windmills but had gained itself a water tower, a railway, an

Storms in 1905 destroyed much of Southwold's sea defences, swept away the beach houses of the longshoremen...

...and demolished many yards of clifftop footpaths. (*Alfred Corry Museum*)

810ft (247m) pleasure pier and a broad avenue leading on to it, and – most crucially for seamen – a tall upstanding lighthouse. Completed in 1890, the year of Maggs's death, its oil-burning lantern shone out across Sole Bay for seventeen miles. In the ten years after the light came into service the number of wreck incidents in Sole Bay fell by 30 per cent. The reduction happened for many reasons – the fast-increasing number of steamships, better training, tighter regulations and so on – but the shining of a seventeen-mile light was one of the more important.

Brightly shining lights had not always been so helpful. In 1848 Southwold had been unexpectedly – so far as occasional passers-by from Whitby were concerned – festooned with them. Instead of feeling their way past an inhospitable coast that was always wrapped nightly in darkness, on their next passage homewards the north-country skippers were suddenly confronted with a segment of Suffolk as brightly lit-up as a middle-size port. The outcome was predictable. Buoyed by a confident belief that the newly erected gas lamps on Southwold cliffs were leading her into Lowestoft harbour, at four o'clock on Boxing Day morning the brig *Leda* ran on to the beach south of Gun Hill, whereupon the bright-eyed watchers on the cliff spat on their hands, winched her afloat again and went happily homeward to carry on with their Christmas beanos £70 the richer. The *Leda* was followed up the strand a year later by the equally myopic *Robert & James* of South Shields, enabling the long-headed salvors of Southwold to pocket a further £5 for their services. Their brilliantly enlightened but darkly irregular source of income was put an end to in 1853 when the sea undermined the cliffs and broke the gas pipes.

By 1910, however, the building of other lights with distinctive and different characters had added to the navigational benefits brought by the lighthouse. There were now flashing lights on each pier at the harbour entrance, two vertical green lights (as well as a fog bell) at the end of the pleasure pier, and three leading lights on Gun Hill to meet the seasonal needs of fishing boats. Nationwide concerns about the increasing number of mariners being drowned in Sole Bay had resulted, from 1826 onwards, in the building of specially designed lifeboats and the provision of life-saving apparatus that could be launched from the beach by rockets. In 1859 Sole Bay had six lifeboats in fifteen miles: two at Thorpe Ness, another two at Southwold, and one each at Dunwich and Benacre. A station at Sizewell had closed in 1851, probably because – like Thorpe Ness No.1 in 1900 and Dunwich three years later – there were no longer enough able-bodied people living nearby to man it. In 1910 Benacre also had a rocket staff, a boathouse and a flagstaff, while Covehithe had its coastguard and its flagstaff, and so too of course did Southwold.

⎯•⎯

The most perilous places in the eighty-eight square miles of Sole Bay are its shoals, which are called either banks or sands, except when they have been charted by Close, who in mapping the bay calls them neither. (Any reader who is beginning to feel queasy about navigating the bay should count his blessings and be thankful. The further south he ventures the more complicated it becomes: if he pushes his luck beyond Thorpe Ness he will be imbrangled in napes, knowls and onions.)

Another source of confusion when looking at depictions of shoals is the fact that chart-makers have had different notions about where to draw the separating contour. A shoal to Master George Thomas was an isolated patch of water less than 4 fathoms (7.3m) deep; the dividing line for Close was sometimes 2 fathoms (3.7m) and sometimes 1 (1.8m), while Imray in 1990 showed a shoal at the 2.7 fathom (5m) contour, with the result that some charted dangers may appear to have diminished over the centuries without ever having done so. The Sizewell bank, for example, shown in 1990 to be occupying only half a square mile and in 1824 as having been four times larger, was really still so extensively shallow to the north of the 1990 contour as to have destroyed thirty ships in the intervening period. Another, the Red Sand shoal, was a wandering will-o'-the-wisp. Depicted in 1693 as lying either far seaward of Pakefield or, perhaps, Kessingland, by 1752 Red Sand had wriggled seven miles seaward of Covehithe church, since when it has vanished without trace (C4, 6 and 7, pp. 16-18.) Closer inshore, the Barnard sand has altered perceptibly, sometimes to the mariner's benefit and sometimes not. Collins described the Barnard and the Newcome as all one sand extending from Covehithe Ness to Pakefield, with a least depth of 3 or 4ft (0.9–1.2m) and having an inshore channel usable by small vessels at high water. Thomas in 1824 found the channel through the southern part of the Barnard was 1¾ fathoms (3.2m), but by 1910 it had deepened to nearly 3 fathoms (5.5m) and become a buoyed channel to the shelter of Pakefield Road, only to shoal up again in recent years – as the cruising club discovered in 2005 (C8, p.19 and C14, p.24.)

Buoys, too, have come and gone or changed their characters. For a time between the late nineteenth and mid-twentieth centuries Sole Bay had nine buoys; today it has only one. A white buoy of indeterminate shape on the eastern edge of Sizewell bank in 1824 was later replaced by a black-and-white can-shaped buoy moored one mile north of it. This can-shaped buoy marked the bank until the entire buoyage system of the British Isles was altered in the 1970s, when the dumpy – and by this time dowdy – Sizewell buoy changed overnight into an attractively tall, yellow-and-black structure with a delicate pointed head and the engaging nocturnal habit of winking at passing mariners every ten seconds, something it continued to do until the killjoy Elder Brethren of Trinity House clasped it back to their withered but magnificently buttoned bosoms in the 1980s and snuffed it out.

The Barnard sand in 1910 was garlanded with a two-mile chain of six buoys marking its approaches and an inside channel (C14, p.24.) Coming southward outside the bank with the flood tide, the mariner would be warned of its presence by, first of all, a conical East Barnard buoy, followed 11½ cables (1.15 miles or 2.16km) later by the SE Barnard, at which juncture he could either keep on steering SW ¼ S, passing the South Barnard buoy off Covehithe church, and press on for a further four miles until abreast of two red or black fairway buoys at the Blyth entrance, where – if the tide was high enough and he felt like it – he could nip upriver and wet his whistle in the Harbour Inn, or, if the tide happened to be ebbing or he'd been given a talking-to by the earnest ladies of the Salvation Army, he might feel minded to turn hard a-starboard after passing the South-east Barnard so as to enter the Covehithe channel, where two black-and-white-striped or chequered buoys would lead him into an unalcoholic anchorage where he could put the tea kettle on the stove and put his feet up.

The Covehithe channel was first buoyed at some time between 1824 and 1840, and in light weather would have been usable by vessels with drafts of up to as much as 15ft (4.6m) until well into the twentieth century. By 1960, however, the Admiralty's *North Sea Pilot* was advising its readers to cross the sand and enter Pakefield Road north of the East Barnard buoy, but by 1973 even this approach had silted up and the six Barnard buoys had been cut down to two. No longer possessing a perceptible channel and marked by just a single buoy winking three times every ten seconds, today the Barnard bank is crossable only by shallow-draft boats with local knowledge in light weather.

An inshore shoal runs northward from the harbour entrance and parallel with the coast for more than three miles. Lying between 50 and 200m offshore at low water, it is between 20 and 50m wide, except near the harbour entrance, where its width is 0.9km, half a mile. The present least depth of 1.2m at the bar is a welcome – but possibly short-lived – aberration. As we have learned from Maggs, the shoal has usually varied between being an occasional impediment, navigable by the deepest-draft (presently 8.5ft or 2.6m) user only after four or five hours of flood, to being an all-too-familiar obstruction that has to be dug through. Close's 1910 chart shows it extending across the harbour entrance and stretching well south of Walberswick. The chart also shows the shoal was by no means continuous, having in 1910 a 0.2-mile-wide gap of deeper water in it that extended from just north of the present white-painted restaurant on Ferry Road and had a least depth of 7ft (2.1m). If the gap had been there in 1858 and been about 50m wider, it might have saved the lives of the curate of Wangford and his two fellow passengers who were drowned when the lifeboat *Harriet II* caught on the shoal while returning from exercise and was rolled broadside by a following wave.

The shoals are Sole Bay's smallest death traps but they are also its most effective. Taking up less than 2 per cent of the bay, they have claimed 20 per cent of its shipwrecks and the lives of unknown thousands of seamen: 700 from the *Royal James*, wrecked near the Red Sands; more than 200 drowned in the sixty-two vessels known to have been driven on to the Barnard and another ninety from the thirty-three lost on the Sizewell are only the losses that have been witnessed and recorded. If the 'certain ship of Prussia' had ended up on Sizewell bank during a rainstorm instead of on Dunwich beach, it is likely that no one would have seen it. Before its loss and later, screened by night or thick weather, the many other vessels wrecked on the shoals would have gone down unnoticed. Their names unlisted in the legions of the lost, they perished unseen, sunk in the few acres of restless water that cover Sole Bay's killing fields.

3

PILOTAGE AND THE *FAIRY*

Pilotage is navigation close to the coast – and there of course lies the rub. 'The nearer the land the greater the Danger,' wrote Captain Greenville Collins in his *Great Britain's Coasting Pilot* of 1693, 'therefore your Care ought to be the more.' Captain Collins was not codding; under a law enacted by Eleanor of Aquitaine in around 1190, the careless pilot could be put to death.

In the last quarter of the nineteenth century the Sunrise Coast had a cadre of forty-five Trinity pilots to guide the wary sea-captains through the treacherous shoals littering the Thames estuary and the equally dangerous banks extending northward from the Barnard to the Wash. Fifteen were stationed at Lowestoft, fifteen at Southwold and fifteen at Aldeburgh. The Southwold pilots usually put out from the beach in fast gigs or luggers like *Reliance, Jubilee, Cricketer, Swiftsure, Bittern* and *Teazer*, but those with larger vessels such as the 50-ton cutter *Cynthia* and the *Providence* went out from Southwold harbour, touting their skills as far afield as Norway in search of custom. One of five deep-draft pilot cutters in service in 1842 was William Easy's 27-ton *Amicitia*, which drew 8ft (2.4m) water. *Amicitia* is the Latin for 'friendship' and if the same quality could have justly been applied to her skipper his character would probably have been unique. According to the poet Crabbe, Sole Bay pilots were reckoned altogether 'artful, surly and savage'. The poet was putting it too mildly. From what Maggs tells us of their behaviour, to cross a pilot in pursuit of his quarry was to become a candidate for instant death. Racing out to a potential customer in 1814, *Jubilee* cut a rival in two; another was sunk when *Swiftsure* rammed *Reliance* in 1855, and again three years later when *Cricketer* locked oars with *Teazer* so brutally that *Teazer* capsized. Tempers were no sweeter when rivals encountered each other ashore. During a scuffle in their lookout on Long Island Cliff in November 1842, Trinity pilot Abraham Girling was knocked off it by Foster Bokenham and instantly died. In spite of (or because of) Maggs's testimony to his good character, Bokenham was sentenced to four months' imprisonment for manslaughter. He too died tragically in 1869, drowned while fishing.

When not guiding customers through sandbanks, retrieving lost anchors, salvaging wrecks or duffing-up competitors, pilot-boat skippers displayed exemplary courage, often risking their lives to assist vessels in distress and save their shipwrecked crews. In January 1831 Trinity pilots from Southwold rescued the crew of the *Cumberland* when it stranded on the Barnard sand, and, as we shall see, their skilfulness and bravery were to characterise the Southwold lifeboat service when it was established in 1841.

If incoming traffic was plentiful, Trinity pilots were outnumbered two to one by uncertificated pilots called Brummagers. Both groups were employed mainly by vessels on passage from middle-distance ports: Baltic traders with timber, ketches from the West Country with tallow, barquentines from Atlantic Spain or the shores of the Mediterranean with esparto grass, iron ore or fruit, or from Bordeaux with hogsheads of wine for the tables of the better-off. However, local skippers and knowledgeable visitors navigated Sole Bay without assistance, working from memory, casting the occasional glance at a rough sketch copied from a chart, only occasionally using pilots to enter the Blyth river.

The most popular English charts used by British captains in Elizabethan times were Anglicised versions of Lucas Wagenaer's Dutch sea-atlas *Spieghel der Zeevaerdt*, published in London as *The Mariner's Mirror* in 1588. Wagenaer showed us the Dutch knew more about the North Sea than we did, and until Captain Collins brought out his survey of Britain's coasts more than a hundred years later, none of our home-grown chart makers could match them. Collins's labours were Herculean. Five thousand miles of coastline, no national triangulation grid on which to base his surveys, using only a compass, a measuring chain and a lump of lead, it was no wonder he took seven years to complete the work. Published in 1693, his *Coasting Pilot* was a long-lasting success which ran to twelve editions. Its forty-eight charts included plans and views of the Sunrise Coast from Orford Ness to Lowestoft. Along with later charts by Hamand (1794), Chandler (1800) and Steel (1803), they were the staple British charts for navigating Sole Bay until the coming of *A Survey of the Coast of Suffolk from Lowestoff* [sic] *to Orford*, done by Master George Thomas RN in 1824, with the assistance of John Frembly and two youthful midshipmen named Lord and Cudlip.

Using recently completed Ordnance Surveys, measuring instruments such as the improved sextant and the newly invented station-pointer, Thomas constructed charts of much finer accuracy than anything Collins could possibly have come up with, plotting the position of Southwold church to the six-thousandth part of a nautical mile, which is 30cm, or – for any reader who is as long in the tooth as I am – eleven and four-fifths inches.

In one important respect, Thomas's chart is better than any chart we can buy over the counter today. Continuing the practice of Greenville Collins, he drew bearings of crucial daytime leading marks, adding helpful information which could be seen at a glance. On a bearing that leads mariners clear of Dunwich bank, for instance, he wrote '*Covehithe Church will open to the Eastward of the low North East end of Easton Cliff*', and, to reduce the head-scratching among navigators approaching Lowestoft, he wrote '*The High lighthouse, its apparent breadth open to the Left of the Low lighthouse*' on a bearing which would lead them into the Stanford channel and Lowestoft roads (C8 & C9, p.19).

Above: All Saints church at Dunwich was built in the fourteenth century and toppled down the cliffs in 1919. This painting by E.D. Philpot is in Dunwich Museum. (Alan Hale)

Left: The Black Mill on Southwold common, 1798-1894. (Pimple Thompson)

'Do come off it!' urges the twenty-first-century visitor who is shamelessly supping foreign lager on Blackshore. 'Things have moved on a bit since then. It's all done by computers now, so there's no call for such bearings today.'

Step forward William Stannard, sailorman, lifeboatman and fisherman, who's been using bearings on and off for fifty-seven years. Fishing Sole Bay in his *Wyenot* or his *Nonsuch*, he uses them all the time. 'Look you here ...' says Billy, clearing away a jigsaw puzzle depicting a Baltic trader with a juicy bone in its teeth, unrolling a sea-chart and putting a finger into a yawning two-mile gullet between the Sizewell bank and the shore that he pleases to call Hell's Kitchen, '... it's like this: you line up the House in the Clouds with a building which was another water tower...or, wait a minute, was it? Cor, I can't be sure!... Anyway, that bearing will take you to two minesweepers. Then you have to come through above the sweepers. One of them lays one side of the line and one is the other of it. Then, when you've got through above the sweepers and have come abeam of the Coastguard cottages and opened them slightly, why then!, you'll be right on to the *Belle Isle* ...'

'So?'

'... which is the very same *Belle Isle* what you've got in your book!'

'Sorry ... Please go on.'

Billy takes his finger out of Hell's Kitchen, raps his knuckles on the table and glares at me severely. '*Therefore*, when you've got the lighthouse right over the outmost corner of the centre cliff at Southwold, *AWAY YOU HAUL!*'

The practice of printing George Thomas's helpful bearings on the chart has long since been done away with. Except for depicting the red-sectored arcs of Southwold lighthouse, which are not the slightest use to anybody in the daytime, modern charts of Sole Bay require the navigator to draw the bearings for himself.

The 1753 edition of Collins showed only forty soundings between Benacre and Thorpe. Seventy-one years later George Thomas was showing 400. The getting of each sounding required him to be aboard a small open boat, firmly anchored fore and aft, stemming a tidal stream running at speeds of up to 2½ mph and often being pushed sideways by wind. Bracing himself against the ceaseless rocking, he would lift a 3lb sextant to his eye and measure the angle between, say, All Saints church tower in Dunwich and Mr Robinson's house a mile to the south of it by moving the arm of the sextant until a reflected image of All Saints was squatting amidst the begonias blooming on Robinson's front doorstep. That done, he would screw down the arm, squint at a microscopic scale engraved on its outer end and announce the angular distance between All Saints church and the blooming begonias to a shivering Cudlip crouched at his feet. The procedure would then be repeated, substituting a third object such as the Preventive house – nowadays called the Coastguard Cottages – on Minsmere cliff in the place of All Saints church. While Thomas was fixing the boat's position, another crewman would be measuring the depth of water, using a 7lb lump of lead with a hollow base that had been filled with tallow. 'Deep six, less six inches … Mud, wiv a fair pepperin' of sand,' chants the leadsman, peering at the sample of seabed stuck to the tallow. Midshipman Cudlip writes the information in his book, wipes his nose on his sleeve and blows into his chapped hands. His shipmates heave up two anchors, each of which is attached to perhaps 30 fathoms (55m) of waterlogged hempen rope, and row to the next sounding position a quarter of a mile down-tide, where they re-adjust the bandages on their blistered wrists and mumble conventional curses.

Eight hours of this health-promoting activity enables Master Thomas and the leadsman to furnish the midshipman – if the weather has been helpful and I am not underrating their abilities – with the results of between twelve and fifteen casts of the lead. Thomas is then rowed to his parent ship anchored in the bay, where he factors into each sounding various allowances for the barometric pressure, the wind's strength and direction, not forgetting the height of tide at the time of sounding, until the leadsman's 'Deep six …' and all the rest of it can be set down on the chart as **5¼ m.s** and Master George Thomas can totter to his cot.

The finished chart would have been sent to Captain Hurd, the Hydrographer of the Navy, for his scrutiny and approval. Hurd was followed in 1829 by Captain Francis Beaufort, who expanded the hydrographic department and systemised the mapping of the seas to further Britain's role as the leading maritime power and 'render the whole useful for the benefit of navigation and the saving of life'. By 1837 Beaufort was directing the work of thirteen vessels and 800 men, whose surveys ranged from the kelp-infested Strait of Magellan to the sandbanks of Sole Bay. Between the ship surveying the Strait of Magellan and the one doing the same work in Sole Bay lay 7,000 miles of water, but their widely separate endeavours are linked together in history by some curious conjunctions: the two vessels were sisters, they began their major work in the same year and their commanders died tragic deaths.

The better-known is HMS *Beagle*, which set out from Plymouth in December 1831 with seventy-four people, one of whom famously went on to map the origin of species, leaving to *Beagle's* commander the tasks of charting the Strait of Magellan and sailing round the world. Captain Robert FitzRoy of the *Beagle* completed his circumnavigation in four years and nine months at the age of thirty-one. Brave, resourceful, humane, highly intelligent, a gifted mathematician, *Beagle's* commander also had a darker side. 'FitzRoy's temper was a most unfortunate one, and was shown not only by passion but by fits of long-continued moroseness,' wrote Darwin in the course of the voyage. His words were ominous. Though he did much to improve the equipment in Britain's ships and elevate the conditions of its seamen, after a lifetime in the service of his monarch and his country, Robert FitzRoy elevated a razor and cut his own throat.

The second vessel was HMS *Fairy*, one of the hundred-strong Cherokee class of brigs and near-identical sister to the *Beagle*. In the same year in which FitzRoy set off to circumnavigate the world in the *Beagle*, Commander William Hewett set out from Harwich to chart the southern portion of the North Sea in the *Fairy*, and, though photographs and documents can be misleading, judging from the smoothness of his forehead and the size of his family, any fits of depression that Hewett may have suffered during the course of his arduous labours were neither long-lasting nor deeply injurious. Eight years later, now ranking as captain but with the survey still unfinished, Hewett departed from Harwich in the *Fairy* and never returned.

The hows, whys and wherefores that followed his disappearance focused on the state of the weather and the ship. Where was the wind? What strength was it? Was the hull sound? Was *Fairy* so stiff that it rolled its masts over the side, or – much worse – was it so tender as to have capsized? And how old, d'you think, was the rigging, how stout the sails?

'I do not and cannot imagine that any thing very serious could have happened to her,' wrote an officer who had served four years in the *Fairy* under all circumstances and in all weathers. But the *Fairy* has never been found, and so the questions continue.

Though lovely to look at, the Cherokee class of brigs had such a poor reputation that they were known as 'coffins'. An architect's drawing shows a flush upper deck running the whole length, very high bulwarks and a deep waist, features which combined to make them dangerous in heavy weather, when the entire deck might suddenly be filled with 100 tons of water that seriously threatened the stability. FitzRoy countered the design defects by raising *Beagle's* deck 12in (30cm) and by adding a raised fo'c'sle and a poop. How far Hewett was able to improve *Fairy* is difficult to say. From his account of his surveying methods we know it certainly had a poop; it is *likely* that it had a raised fo'c'sle, but whether or not *Fairy's* upper deck had been raised is still to me an open question.

In spite of the shortcomings in their design, both 'coffins' had come through many days and nights of heavy weather without serious damage or loss of life.

The dinghies have raced to the East Barnard buoy and are beating towards Southwold in light winds. Helped by the flood tide, they will travel the seven miles to the finishing line in about forty minutes. (Southwold Sailing Club)

This 1910 compass rose favours the older ways of thinking. Thirty-two compass points, each divided into quarters, are given greater prominence than the modern notation in degrees, the command 'Steer Sou'west by South three-quarters South' sounding more agreeably Nelsonic than 'Steer South twenty-five West'. How an Edwardian helmsman would respond to a twenty-first-century commander who bade him to 'Head Two-Zero-Fiver', one trembles to think.

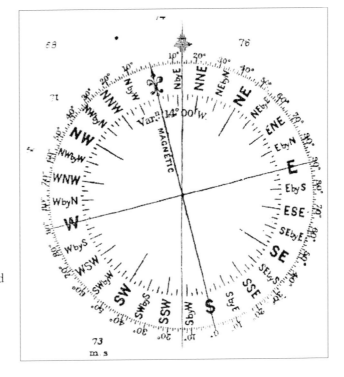

Describing how *Beagle* weathered a gale near Cape Horn, FitzRoy wrote:

> At three in the morning ... the vessel lurched so deeply and the main-mast bent and quivered so much that I ... took in the main-topsail ... leaving set only the storm-trysails ... and fore-staysail. At ten, there was so continued and heavy a rush of wind that even the diminutive trysails oppressed the vessel too much, and [so] they were still farther reduced. [Three hours later] the sea had risen to a great height, and I was anxiously watching the successive waves, when three huge rollers approached, whose size and steepness told me that our sea-boat, good as she was, would be sorely tried.
>
>   Having steerage way, the vessel met and rose over the first unharmed, but, of course, her way was checked; the second deadened her way completely, throwing her off the wind; and the third great sea, taking her right a-beam, turned her so far over that all the lee bulwark ... was 2 or 3ft under water. For a moment our position was critical; but, like a cask, she rolled back again, though with some feet of water over the whole deck. Had another sea then struck her the little ship might have been numbered among the many of her class which have disappeared: but the crisis was past – she shook the sea off her through the ports and was none the worse – excepting the loss of a lee-quarter boat, which ... was dipped under water and torn away ... [and] Mr Darwin's collections in the poop and forecastle cabins on deck were much injured ... The roller which hove us almost on our beam ends was the highest and most hollow that I have seen ... yet so easy was our little vessel that nothing was injured besides the boat, the netting (washed away), and one chronometer.

The seas off Cape Horn are higher and longer than any Hewett could possibly have met with – but they are no less steep. If a force nine North Sea gale comes up against a 2-knot tide it will push up the water into vertical slabs. When the 8,000-ton tanker *Nuculana* encountered these conditions off the Kentish coast in 1947, it needed only one toppling megalith to crush its windward lifeboats into matchwood.

    The 233-ton *Fairy* was 90ft long, 25ft broad, and drew 11ft water. Her mainmast was about 130ft (39.6m) tall and her jib-boom projected about 40ft (12m) ahead of her bows. Both *Fairy* and *Beagle* were fitted with a third (mizzen) mast to improve their manoeuvrability. Built in 1826, *Fairy* was still a fairly youthful vessel in 1840 and so her frame would not have been seriously weakened by the ravages of age. Though she would have been worked hard from April to December during the eight years of her North Sea survey, any incidental damage would have been repaired during her annual winter lay-up at Woolwich, and any lost gear – such as 'Christopher's anchor' which disappeared in 1836 off Lowestoft – would have been quickly replaced. So we can confidently assume that *Fairy* was a strong, well-tried vessel in sound condition, adequately equipped to meet the challenges of the North Sea. Apart from being very deep-waisted, everything about her structure argued strongly for her safety.

    The same was true of *Fairy*'s officers and crew. Captain William Hewett knew the character of the North Sea and the coast of East Anglia better than any man alive.

Between Yarmouth and the Texel he had discovered curious tidal nodes where the sea level scarcely altered with the ebb and flow of the tide. He had mapped the approaches to Yarmouth and the dangerous Hewett Ridges twelve miles offshore. Closer to Sole Bay he had charted the gatways leading into Lowestoft roads and had instigated the mooring or re-positioning of the fifty-seven lightships and buoys that would mark the dangers of the Sunrise Coast. His well-experienced officers included his very capable brother-in-law Richard Stevens, who ranked as master, and the long-enduring Frederick Cudlip, now a lieutenant, who were assisted in their duties by midshipmen like the captain's seventeen-year-old son William B. Hewett, who had already logged more than thirteen months' service in *Fairy* when she departed on her final voyage.

Accompanied by the support tender *Violet* and helped on her way by an ebbing tide and a light north-westerly breeze, *Fairy* left Harwich at midday on Thursday 12 November 1840 on passage to Yarmouth, where Hewett was to inspect a new device for dredging the Stanford channel. According to Cudlip, he expected to complete the 130-mile round trip before midnight on the Saturday.

Outside Harwich the wind fell calm. Thinking the weather looked favourable, Hewett instructed his lieutenant to go aboard *Violet* with two of *Fairy*'s crew and survey the waters off nearby Felixtowe. The order saved Cudlip's life. He anchored the tender off Felixstowe at four in the afternoon, leaving *Fairy* drifting slowly towards Orford Ness, where he expected Hewett would also anchor for the night when the tide set against him at six.

The lieutenant turned in with every hope of passing a restful evening but it turned out to be anything but. At ten the light offshore breeze swung to the SE and strengthened, transforming the coast between Harwich and Yarmouth into a dangerous lee shore. Weighing anchor at midnight amid a gusting wind and difficult seas, Cudlip struggled back to Harwich, arriving there at three on Friday morning with torn sails and a broken anchor – and the great gale fell upon the Sunrise Coast.

It had already devastated shipping far to the west, sinking an unknown number of vessels off Bideford, driving three others ashore at Brighton, swamping the Isle of Wight ferry and causing immense damage among the craft moored at Southampton. To Beaufort at the Admiralty, the news coming from the eastern coast was even more disquieting. At Sunderland the gale had been described as a hurricane, a brig had been driven ashore at Walberswick, another sunk off Lowestoft and a third wrecked near Yarmouth. Six Dutch skutes had gone ashore between Kessingland and Pakefield, a Humber keel had been wrecked on Southwold beach and a brig had been lost on the Barnard sand. An anxious Beaufort wrote Lieutenant Cudlip for information.

Cudlip penned a four-page reply, describing the gale and giving Hewett's probable reactions. At Felixstowe, he wrote, the gale had started at SSE, had later veered SW and had blown from that direction with increasing violence through the whole of Friday. He thought Hewett would have headed eastward from

Orford Ness so as to clear the coastal shoals and would have subsequently run downwind with the SW gale to seek shelter at some port in Norway.

On both counts he was wrong. Synoptic weather-charts were still in their infancy, so Cudlip was unable to see a larger picture. Thirty-five miles north of Harwich James Maggs recorded the 'tremendous gale' had blown on to Kilcock Cliff from a crucially different point, the ESE, 112½ degrees away from SW. One hundred and twenty-five miles farther north it had blown force twelve from seaward, making Norway unreachable. So, if *Fairy* had indeed run before the wind from a latitude just a few miles above Orford Ness, she would have been driven into Sole Bay and run aground on the Sunrise Coast.

Notwithstanding his hopeful thought about Norway, in the weeks following the gale Cudlip and his superiors hedged their bets by searching both far and near. No source of information went untapped, no sleeve went unplucked, no rumour went unqueried. A paddle steamer was dispatched to Norway; revenue cutters scoured the Leman and Ower banks; incoming fishing smacks were questioned, and Cudlip hastened to Aldeburgh to interrogate a Mr Fuller about certain items of wreckage said to have been found on the beach.

For six weeks Beaufort sifted through a mountain of reports. Some were baseless rumours; Cudlip learned that no wreckage had been washed up at Aldeburgh for months; some told of sightings of the *Fairy* that proved to be mistaken: a vessel anchored off the Leman bank turned out to be a timber ship repairing its damaged spars. Among the very few certainties was the sombre information that a distinctive piece of grating picked up thirty-five miles ESE of Lowestoft was definitely from the *Fairy*, and that it could only have come adrift if the ship had been breaking up. 'These circumstances,' wrote the harbourmaster at Harwich, 'afford a melancholy presumption of the ship's fate.' By the end of December it was impossible to disagree.

Why did she founder? Cudlip had written gloomily that, 'Being so very deep waisted', *Fairy* had probably sunk under a great weight of water. He was almost certainly right. The high swells from the north and the cross-seas from the east would have thrown up slab-sided, irregular crests. Although a fourth huge roller off Cape Horn just 'might have' sunk FitzRoy's *Beagle*, the same number of smaller North Sea storm-waves would have been more than enough to crush the *Fairy*.

But where was her wreck? Anxious to retrieve Hewett's invaluable charts and the Admiralty's expensive surveying equipment, the paddle steamer *Lightning* and a cutter swept the seabed between four miles south of Lowestoft and one mile north of it, but *Fairy* was not found.

Looked at a century and a half later from a reclining armchair, Cudlip's information suggests that the steamer ought to have swept much farther afield. He had told Beaufort the débris had been picked up thirty-five miles from Lowestoft, which implies that if *Fairy* had indeed sunk 'near Lowestoft', the wreckage would have had to travel at a speed of 1½mph *against* a force ten gale and *across* the tidal streams. Wouldn't she more likely have sunk farther offshore, nearer to where the floating wreckage had been found? The armchair historian leafs through his tidal atlases, feeds figures into his computer, and unfolds a copy of a deposition from the Seamen's Loyal Standard Association stating that at ten o'clock on the Friday morning the crew of the brig *Alpha* had seen 'a warlike vessel' roll on her side, come briefly upright and straightaway sink in 17 fathoms of water 'between East Ness & Southwould'. The amateur analyst unrolls Hewett's chart (C10, p.20), moves his pencil to a position seven and a half miles seaward of Easton Bavents and draws a small black cross to mark what seems a more likely area for the North Sea to have taken the life of its greatest surveyor and deprived a grieving woman of her husband, her eldest son and her brother.

A padded hessian parcel, 4ft square and some 6in thick, supposed by the maidservant who received it to be either a picture or a mirror, was delivered to a house in Harwich in the spring of 1842, together with the following letter:

My Dear Madam,

The engraving of the southern sheet of the North Sea has been at length completed, and is this day published; and every copy of it that circulates throughout this empire, or finds its way among Foreign nations will carry with it irresistible proof of the ardour, sagacity, and perseverance which your lamented husband lavished on its construction; and while it revives our grief for the loss of such a man, we cannot but feel gratified in knowing that the innumerable copies which will go down to posterity will each of them be the most appropriate and most eloquent monument that could be devised to perpetuate his fame.

The parcel contained a framed presentation copy of the chart, and the letter concluded with an assurance of the faithful friendship of its sender, Francis Beaufort.

4

SHIPS AND CARGOES

As a boy living far inland, my chief source of shipping information was E. Keble Chatterton's *Ships and the Sea*, an inflammatory black bible that pictured seas thronged by vast trading fleets powered entirely by diesel or steam. So far as the North Sea was concerned, the picture was untrue.

Steam power came late to Sole Bay. The world's first commercial steamship had appeared on the River Clyde in 1802 but half a lifetime later Maggs was still recording that every one of Southwold's vessels was going about its mostly lawful business under sail alone. Not until the first decade of the twentieth century could the harbourmaster at Blackshore point to a steamer with Southwold as its adoptive home port, and even then it would have not have been a merchantman but a tug.

Though the tonnage of foreign-going sailing ships entering and leaving British ports fell from 80 per cent of the total in 1860 to only 8 per cent in 1900, in the home-trade fleets the decline of sail was much less rapid. Indeed, in some North Sea ports the national downward slide was corrected by the spectacular local revival witnessed by the Northumbrian Walter Runciman in 1851–74, when the number of sailing colliers trading from Blyth almost doubled, shooting upwards from 118 to 201. And even at the outbreak of the First World War forty years later, sailing ships were not uncommon sights. Three hundred and fifteen pages of beautifully penned but terribly sombre figures in *Lloyd's War Losses* testify that almost one in four of the 6,927 vessels sunk by the Germans in the First World War were under sail. Yet, in spite of the very many sinkings and the dominance of steam, in the Baltic and the North Sea the sail-trading tonnage survived until the 1970s.

'Sir! I never know where I am with tonnage, sir!' wailed a borrower of *Ships and the Sea* before he absconded to Australia with it. 'There's so many sorts! What's the difference, sir, and why?'

'It's all to do with making money. Anyone with eyes can see that even the boxiest-looking seagoing hulk has a number of curves in it, especially in its foreparts and rear. However, in order to maximise their money-making the foxy medieval tax-gatherers pretended that the hull was shaped *exactly* like a box, so enabling them to maximise its 'tunnage' or 'tons burthen' – and, of course, their personal rake-offs – by simply multiplying its length by its extreme breadth and depth of hold in feet and dividing the result by a hundred. This practice went on almost unaltered until 1773, when a more complicated formula was introduced. The new formula, confusingly known these days as Builders' Old Measurement, lasted until the building of slimmer, sharp-ended clipper ships and transatlantic steamships in the mid-nineteenth century prompted further political twiddles whereby a merchant ship was measured either by its gross tonnage, which is the total internal volume of the hull and its above-deck cabins etcetera reckoned at 100 cu.ft to the ton, or by its nett tonnage, which is its cargo-carrying capacity …'

'But, sir! How *heavy* was a Ton Burthen compared with a Gross Ton?'

'It depended on the nature of the cargo. The Victorians reckoned they could usually stow about 2 tons weight of cargo into every measured ton of ship.'

At this moment the swelling tide of nautical history was diverted by the sight of a tea lady under full sail with a cargo of biscuits.

'However,' I went on, when she had discharged it and breezed on to her next port of call, 'since you will be more interested in comparing the sizes of ships than in taxing their contents, we'd better ignore nett tonnage and just remember that the standard indicators of size are Tons Burthen for any vessel built before 1773, Builders' Old Measurement Tonnage for anything between 1773 and about 1860, and Gross Tonnage after the 1860s.'

My inquisitor jiggled his pencil at arm's length above his head and clamoured, 'But what about Displacement Tonnage and Deadweight Tonnage and Panama Tonnage and – COR! LOOK WHAT IT SAYS ON THIS YACHT PHOTO, SIR! – "*Brave Puddleduck of Leptis Magna*, built 1962, 9 tons Thames Measurement", sir! – WHAT'S THAMES MEASUREMENT, SIR?' – at which moment I could have strangled him.

A typical vessel crossing Sole Bay in medieval times would have been a flat-bottomed workhorse called a cog. Built in the 1320s and measuring about 50 tons burthen, the Dunwich-built cog *Margarete* had bottom planking laid solidly edge-to-edge, though its upper planks would still (because habits die harder in Suffolk) have been overlapped at their edges in the clinker system used by the shipwrights who built the Buss Creek longboat. The cog was driven by a single large squaresail hung from a horizontal yard that could be swivelled about the mast according to the direction of the wind. Perhaps steered by an innovative rudder that had appeared in northern Europe during the last half of the twelfth century, a rudder that hung solidly on the centreline instead of dangling limply, as in Beowulf's day, from the side, the fourteenth-century Sole Bay cog was built to carry mainly corn, wine, wool or hides, with added fore- and stern-castles to house a bristly phalanx of archers in the likely event of her being commandeered by the reigning monarch to prosecute his everlasting squabbles with the French. The archers may have been happy with their castles, but it is likely that the added windage would have aborted many a sailing sally against fair France.

Borne on the varnished wings of history, by the time we arrive at the Battle of Sole Bay in 1672, cogs and their capacious but clumsy successors such as hulks and carracks had given way to larger vessels with somewhat handier rigs. One of the most commercially successful types was the Dutch *fluyt*. Here in the *fluyt*, the cog's impressively large but sometimes uncontrollable squaresail has been replaced by a proportionally smaller sail and, hanging from a yard above it, a supplementary rectangular topsail. Triangular fore-and-aft sails in front of a foremast and another on a lateen yard on a third mast near the stern enabled *fluyts* to work to windward more effectively than cogs – and do it more cheaply too, leaving Sir Walter Ralegh complaining bitterly that whereas an English 100-tonner needed thirty sailors to handle it, a *fluyt* of the same size could hurtle past him crewed by only ten. The bulbous hulls from the Land of Tulips collared a large share of European sea-trade, and their tremendous tumblehome and closer-winded rig are paralleled in the work of English architects like Sir Anthony Deane, MP for Harwich and designer of the 70-gun *Resolution*, which fought in the Battle of Sole Bay alongside the doomed flagship *Royal James*.

The most numerous listing in the shipwreck chronology is the brig. Between their first appearance in 1802 and their last in 1895, brigs and snows, their near-identical sisters, comprised 27 per cent of the bay's shipwrecks. The earliest is the *Fire Ship*, which Maggs records as sinking 'opposite Sand Pit', which was probably at Easton, but it is likely that many earlier, unclassified wrecks in the Larns' *Shipwreck Index of the British Isles* were also brigs, particularly if – like the *Elizabeth* wrecked in 1743 – they were trading from Newcastle with cargoes of coal.

Two-masted, square-rigged and wide-hipped, North Sea collier brigs were the legendary mothers of the nation's seamen. James Cook learned his basic skills in them, and quite a few of the world's navies were using brigs to train their boy intake well into the first decade of the twentieth century. Their work as survey ships has been touched on in Chapter 3; an insight into their more usual mercantile role is given in a newspaper clip about the brig *Victoria* that Maggs inserted into his diary.

The *Victoria* had left England in the late spring of 1852 on a 3,500-mile journey through the Mediterranean, the Sea of Marmora, the Bosphorus and the Black Sea to the Russian port of Tanganrog on the Sea of Azov, where she loaded a cargo of linseed before setting out on her homeward voyage on 28 July. Buffeted by adverse Mediterranean winds and currents, *Victoria* averaged only seventeen miles a day. Three months after leaving Tanganrog she ran into a heavy westerly gale in the Bay of Biscay and was thrown on to her beam ends by tremendous seas. The linseed cargo shifted, listing her 'several streakes' of planking to starboard, and it was in this perilous condition that on 31 October the *Victoria* struggled into Falmouth, where her cargo was re-stowed and secured before she set off again for Hull. After rounding the South Foreland the master headed northward through the Downs to make a night passage between the Kentish Knock and Galloper lightships. Unable to pick out the Knock light among the lanterns displayed by numberless other ships, the *Victoria* ran aground in strong winds on the Knock bank. With the vessel bumping heavily on the sand and lurching wildly amidst the breakers, the crew succeeded in nursing the ship over the shoal and letting go two anchors in deeper water, though

Above: The side rudders salvaged from Sole Bay probably came from vessels such as the cog depicted on this seal of a merchant of Dunwich dated 1199. Perhaps Osmond Ferro's ship was steered by a centreline rudder shown on an Ipswich town seal of the same date. The two rudder systems co-existed for more than 200 years.

Right: Modern replica of a cog, with a Viking cargo-carrier lying alongside. Both are equipped with centreline rudders. (Mike Stammers)

not before the seas sweeping across the hull had carried away all the movable items such as boats, pig pens, chicken coops and the customary 'Little Somethings for My Darling' that had been lashed down on deck.

At daylight, even worse conditions of wind and tide compelled the master to cut the anchor cables and allow his vessel to be driven northward. Damaged and leaking, her crew exhausted by continual spells at the pumps, *Victoria* was sighted off Southwold on 7 November flying signals of distress. The yawl *John Bull* put out from the shore with a party of beachmen who took over the pumping and piloted the stricken vessel into Lowestoft harbour. Five days later *John Bull* and the beachmen were paid £400 for their services, each receiving £9 – the equivalent of three months' wages.

The last brig to be wrecked in Sole Bay was the *James & Eleanor* in 1895, though a number of these rugged craft were still trading as lately as 1976.

Why then, the reader is entitled to ask, did these versatile vessels disappear? The dominance of steamships was not the only reason. Fore-and-aft-rigged vessels were cheaper to build and maintain, their gear was lighter to handle, and they were more efficient to windward than square rigs. Changes in the nineteenth-century weather pattern may also have worked against the brigs. Robert Simper suggests that in the first half of the century the prevailing winds on the East Coast were more often north-easterly, which would have favoured the square-rigged collier brigs on their laden southbound passages. However, argues Simper, gradual

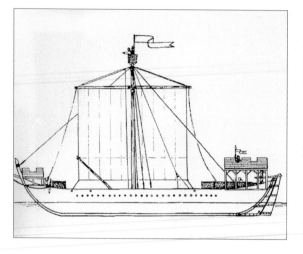

Left: Built at Newcastle about 1294, this huge 120ft (36.5m) galley was one of twenty ordered by Edward II from various ports in his kingdom, including Dunwich.

Below left: Fifteenth-century Sole Bay fishing boat.

Below right: Tudor cargo carrier. Note the rotund stern.

Seventeenth-century herring buss. (Pimple Thompson)

Above: Revenue cutter, 1750.

Left: The bulbous stern of this Dutch *fluyt* would have been a familiar hull-shape on the Sunrise Coast during the sixteenth and seventeenth centuries. (From an engraving by Frans Huys in 1565, after Pieter Breughel the Elder)

changes in the weather during the latter half of the century shifted the prevailing wind-direction towards the south, which would have favoured the building of closer winded fore-and-aft rigs.

Shipowners took the opportunity to drive down costs even further by manning their vessels with ever-smaller crews, a practice which culminated in the coasting barges of the late nineteenth and early twentieth centuries. The barge *Topaz*, wrecked on passage from London to Yarmouth in 1885, carried a crew of three, and by the last half of the twentieth century Sole Bay seamen like Billy Stannard were handing, reefing and steering 'Channel-bangers' of up to 200 tons which sailed the coasts in charge of only two men and a boy.

Their spritsail barges have a lasting place in the maritime history of East Anglia. Descendants of Captain W. Ling, who was tragically lost in the *Topaz*, are still associated with barge-chartering in Essex. Dick Durham at *Yachting Monthly* tells of drinking with Spiro Ling in the Butt & Oyster at Pin Mill on the River Orwell. Asked during a visit from Canada what he thought of the brave new world outside the county of Essex, the old man replied: 'Well, thass a wonderful place. You can stand on the top of a mountain and see for a hundred miles … and there's nuthin' to look at.'

To the passengers and crew in the barge *Martin Luther*, the views from the lowlier hills of Suffolk must have seemed more seriously attractive. Fleeing from Nazi persecution in Germany, a shipload of Jewish refugees reputedly sailed the *Martin Luther* into Southwold in the spring of 1939 to escape the impending holocaust.

One hopes they prospered here. Had they crossed the North Sea fifty years earlier they would have found themselves among British crews who were closely fettered by grinding poverty and toil. For although the fore-and-aft-rigged vessels crossing Sole Bay are said to have carried fewer crew per ton than square-riggers, sporadic details of crew numbers in the Chronology show that this was by no means always the case. The wages bill for the 100-ton schooner *Margaret* with its crew of five may have been 50 per cent smaller than that of the brig *Henry's*, which was about the same tonnage but carried ten seamen, but other brigs were plying the North Sea with proportionally smaller crews. The bigger the brig, the heavier the workload. A sailor in the schooner *Margaret* would have worked just 20 tons of ship, but aboard the 233-ton brig *Pallas* and the 263-ton *Sheraton Grange* he would have been required to work almost 30 tons, and if he had the fatal misfortune to have shipped in the *Reindeer* that was wrecked on the Barnard in 1878, he would have been working more than 33 tons.

Some of what is now called 'the downsizing of the workforce' was brought about by the genius of Victorian engineers, whose steam-driven donkey engines could pump the bilges, winch cargo from the holds or turn the capstan with much greater gusto than could a dozen wet and weary foredeck hands who had little more than porridge in their stomachs. With occasional help from a donkey engine and devices like Jarvis winches for bracing the heavy steel yards – the largest of which was 95ft (29m) in length and weighed 5 tons (5,080kg) – by the 1930s each of the twenty-eight men and boys in the 3,116-ton *Moshulu*, built 1904, were working an incredible 111 tons of ship, an achievement which far outstripped that of steamer crews during the period 1914-18, when the eleven cargo steamships sunk in Sole Bay averaged the much inferior tons/crew ratio of just 86:1.

The benefits of mechanisation were often cancelled out by overloading and under-manning. In spite of three Merchant Shipping Acts between 1854–76, palm-grease and peculation meant that the regulations were only patchily enforced. Why else was the 233-ton *Content* allowed to put to sea in 1861 with only a five-man crew when other ships of the same size were carrying eight or ten?

Among the more comely fore-and-aft rigs were schooners. Their two or more tall masts untrammelled by many cross-yards, schooners offered smaller angles to the wind than brigs did, even when they carried rectangular topsails on their foremast. Though the type is said to have originated in Massachusetts as early as 1713, the first wrecking of a schooner in Sole Bay did not happen until 1841, when the *Star* of Perth foundered after being driven many miles south on a passage from Yarmouth to Sunderland. In the fifty years following *Star's* sinking, fourteen more schooners were lost in the bay. One is described by the lifeboat historian Ernest Cooper:

At 4 a.m. on the 4th December 1848, during a sou-west gale, the schooner *Ury* of Sunderland, bound to Dunkirk with coal, struck on the Barnard, and at 8 a.m.

The brig *Berbice*, built in 1816 at Southwold for a local owner engaged in the Mediterranean trade, coming up in a quartering breeze under topsails and jib. The Mediterranean connection is emphasised by the lateen-rigged feluccas. A windlass from the *Berbice* was trawled up in the 1970s and lay for a time on Blackshore. (Great Yarmouth Museums)

she was observed from Kessingland dismasted. The men there tried to launch their yawl but found too much sea and a man was sent on horseback to Southwold. The Lifeboat [*Solebay*] was launched and reached the wreck in about half an hour. She was on her broadside with the decks blown out and a tremendous sea breaking over her. The Lifeboat anchored to windward and veering down rescued a man fast to a rope amongst the wreck. Another man was seen and ropes thrown to him, but ineffectually, as he was in a state of insensibility; thereupon John Fish, one of the lifeboatmen, got on to one of the masts which was floating attached to the wreck and *running along it* [my italics] succeeded in rescuing the man in the circumstances of the greatest peril, having the utmost difficulty in breaking his grip of the rigging. During this service the lifeboat struck heavily on the sand and was nearly swamped with water. There was too much sea to land at Kessingland so the lifeboat made for Lowestoft, arriving there at 11 a.m. with the two men in a very exhausted state. The captain and two others had been drowned and shortly after the rescue the wreck wholly disappeared.

Ten days later Ben Herrington, coxswain of *Solebay*, received the following letter:

Dear Friends,
I have taken this favourable opportunity of writing to you these few lines hoping this will find you all in good health as leaves booth of us a great deal better than we

The 56-ton barge *Marjorie* on the River Thames. (Philip Kershaw)

The boomie barge *Harwich* navigating the shoal at the harbour entrance. The taut line from her bows is attached to the paddle tug *Pendennis*, which was owned by Billie May. (William Stannard)

The *Pendennis* was a permanent resident during the building of the harbour in 1906–8. (*Alfred Corry Museum*)

A Sole Bay beach punt of the 1890s. (Robert Malster)

was [.] When we got home we was very stif with the bruses we had about us ... We have had a letter saying the master is picked up [;] his brother went away directly to see him buried [.] If ever you go to lowstoft give our kind love to the landlord for his kindness to us [.] I hope god will reward you all ...

Give my kind love to that man that took me of the wreck, but not to him alone but to you all. So no more at present but ever remain your wellwishers.

Charles Holley and John Courtnell

Though brigs appear in the wreck list more often than any other type of trader, the most numerous losses were probably sustained by the fishing fleets, which were made up of several different sizes and types. Small Sole Bay punts, clinker-built, single- or two-masted luggers with quadrilateral fore-and-aft sails, were launched from the beach. At sea, attached to their drift-nets or trawling, unable to react quickly to changes of wind, they were liable to be capsized by sudden gusts. An unnamed Walberswick boat was upset in this way by a squall in 1802 with the loss of two men, another was lost in 1832 off Easton, and a third went down in 1845, drowning the skipper's two young sons. The sinking of these three nameless punts was at least itemised and noted. How many more beach boats were wrecked is impossible to say, but it is likely that a great many of the 250 vessels lost between Cromer and Thorpe Ness in the storms of 1770 and 1789 were small boats like Southwold punts.

Larger fishing vessels like smacks and dandies from Yarmouth and Lowestoft usually worked the offshore grounds such as Smith's Knoll and the Dogger Bank rather than Sole Bay but they too were often driven inshore and wrecked. Though gale-force easterlies sank the dandies *John & Susannah* and *Olive Branch*, heavy winds were not the only cause of fishing-boat disasters; heavy eyelids played a part in them, too. The 'Wakey-wakey!' bellowed into my sixteen-year-old ears by a First Mate who was vigorously kicking my backside in 1946 for not reporting the glimmer of a light while supposedly on lookout was the sort of high-quality remedial education which might have saved fourteen ships, five of them fishermen, run down and sunk in light or moderate weather between 1856 and 1907 by vessels that were neglecting to keep their eyes peeled.

In times of war, fishing fleets were sitting ducks. One in four of the 772 vessels sunk by the Germans in 1915 was engaged in fishing, as too were thirty-two (out of the worldwide total of forty-five) sunk off Scarborough and Spurn Head on three of the worst days of the First World War in September 1916. By this date, most boats in the fleets based at northerly ports such as Grimsby were steam-driven vessels of between 110-170 tons. Further south on the Sunrise Coast, fishing fleets comprised smaller craft that were increasingly driven by steam, though even as late as the 1920s they still numbered a sprightly cavalcade of sail-powered smacks and dandies as well as sprinkling of zulus and fifies that continued to make the traditional autumn migration from Scotland to harvest East Anglian herring.

The largest sailing vessel wrecked in the bay was the 106-gun *Royal James*, 1,416 tons, 131ft (40m) long, crippled by gunfire from Admiral van Brakel's *Groot Hollandia* during the Battle of Sole Bay in 1672 and sunk later in the day by the fireship *Vrede*.

The battle was a bloodbath. Never before or since has anyone on Kilcock Cliff seen so great a fleet of warships nor so many deaths. Between dawn and dusk on 28 May, 45,000 human beings gave each other hell. A combined English and French fleet of 128 ships carrying 5,500 guns and 24,000 men had been surprised by a Netherlands fleet of 106 ships with 4,484 guns and 20,732 men. The English had been literally caught with their pants down. Many ships were lying on the beach, having their bottoms cleaned, their crews camped on the dunes, shitting among the sandhills. When the English had buttoned up their breeches and sailed north to do battle, they beheld their Gallic brothers-in-arms hurrying south in obedience to secret orders from Catholic Louis XIV to leave their Protestant English allies in the lurch. It was 172 years before the two nations could patch up the *entente cordiale*.

There was lots of smoke in Sole Bay on that fateful day in 1672, most of it coming from 10,000 cannon belching flames and sixty-six kamikaze fireships trying to immolate themselves by wilfully crashing into the largest enemy vessel in view. With visibility less than 200m in the smoke, not many did. Enough, however, for the cannon and the fireships to sink a dozen vessels, kill 4,750 men and injure 800.

The English sank the 54-gun *Josua* and two fireships, and captured the 48-gun *Stavoren*. Another hefty Dutchman blew up while making repairs. The Dutch sank HMS *Royal James*, the newest and largest warship in the navy, along with six smaller vessels, including at least three fireships. *Royal James* is said to have sunk near the Red Sand but no remains were ever found. On balance, it was victory to the Dutch.

Naming the largest merchant-sailing vessel to be wrecked in the bay is more difficult. Judged by the size of its crew, it could have been the Genoese barque *Rosette Patrone*, tonnage unrecorded, driven ashore in 1881 at Minsmere by a force eleven easterly that drowned all fifteen aboard. On the other hand, the 520-ton barque *Palestine*, wrecked in the same gale with only a nine-strong crew, may have been larger, for *Rosette Patrone* had been attempting a difficult 1,500-mile passage from North Shields to Genoa in the depths of winter, so her master may have shipped a proportionally larger crew than did the *Palestine*, which was on a much shorter passage from Dover to Hartlepool. A much likelier candidate is the Norwegian *Nordhavet*, wrecked below Gun Hill in 1887 with a crew of fourteen. Given a nett tonnage of 607 by the Norwegians yet *grossing* only 610 in the *Shipwreck Index*, *Nordhavet* still appears to have been far larger than any other sailing merchantman lost in Sole Bay. However, doubts begin to arise if we compare her linear measurements with those of the *Idun*. The *Index* gives *Idun*'s length as 130ft (39.6m), beam 30ft (9.1m), and gross tonnage as 395, yet according to Norwegian records she measured 139.7ft by 30.7ft (42.4m x 9.4m), only 3m shorter and 1.2m narrower than *Nordhavet*, and had a compensatory depth that was somewhat greater, which makes it hard to believe that *Nordhavet* could have been half as large again as *Idun*.

However problematic it is to compare their sizes, we can at least be fairly certain that the largest sailing merchantman to be wrecked in the bay must have been a three-masted barque. Square-rigged on the fore and main masts and gaff-rigged on the mizzen, middle-size three-masters like *Idun* and *Nordhavet* commonly sailed the routes from the Baltic to the Mediterranean, though others made long-distance passages that began in the Americas, Africa or the Far East and ended thousands of miles later with their crossing Sole Bay on the way to North Sea or Baltic ports. Among them was the 411-ton *Elissa*. Built in 1877 at Aberdeen for Liverpool owners, *Elissa's* worldwide trading career lasted more than seventy years, under a motley of rigs, names and nationalities until she was sold out of the Swedish merchant marine in 1966 to Greek owners as a motor vessel. (Impeccably restored, *Elissa* now sails under the Stars and Stripes from Galveston.) The much larger early twentieth-century barques like the 1,849-ton *Mount Stewart*, the 2,196-ton *Chelmsford* and the 3,116-ton *Moshulu* plied the trans-ocean routes between Britain and South America, Australia and the Far East, and so they crossed Sole Bay more rarely, returning in ballast to their home ports in Britain, Germany or Finland only for their autumnal lay-ups. Except for the *Olivebank*, mined and sunk off the Danish coast in 1939, these twentieth-century trans-oceanic barques crossed the North Sea without loss.

Compared to some steamer wrecks, *Nordhavet* and *Idun* were small fry. At 473ft (144m), three-quarters the length of Southwold's latest pleasure pier, the 8,641-ton SS *Magdapur* is not only the longest wreck in the bay, but, being twenty times bigger than *Idun*, it is also by far the largest. With dozens of wiry Lascar stokers shovelling tons of best Tyne coal into her boilers every four hours to keep her steaming along at her maximum speed of 13.5 knots, the Brocklebank liner *Magdapur* was sunk off Thorpe Ness in the first days of the Second World War. The second mate, probably on watch on the bridge, and five Lascars in the boiler room were killed by the explosion, but seventy-four of her complement were rescued by two steamships and the Aldeburgh lifeboat *Abdy Beauclerk* in the first wartime service by a British lifeboat.

Though ships varied widely in their sizes, it was as nothing when compared with their cargoes. For smelliness and sheer variety, the really ancient North Sea cargoes took some beating. In 1293 eleven ships from Friesland put into Scarborough with 20,000 resinous, sweet-smelling boards, ninety-nine barrels pitch, 261 casks acrid wood ash, forty-five barrels butter, twenty-two lasts malodorous seal blubber, twenty-three lasts herring, fifty-two lasts and nineteen dickers of hides from odiferous oxen, horses, goats, seals, calves and lambs, 500 hare skins, fifteen and a half bundles of popel and strandelin (kinds of fur), 2,800 dried stockfish, 300 bowstaves, four crapping goshawks and a barrel of wax.

'SIR! WHAT'S A LAST AND A DICKER?' hooted a ghostly Australian from half a world below my pillow.

'It all depended,' I heard myself murmur. 'As a straightforward measure of weight, a last was 2 short tons, 4,000lb or 1.81 metric tons, but if you were dealing

Wearing a discarded bowler hat liberally coated with tar, the skipper has been out a-catching sprats. (Sailors' Reading Room/Alan Hale)

Shorn of its topmasts, a schooner lies at Walberswick quay. At the left end of the trees a tall marker, still in place in 2008, warns that anchoring is forbidden because a telegraph cable lies across the riverbed. The bridge in the foreground spanned Salt Creek. (*Alfred Corry* Museum)

A single steamer and two spritsail barges among this thicket of masts on Blackshore are outnumbered by scores of zulus that have followed the herring down the coast from Scotland. The all-black vessels first appeared during the Zulu War of 1878-9, hence their name. (Robert Malster)

in wool it was 4,368lb or twelve sackfuls, and if you were buying or selling grain or malt it was ten quarters, which was eighty bushels …'

'Are you making this up, sir?'

'… but if you were trading in fish, a last would be twelve barrels of herring, though if they happened to be red herring or pilchards, the figure would have been somewhat larger …'

'How much larger?'

'It depended on where you were doing the deal and the century you were doing it in. Sometimes they reckoned 10,000 herring to the last but at other times it varied between 12,000 and 13,200 …'

'You *are* making it up!'

'Hang on a bit … but a dicker of hides was always, so far back as I can discover, always just ten.'

'Strewth! No wonder we had to send you Rupert Murdoch.'

Coal was arguably the filthiest but certainly the commonest cargo to cross Sole Bay or to sink in it. In 1830, well over 2 million tons of the stuff was shipped from the Tyne in 11,226 coastal voyages. By luck and good seamanship, none was lost in the bay during that year, unlike in 1852, when eight of the eleven vessels wrecked were carrying coal. Most of it would have gone straight to the bottom and stayed there but marketable quantities must have been washed up on the beaches, though Maggs doesn't say so. In fact, it wasn't often that James Maggs named any goods that he auctioned; 'effects', 'furniture', 'wreck and stores' more common entries in his diary than the intriguing medley of *papier mâché* goods and firearms he sold for a shadowy (but not shady) gentleman bearing the name of O'Hare. However, though Maggs merely records that he 'Sold coals' salved from the schooner *Spring* that was wrecked in 1852 on Southwold bar, he attaches a newspaper clipping that paints a fuller picture, from which we gather that the *Spring* had sailed from Middlesbrough with a cargo of coal for Messrs Stratbarn and Paul of Halesworth in the depths of winter. Arriving off Southwold on 29 December but unable to enter 'for want of water', her master turned back into Lowestoft roads, sheltering for nine days in wintry, unsettled weather before trying again just before high tide on the morning of 7 January.

It is not difficult to picture what happened next. Under the eyes of the longshoremen mustering on the pierheads and the scrutiny of the spyglasses on the clifftops, the pilot would have directed the helmsman to make for the harbour entrance. Under topsails and jibs, heeling to a favourable wind, the *Spring* would straightaway have headed for the narrow gap between the piers, a course of action which would have had some beachmen sucking their pipes in approval while the more demonstrative would have leaned a couple of inches seaward and eyed the water. Heading NW by N against the last dribbles of the flood, *Spring* would have slithered on to the sandbar at the harbour entrance and come to a halt. 'Told yer so,' would have rumbled the doubters, readying their heaving-lines. Dottle would have been spat, clay pipes pocketed, heaving-lines hove, and soon a tow rope is being hauled up to the capstan on the south pier. 'Quickly does it!' calls the pilot. 'We've twenty minutes at most, my lads!'

'Hooley-my!' pipes an unladylike veteran of Trafalgar as the wringing hempen hawser dribbles water into his boots.

'Hooley-tie!' respond fifteen lusty sons of the sea, taking up the shanty as they lean on the capstan bars. Their heads go down and their legs strain but the *Spring* moves not an inch.

'A *leetle* harder, if you please, pilot,' urges the captain, 'or else we'll be bloody well stuck.'

'Put your backs into it, boys!' cries the pilot. 'Show them what we're made of!'

'We'll sing, aye!' quavers Nelson's hero.

Left: In contrast with the many fore-and-aft-rigged vessels then plying the Sunrise Coast, this bluff-bowed billy boy moored on the Blyth about 1900 is rigged to carry square sails. (Robert Malster)

Above: SS *Abercraig* enters harbour in 1908 with 490 tons of granite. With her smoky funnel, gritty decks, parcelled mizzen sail and an open bridge, she could be the 'Dirty British coaster with a salt-caked smoke stack' of Masefield's *Cargoes*. (Southwold Museum)

HM torpedo boat *119* leaving Southwold in 1909, five years before the outbreak of the First World War. Unlike the windowed wheelhouse of the nearby tug, its conning tower offered no protection from the elements. (Southwold Museum)

'We'll heave, aye!' roar the sweating longshoremen. 'An' we'll hang Paddy Doyle for his boots!'

Shanty or no shanty, *Spring* stuck fast on the bar. As the tide began to fall, the master would have tried to hire lighters to off-load some cargo so the unburdened schooner might be warped over the bar on the evening tide, a course of action that would probably have saved his ship. But such was not to be. Before any lightening could be done the wind veered SSW and increased to gale force nine. The tide began to make, bringing high waves that swept over the vessel, breaking the lines attached to the piers and shattering the bulwarks protecting her decks and hatchways. With daylight gone and their spyglasses closed, the unsleeping watchers on the cliff trundled Captain Manby's life-gun down from the town and by midnight the master of the *Spring* and his four crewmen clinging to the rigging had been hauled to safety. Fourteen days later Maggs sold the coal salvaged from the wreck, together with the remains of the schooner's hull and gear, knocked down on the quayside to Willie Magub and unnamed others for £82.

Though most Tyne coal carried across Sole Bay in the nineteenth century was consigned to the east or south-east of England and the Channel coasts, from around 1830 onwards the Empire's worldwide trade routes were rapidly populated with coaling stations to feed the growing appetites of marine steam engines and the blood-red furnaces of international conflict. *Lloyd's War Losses* reveals that by the end of the First World War hundreds of Masefield's 'dirty British coasters' and ocean-going tramp ships crossing Sole Bay were transporting Tyne coal to sixty-one destinations: nineteen on the northern and western coasts of embattled France, twenty-one in the Mediterranean, the remainder as far distant as Lobito Bay, Buenos Ayres and Bombay. Other cargoes came past Southwold from nearer places: iron ore from Algiers, Almeria, Benisaf, Bilbao and Bizerta, Castro Urdialles, La Goulette and so on through the shores of the Mediterranean, including little-known harbours like Villaricos in Andalucia and Wabana on the Adriatic. Decks were stacked high with Scandinavian timber destined for ports as far distant as Melbourne, returning piled equally high with esparto grass from Arzew in Algeria; holds were filled with bulk grain from Baltimore, Bahia Blanca and Rosario, oilcake from Galveston, phosphate from Savannah, sulphur from Freeport, bagged peanuts from the Gambia and carobs from Cyprus. But, though carrying homogeneous cargoes of pitch to St Nazaire or bagged jute to Dundee makes good commercial sense, some of the very mixed cargoes listed in *Lloyd's* read like nonsense verses by Edward Lear. 'Teapots and Quails / Snuffers and Snails,' warbled Lear, writing at Knowsley Hall on Merseyside; 'Set him a-sailing / and see how he sails!' Did he but know it, life was imitating art as slavishly in sandy Sole Bay as on the murky Mersey, with such ill-matched commodities as cottonseed and onions, iron ore and grapes, willow hoops and tiles, hats, jackets and wainscot boards whirling past the Sunrise Coast even as he wrote. What would he have made of the sinister triumvirate of lead, manganese ore and arsenic that went to the bottom when the SS *Gartness* was torpedoed, years after his death, while on passage to Middlesbrough? 'She's down by the head / With arsenic and lead! / Set her a-sailing, / And glug-glug, you're dead!'?

Importing hides from Archangel to be made into boots for Tommy Atkins fighting the Boche or barrel staves from Tonsberg for casking Lowestoft herring and Southwold ale may have seemed a tolerable commercial risk even when the enemy were sinking 200 vessels a month, but how could an opportunist in Tunis hope to

Above: During a visit by the destroyer HMS *Solebay* in 1946, one of her picket boats foundered off the town. (*Alfred Corry* Museum)

Left: Belgian refugees entering Southwold during the First World War. (Pimple Thompson)

Old longshoremen say the barge *Martin Luther* carried Jewish refugees into Southwold shortly before the outbreak of the Second World War. In Summer 1939 she was bought by Victor and Jenny Knowland at Rochester and sailed to Southwold. Twice vandalised and sunk during the war years, here in 1965 *Martin Luther* lies derelict at Blackshore. (Dick Durham)

The neater, cleaner paintwork of the diesel-engined *Ordinence* in the 1950s is a far cry from the grimy, smoke-stacked coasters of earlier years, though her cargoes were every bit as dirty. (William Stannard)

sell a cargo of *480 million* imported matches except by infusing the entire population of the African continent with a lifelong addiction to cribbage?

Whatever his master plan, it never came off. After giving the slip to German submarines lurking in the English Channel, the 100 tons of so-called 'safety' matches loaded into the SV *Kirstine Jensen* at Gothenburg went up in smoke the instant she was torpedoed off distant Cape Tiñoso.

Among the more singular cargoes to cross Sole Bay in 1939 was a quantity of infantry boots, left ones only, made by the residents of Parkhurst Prison and conveyed by the barge *Second Apprentice* towards the army camp at Catterick, where it conceivably drove the recipients hopping mad.

Less mysterious was a cargo of isinglass, a semi-transparent form of gelatin obtained from the air bladders of sturgeon, towed ashore in the *Ceres* in 1829 and likely to have been snapped up at knockdown prices by William Crisp for his East Green brewery to clarify Crisp's Very Own (later Adnams') Ales & Stouts.

The most valuable cargoes landed on the Sunrise Coast in the eighteenth or any other century were – and still are – brought ashore by smugglers. Recording their activities, Stan Jarvis writes that in just eight months in 1745–6 they landed at least twenty-one contraband cargoes of brandy, gin and tea, seventeen of them at Sizewell and Benacre, the remainder at Thorpe Ness, Dunwich and Kessingland. It was a risky but lucrative occupation, employing, according to one MP of the time, '... all the young, clever fellows in Suffolk, [for] ... 2s 6d a day while waiting and, when on horseback and going about the country to dispose of the goods, they have a guinea a day and are well entertained'.

Forty years later, William Goodwin of Earl Soham calculated that 1.5 million of the 8,600,000 gallons (39 million litres) of spirits lately smuggled into Britain (sufficient to dampen the throats of every adult then inhabiting England and Wales with four large bottlefuls of brandy) had come across the beaches of Essex, Norfolk and Suffolk, much of it at Sizewell, where 2,500 gallons were loaded into twenty carts in February 1785, followed days later by a further 600. The landings sometimes took place in broad daylight but, though much talked of and noted, they commonly went unchallenged. In July 1789 the *Ipswich Journal* reported a large smuggling cutter with twenty cannons and eighty crew had landed a cargo near Southwold 'in sight of three or four hundred people and several revenue officers'. Before the beefing-up of the Preventive service in 1829, two of the few successes on the Sole Bay coast were notched up in the summer of 1810 by Southwold customs officers who seized an open lugger on Sizewell beach with 187 half-ankers (779 gallons or 3,541 litres) of gin on board, together with a further 196 gallons (891 litres) discovered in a barnyard at Leiston by two sharp-eyed riding officers who bore the disarming names of Gildersleeves and Easy.

The ending of the Napoleonic wars in 1815 allowed the government to deploy more resources against the smugglers. Martello towers, built to counter the threat

Left: No call for shanty-singing here. Aided by a steam-powered capstan made in nearby Beccles, a herring drifter warps into a convenient berth where she will be stemming the flood. (Robert Malster)

Below: Southwold harbour about 1910. Two hundred barrels on the quayside argue for the ongoing employment of coopers. (Robert Malster)

of French invasion, formed the southern arm of a lookout system which extended northward beyond the Suffolk border and was manned after 1829 by the newly formed coastguard service. Aided by a strengthened squadron of revenue cutters and backed up ashore by army dragoons, the officers speedily reduced the flood of contraband to a mere trickle. Their campaign is filled with tales of the savage beating of informers and battles with armed banditti that were thunderously echoed at sea by furious broadsides between revenue cutters and smugglers. Stakes were high and bloodshed frequent. During one encounter in 1817 in which

The Sole Bay Inn was opened in 1868 by Samuel Hayden Finch, landlord for forty-two years until his death in 1910.

five men were killed and seven wounded, the cutter HMS *Ranger* captured the smuggler *Folkestone* and its illegal cargo of brandy, silk, tea and tobacco that were together worth more than £250,000 at today's values.

At the lower end of the scale, an attempt to smuggle seven pints of whisky from the *Isabella* of Southwold in 1851 resulted in the confiscation of the boat, which was a heavy penalty. The *Isabella* belonged to one of the many brave Southwold Palmers who sometimes seem to have been a wee bit overly bold and cheeky, because four years later Maggs records the same Palmer had a second boat seized by the Customs for bringing ashore just one measly bottle of brandy.

A newspaper account of the loss of the smugglers' opponent HMS *Ranger* on the Haisboro Sand in 1822 is not matched anywhere in Maggs by a mention of a smuggling vessel being wrecked in Sole Bay, which is only to be expected. After all, what survivor in possession of his senses would admit to being a smuggler? Like death and taxes, smuggling will always be with us, trailing lies and evasions as well as a wealth of stories, among the more recent of which is the true tale of two black men who entered the Sole Bay Inn wet to the waist and enquired the way to the town railway station. Told that the nearest was seven miles down the A12 at Darsham, they squelched off into the night, leaving behind a couple of quivering puddles and a larger number of raised eyebrows.

THE LIFEBOATS

Commercial boatwork on the Sunrise Coast in the nineteenth century was largely controlled by companies of beachmen, made up of mariners, fishermen and pilots. At Lowestoft, Southwold and Aldeburgh the dominant members were the pilots, who managed their sometimes riotous followers from watch houses, which at Southwold took the form of eyries cut into the cliffs: Long Island at the end of East Street, New York to the south and Kilcock to the north. Until they were swept away by storms, huddled below on the beach lay a lifeboat house, a coastguard station, the huts of the longshoremen and the all-important workshop of James Critten, who built their beach punts, pilot yawls and gigs.

Between 1836 and 1870 Critten was the main builder for the two most vigorous companies, providing thirteen of the sixteen vessels they acquired during those years: four gigs and three yawls for the Long Islanders, and three gigs and three yawls for their rivals glowering at them from Kilcock Cliff. The Critten boats ranged in size from the 35ft (10.7m) gig *Mayflower*, built 1838 for the Kilcock men, to the three-masted, 55ft (16.8m) *John Bull*, constructed in 1849 for Long Island.

Many of the so-called huts below the cliffs were in fact built of substantial brick and roofed with Suffolk pantiles. At least one – that belonging to Benjamin Herrington, for twenty-four years a lifeboat coxswain – was the permanent residence of its owner, housing not only his fishing gear but also a shoreside life-support system that included a couple of pigs. Adorned with salvaged figureheads and handsomely carved name-boards, reeking of cut-plug tobacco and cough drops, the huts were the longshoreman's home from home.

The oldest company was probably the New York Cliff Co., original owners of the 50ft (15.2m) yawl *Jubilee*, which they sold to the newly incorporated Long Islanders in 1810. The following decades saw the decline of the New Yorkers and the rise of the Long Islanders and of a third company at Kilcock Cliff, known also as North Cliff, who built their lookout in 1829 and acquired the newly built yawl *British Tar* a year later. For more than seventy years thereafter the companies co-existed in an atmosphere of intense rivalry. Go-getters to their itchy fingertips, pilots depended for success on their ability to respond speedily to whatever money-making opportunities came into view. Whether their objective was navigation or salvage, dash was essential: 'Pilot! Russian brig's bin sighted orf

The *Lily Bird*, last of the Dunwich lifeboats, built in 1894 by Forrestt of London. Unlike most other crews serving Sole Bay in the nineteenth century, the Dunwich men chose self-righting boats, which had their buoyancy cases high up in the bow and stern. *Lily Bird* served until the station's closure in 1903, by which time the lifeboatmen of Dunwich had saved twenty-one lives. (Dunwich Museum)

of Benacre!' might pant a bootless tubercular urchin from the Long Island watch house, where *Jubilee*'s bows were already halfway into the sea.

'Palmer…? Where's Palmer…?'

'Down with a fever.'

'Bugger it, let's get launched!'

'Christ alive, pilot! The Kilcocks are goin' orf to the Ruski, too!'

'Give way tergether then, boys! Put me aboard her!'

Who dared, won. The Kilcock's *Swiftsure* may not have intended to cut a rival boat in two but more often than not they were the first to be alongside potential customers; and, as well as bringing in a living, their derring-do saved lives. Forty years before Southwold had its own dedicated lifeboat service, pilot yawls were saving people from the waves. Maggs records only three instances, though there were probably many more: the crew of the shallop wrecked on the Sand Hail in 1802, saved by the pilot boat *Dove*; the people in the galliot *Zeland* who were brought ashore at Yarmouth by John Waters and his six-man crew in the *Samuel*, and the survivors from the *Cumberland*, rescued in 1831 '… thro' the speedy exertions of Mr John Montague and Mr John Lowsey of this place – Trinity Pilots'.

The most intriguing entry is a note written by another Long Island pilot, telling what he did on 9 March 1814:

Retoke a Collier brig with Jubilee pilot boat from a French luger Ben [Benacre?] a Bout three miles a Head Put 5 Frenchman on shore at Southold it came on to blow at N.E. and i toke the Brig to Harwich. W. Woodard.

What are we to make of it? Trafalgar had been won but Britain and France were still at war; so here we have half a dozen Englishmen in a fast but puny open boat who pursue and re-capture a hefty prize from under the noses – to say nothing

Even in light weather, the shoal at the harbour entrance can kick up lively seas. Harbourmaster Wally Upcraft crossing the bar in the 1950s. (*Alfred Corry* Museum)

of the pistols – pointing at them from an enemy lugger. Were they tit-for-tatting the same cunning *matelots* who had captured the *Providence* in 1805? Did Woodard land the Frenchmen as distressed seamen or as prisoners-of-war? Saving them from the sea or sending them to the slammer? Just seventeen at the time, Maggs returns to the note in later years but, reticent as ever, adds no comment.

The more usual work of the beach yawls is characterised in part by an earlier note, written in the same hand:

1808 Dec 28th Towed a Swade ship a Shoar at Southwold with Boats, called the Marriar Charlotte – Captn Blomer master, no one on board. W Woodard

Woodard was probably one of the two pilots in the *Jubilee* when she went to the assist the *Eliza Frances* on 5 March 1818, a typical incident where pilotage and salvage went hand-in-hand. The vessel had parted from her anchors during a SSW gale in the Downs and had eventually brought up off Dunwich. The *Jubilee* put aboard the two Southwold pilots who navigated her safely past the Barnard and through the gatways into Yarmouth roads, where *Jubilee* was waiting with a replacement anchor and cable. The gale raged unabated, driving several vessls ashore and sinking three others, but the replacement tackle provided by *Jubilee* was equal to the task and *Eliza Frances* survived.

William Woodard was still employing his pilotage skills thirty years later when Maggs clambered aboard the 700-ton Russian ship *Caster* from the gig *Princess Victoria*, nine miles out from the shores of Sole Bay, hoping for some nautical chit-chat and refreshment, and obtaining pleasing amounts of both.

The Dutch schooner *Voorwaartz*, driven ashore in 1912 at Minsmere sluice by the same gale that wrecked the barque *Idun*. This is a unique photograph, because *Voorwaartz* was one of the few stranded vessels to be refloated, whereas the majority were broken up where they lay. (*Alfred Corry Museum*)

How much light-hearted chit-chat the ageing pilot was able to contribute is open to speculation. The bold salvor of ships and resolute saver of other people's children had lost two of his own sons at sea, the latest only months previously, drowned near the Barnard at the age of twenty-two.

Some historians record that the Southwold pilotage service provided by Woodard and others went into decline after Lowestoft harbour opened in 1831. If this was so, Southwold must have later regained its strength, for Cooper writes that round about 1885 Southwold, Aldeburgh and Lowestoft were level-pegging, each having fifteen Trinity pilots who served the North Channel, the part of the Thames pilotage district extending from Orford Ness, past Harwich into the Thames estuary. Pilots did not stay at this strength in the three towns for much longer however, for in 1899 all North Channel pilots were posted to Harwich and vessels were compelled to embark them at the Shipwash light vessel. The departure of the pilots brought about the steady demise of the beach companies, with the Long Islanders' *Reliance* performing her last service in 1894, and although the Kilcock Cliff's *Bittern* won the 1910 Yarmouth regatta and their watch house survived till 1926, pilotage in Southwold was by then a distant memory, leaving Trinity pilots Griffiths and Magub to gaze on its dissolution from their fading sepia photos on the mantlepiece.

Long before they upped sticks and moved to Harwich, the pilots' legendary verve had made its mark among the beachmen crewing the Southwold lifeboat service, inaugurated in December 1840 in response to the terrible losses of the previous November, the worst month in living memory, when six vessels had been wrecked in the bay and more than eighty men drowned.

Though delivered in 1841, the earliest lifeboat, the 40ft (12.3m) *Solebay*, did not make her first recorded launch until November 1844, when Coxswain Isaac Jarvis was paid £4 5s for attempting to save the crew of an un-named vessel, possibly the *Lord Nelson*, that had been wrecked near the South Pier.

Voorwaartz crew, with Captain Laan, his wife, and Mate Coetzee standing in the doorway. (Pimple Thompson)

The 133-ton brigantine *Isabellas*, wrecked off Covehithe Ness on 22 December 1884 while on passage from London to Middlesbrough with wood. The photo was taken on Christmas Day, by which time the vessel had been stripped of her sails and, very likely, her cargo. Discernible amidships is Plimsoll's life-saving loadline. (Courtesy George Eastman House)

Trinity pilot Griffiths worked the Sunrise
Coast between 1879 and 1908.
(Southwold Museum)

Trinity pilot George Magub came from
a family with wide seafaring experience.
John Magub was drowned in Cardigan
Bay from the *Perseverance*, another Magub
commanded the 74-ton *Dispatch*, and two
other Magubs captained larger vessels.
(Southwold Museum)

Her next call-out in July 1845 was precipitated by a tragedy. Several longshore
boats had gone out at daybreak to trawl for soles and a south-west gale had blown
up, capsizing Robert English's punt on the offlying sandbank as it was heading back
for the beach. English survived by clinging to a pair of oars but his two young
sons were kicked into eternity by their struggling father, who was borne seaward
by the ebbing tide and picked up by two men in the *Dart*, a second punt, which
was running up from the south. Rather than attempt a beach landing, they made
toward a pilot cutter that was riding out the gale, at anchor to windward. Unable
to reach her against the strong wind and ebbing tide, *Dart* threw out an anchor,
plunging bows under and looking to be in danger of swamping beneath every
breaking crest. Meanwhile, the lifeboatmen had launched *Solebay* through the
breakers 'in a most admirable and gallant style' to attempt rescue. Heeling to the
blasts, her twelve-man crew baling, playing the sheets, luffing through the gusts but
gaining next to nothing over the ground, *Solebay* was herself obliged to anchor,
brought up 'with great dexterity,' downwind of *Dart* and in line with her.

What happened next called up a magnificent mix of seamanship skills from the
lifeboatmen and a scintilla of telepathy from a female ghost. Ernest Cooper wrote:
'A signal was then given from the lifeboat to the two men in the trawl boat to let
slip from their anchor, which they did and were thus driven towards the lifeboat

from which communication was obtained by means of ropes through the activity and energy of the crew.' In short, John Bedingfield Hurr, James May and Robert English were saved from drowning by a lifeboat crew who received £21 19s 6d for their services. The telepathic ghost came into the action through the agency of Hurr and May, who swore blind that they had been forewarned of their danger at two o'clock that morning during an encounter with a speechless female spectre that had lost its head.

Solebay was not the first lifeboat to be stationed in the bay. Since 1826 the Suffolk Association of the Royal National Institution for the Preservation of Life from Shipwreck had maintained a boat at Sizewell Gap, and from 1870 to 1936 the Royal National Lifeboat Institution operated boats from three stations at the northern extremity of the bay: Nos 1 and 3 invisible beyond Covehithe Ness at Kessingland beach, and No.2 at Benacre, close to the Barnard sand. An RNLI station established at Thorpe Ness in 1853 was followed by a second in 1860, and Dunwich acquired a lifeboat in 1873. Thus, for much of the nineteenth century Sole Bay had no fewer than seven stations in fifteen miles.

'Why were they so very close to each other?' enquires a hypothetical visitor from Meriden, Warwickshire, the very middle of Middle England, to which the answer of course is wind. However expertly it was handled, a sailing lifeboat could scarcely make progress into the teeth of a heavy gale unless the tide was helping it, and even then its progress would be minimal. Wind-direction was crucial, for the lifeboat needed to have the weather-gage of her objective, be upwind of it; so a five-mile run by a still invisible crew who had the gale at their backs and preferably a fair tide under their keel had a much better chance of effecting a rescue than any number of attempted launchings from a beach that was only half a mile away but where an all-too-clearly-impotent lifeboat crew had the gale blowing into their faces.

Solebay was a non-self-righting boat whose design sprang from the beachmen's tried and tested pilot yawls and punts, and except for the 'evil-disposed person' who cut the haul-off warp in March 1842, the boat was well liked by the majority of lifeboatmen. Its last recorded service was in aid of the schooner *William Cook*, wrecked off the town in 1852. The lifeboat crew made four attempts to reach the stranded vessel, first with oars and then with sails. Although at the third attempt they succeeded in saving the master, the boat's air tanks were leaking so badly by then that she was obliged to come ashore. Three crewmen in *William Cook* were later rescued by lines fired from the beach but a fourth was drowned when he dropped from the bowsprit.

Damaged and needing expensive repairs, *Solebay* was sold to Kessingland in 1855 and replaced by a new boat called *Harriett*. Built on the most up-to-date scientific principles, the self-righting but upsettingly disliked boat and her more popular successor *Harriett II* were the mainstays of Southwold lifesaving for thirty-eight years, rescuing more than seventy-eight people from nine shipwrecks, including

1 The Harbour Inn at Blackshore on the River Blyth, depicted by an unknown artist at the end of the nineteenth century. Variously named the Fishing Buss and the Nag's Head, the inn offered stabling for ten horses and imported grain and coal to supply three malsters in the town. (Colin Fraser/Alan Hale)

2 The House in the Clouds at Thorpe Ness, a water tower disguised as a bijou residence, is a useful landmark to fishermen.

3 The lookout at Long Island Cliff, where Abraham Girling was knocked over the rail by Foster Bokenham and instantly died. If the vessel coming from the south-east is seen to be requesting a pilot, the young crewmen will clatter down the steps and endeavour to launch

the company's yawl ahead of their rivals glaring at them from Kilcock Cliff. This study by Thomas Smythe was painted about 1880. (Rupert Cooper)

4 A modern replica of a Viking coastal trader in her Norwegian home waters. (Sue Crowther)

5 More than a century after she was launched in 1907, the barge *Marjorie* is still racing on the Essex rivers. (William Stannard)

6 The *Lily Bird*, last of the Dunwich lifeboats, built in 1894 by Forrestt of London. Unlike most crews serving Sole Bay in the nineteenth century, the Dunwich men chose self-righting boats, which had their buoyancy cases high up in the bow and stern. *Lily Bird* served until the station's closure in 1903, by which time the lifeboatmen of Dunwich had saved twenty-one lives. (Dunwich Museum)

7 Beached and possibly benighted, the crew is laying out anchors. (Ernie Childs)

8 This figurehead from the schooner yacht *Wildflower* graces the interior of the Southwold Sailing Club.

Opposite above: 9 The Reading Room was built in 1846 to the memory of Captain Francis Rayley RN. (Alan Hale)

Opposite below: 10 The 83ft (25.3m) barge *Martin Luther* ended her days on the banks of the Blyth as a derelict houseboat and was broken up in the late 1960s. (Colin Fraser/Alan Hale)

11 California Sands, Southwold, where the more humorous inhabitants will demonstrate that the Pacific coast of the USA is merely a pebble-cast from New York and Long Island. (Alan Hale)

12 Southwold from the North pier. The November gale of 1855 drove the brigs *Cape Horn*, *Ocean* and *Emma* on to the shingle in the foreground and the California Sands beyond it. (Wells Photos)

13 Landing the night's herring. (Ernie Childs)

14 1 November 1891, and the ketch *Richard L. Wood* of Goole, Master H. Sweeting and manned by a crew of three, is about to be driven on to Thorpe Ness by a force nine gale. (John Robbins)

15 Altogether armless, this figurehead from an unknown wreck was cast ashore at Southwold. (Sailors' Reading Room/Alan Hale)

16 Southwold from the pleasure pier. Kilcock (alias North) Cliff is nearest the camera, with Sizewell power station on the far horizon. (*Alfred Corry* Museum)

17 Southwold lighthouse lantern. The dioptric lenses devised by Augustin Fresnel concentrate the light from two bulbs, each the size of a goose egg. The red glass on the left marks the limits of the Barnard Sand. During the decade after the light came into service in 1890, the incidence of shipwreck in Sole Bay fell by 30 per cent. (Alan Hale)

18 Last of the many brigs to founder in Sole Bay. The crew of the *Alfred Corry* row through the raffle towards the stricken *James & Eleanor*, wrecked in 1895 on the Easton shoal. (Ernie Childs)

19 Built 1921, the Lowestoft smack *Excelsior* is still sailing Sole Bay in the twenty-first century.

20 Martina Maria, wrecked on 18 January 1881 while on passage to Monaco with a cargo of coal. Nine of her twelve-man crew were drowned. (Sailors' Reading Room/Alan Hale)

21 Figurehead salvaged from *William IV*, wrecked 1856 on Walberswick beach. 'The Sailor King', known by his less respectful subjects as 'Silly Billy', joined the navy in 1779 and saw service in America and the West Indies, where he befriended 'a mere boy of a captain' named Horatio Nelson. (Sailors' Reading Room/Alan Hale)

22 Alfred Corry makes out of harbour during a NE gale in December 1911 to aid a schooner in distress. Visible ashore are the fish market at centre and, extreme right on the dunes, a redundant Low Light which had been supplanted in 1890 by the newly built lighthouse in the town. (A painting by S.J. Martin, loaned to the *Alfred Corry* Museum by Wendy Coleman)

23 Launching the surf lifeboat. (Ernie Childs)

Opposite above 24 High Water Springs at Southwold seafront. (Wells Photos)

Opposite below 25 Breakers on The Hale mark the southernmost end of the notorious inshore shoal that lies parallel to the beach and in 2008 extended almost as far as Covehithe, four miles to the north. (Alan Hale)

26 Two chastened longshoremen avert their eyes from this Victorian schoolmarm and her fearsome brolly. This figurehead from an unknown vessel maintains discipline in the Sailors' Reading Room. (Alan Hale)

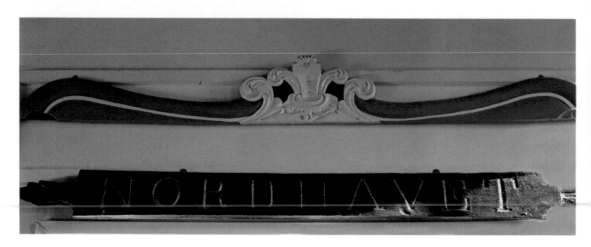

27 Gone, but not forgotten. An *envoi* to a fine ship. (Alan Hale)

The second Southwold beach yawl named *Bittern* won the Yarmouth regatta in 1910 for the Kilcock Cliff Co. Her rudder was saved from destruction when she was broken up in 1926 and now stands outside the Sailors' Reading Room. (*Alfred Corry* Museum)

On a Saturday afternoon in 1858 the yawl *Reliance* put out to aid *Harriett II*, which had capsized on the off-lying shoal that had wrecked Robert English. Here, five of the lifeboat's crew are struggling ashore in their cork lifejackets but three unjacketed passengers will be found drowned. (*Alfred Corry* Museum)

A light wind and only a slight sea, but the moderate swell breaking on the shoal could be a death trap. (Wells Photos)

The 32ft *Rescue*, Southwold surf lifeboat 1897–1920, with Coxswain Sam May towering above. (*Alfred Corry* Museum)

Four years after her tragic accident, an improved *Harriett II* set out on 28 January 1862 to aid the Ipswich schooner *Princess Alice*, wrecked on Sizewell bank with a cargo of coal. The lifeboat rescued its five crew and a dog from the ship's boat. (Robert Malster)

Sheraton Grange in 1853, *Princess Alice* in 1862, *Alma* and *Pandora* in 1874 and the barque *Nina* in 1894.

Like *Solebay*, the second *Harriett* was a non-self-righting boat, fundamentally different from *Harriett I*, which was described by Cooper as having:

> high air cases at the ends, low waist, and narrow section … never enjoying the
> confidence of the Solemen … who prefer a big, beamy, heavily ballasted sailing-boat,
> rigged just like their own fishing punts, and with large sails, capable of driving them
> long distances to outlying sands.

Twenty men pushing on sett poles have assisted this launching. (*Alfred Corry* Museum)

The crew are hauling on the warp that was permanently attached to an anchor, while the beach party pushes on setts. (*Alfred Corry* Museum)

The *Alfred Corry* races to aid the barque *Nina*, run down off Dunwich by a steamer at the height of a force eight gale in October 1894. (*Alfred Corry* Museum)

With a dead straight luff and equally serious sou'westers, the crew set off to exercise their life-saving skills in light weather. (*Alfred Corry* Museum)

The ballast tanks held 5.3 tons of water, admitted through eighteen tubes, eight of which are visible here in the floor of the well. The tubes also drained away any seas that came aboard. Beneath the side decks are the air cases. The four crutches housed sixteen oars. (*Alfred Corry* Museum)

Corry beats across the off-lying shoal against a strong south-easterly wind. (*Alfred Corry* Museum)

Beaching was often more dangerous than launching, for a following sea of this size could strike the quarter and roll the lifeboat broadside in the surf. (*Alfred Corry* Museum)

Solebay and *Harriett II* – which was re-named *London Coal Exchange* in 1869 in tribute to the coal merchants who had donated £700 to the lifeboat funds – and her successor *Alfred Corry*, were what was known as the 'wet' type of lifeboat, with air cases low down in the hull at their sides and ends, and a water-ballast compartment in a deep well on the centreline. As soon as the boat was launched, about 5 tons of water gushed into the ballast compartment through a number (eighteen in the *Corry*) of 4in- (102mm-) diameter tubes, so the boat would then be kept afloat only by the air cases. In moderate conditions the crew would have been doused with spray as soon as they set out; in the roughest weather they were often immersed to the level of their waists. Unlike the self-righters, *Solebay*, *Harriett II* and *Alfred Corry* went through the waves rather than over them, 'completely waterlogged,' wrote Cooper, with tons of ballast sloshing about in the well.

After thirteen months' service during which they had pumped out a sinking brig and earned £38 12s salvage money, the crew's confidence in *Harriett II* was severely punctured on an otherwise delightful Saturday afternoon in February 1858 when she was returning from exercise with the curate of Wangford and two other passengers. With most of the ballast pumped out in readiness for beaching, Coxswain Francis Cooper headed for the shore, setting a course across the same offlying shoal that had capsized *Robert English*. Surfing under reduced sail in a brisk wind from abeam, the boat lifted up her stern to a breaker and straightaway thumped down on to the sand, damaging the rudder. Another wave lifted the stern, cascading tons of water into the bows. A sea broke aboard, filling the sails, rolling her on to her side and throwing the crew and two passengers into the sea. Buoyed up by their cork lifejackets, five crew members were able to swim ashore and the remainder were rescued by the yawl *Reliance*, but all three passengers were drowned.

A report in the *Norfolk Chronicle* highlights the paralysing emotions that could grip members of rival companies when they found themselves side by side, potential rescuers but traditional enemies, and all in danger of drowning. After praising the crew of the Long Island *Reliance* for their gallantry in rescuing the lifeboatmen, the reporter castigates the Kilcock cliffmen, 'who appeared either paralysed or frightened', for not launching their own yawl to aid their Kilcock comrades – 'of which the lifeboat's crew was composed'. Written only three years after the *Reliance* had been cut in two by the aggressive behaviour of a Kilcock yawl, the report makes interesting reading.

A high-level court of enquiry found that the lifeboat had been running too fast before a breaking sea in shoal water, and that the error had been compounded by the ballast rushing loosely to the bows – '... one of the defects of that class of boats,' observed the presiding admiral. As a result of his finding, bulkheads were built across *Harriett*'s ballast compartment to restrain the rushing waters. The crew's confidence was fully restored in May of the same year when they made the heartening discovery that even with thirty-two fully grown men standing on one gunwale and another thirty-six heaving on a rope from the masthead, *Harriett* absolutely refused to capsize.

The improved qualities of *Harriett II* and the stamina and discipline of her crew were put to a severe test during a northerly gale in September 1859, when she went to aid a vessel driven ashore at Minsmere, only two miles north of Sizewell Gap lifeboat house but twice the distance downwind of the Southwold station. With the signal mast at Dunwich hidden by darkness and an electric telegraph not yet installed, a messenger would have taken more than two hours to get from Minsmere to Southwold on the back of a horse. The crew launched at 10.30 p.m. and soon were scudding five miles downwind – but against an ebbing tide – in *Harriett II* to accomplish a hazardous midnight rescue of ten men and the captain's wife from the Prussian brig *Lucinde* amid seas that were breaking over the ship's masthead and burying the lifeboat in surf. While landing the survivors, Acting Coxswain John Cragie was swept over the side but managed to heave himself aboard again, the finale to an heroic feat of seamanship that earned Cragie and Ben Herrington silver medals as well as a share of the double pay (£30) awarded to the crew by the RNLI, another £30 from the Prusssian consul and a further £20 from a collection made in London. On the debit side, two crew members who had broken the lifeboat rules by setting off for the wreck on foot instead of in the boat were awarded the everlasting order of the boot.

Such rules related not only to the operational efficiency of the boat but also to the proper remuneration of its crew. Some rules – such as those regarding the

Driven ashore in 1905 at Covehithe during a force eight gale, the crew of the Dunkirk smack *Joseph et Yvonne* prepare to climb into the breeches buoy they have secured to the mast. (*Alfred Corry* Museum)

firing of rockets and the operation of life-saving apparatus – came into being with the introduction of new equipment but others had been passed down from the ancient traditions of the beach boats. For example, the first boat to get a line aboard a stricken vessel thereby secured its claim to the vessel's salvage, and any man who was involved in a successful launch was thereby entitled to a share of the proceeds. As we have seen, the over-zealous interpretation of this rule caused several disastrous collisions between rival pilot yawls. It also resulted in people risking their lives by recklessly dashing into the breakers to lay a hand on the boat and thereby establish their claim to future payment even after it had been successfully launched.

The No.1 boats were large, heavy craft, up to 46ft (14m) in length and weighing up to 8½ tons (9 metric tons) without ballast, requiring the combined efforts of fifty men to launch them. Photographs show the eighteen-strong crew of *Alfred Corry*, the successor to the *Coal Exchange*, hauling on a four-strand warp attached to an anchor buried far out beyond the breakers, assisted in their labours by another twenty pushing on poles from astern while a further unphotographed dozen struggle to align the cumbersome launching rollers beneath her keel.

Though capable of going far offshore and enduring the roughest weather, the No.1 boats were not best suited for working close to the beach, and so in 1866 they were supplemented by the first of three smaller surf boats: two named *Quiver* and latterly the 32ft (9.8m) *Rescue*, which could be trundled across the sand on wide-tracked, 6ft-diameter wheels to a position where it could be launched upwind of a stranded vessel. Two years after its ceremonial launching, the first *Quiver* earned

The breeches buoy and its rocket launcher were operated by the Coastguard service, set up in 1822 by HM Customs and taken over by the Admiralty in 1856. (Robert Malster)

£9 11s 6d by salvaging the brig *Phoebe*, which had been driven ashore in the Covehithe bight. However, in spite of this money-making exploit, the first *Quiver* proved to be another disliked self-righter, and so it was replaced in 1882 by a non-self-righting boat of the same name. In 1892 *Quiver No.2* was launched from a horse-drawn carriage that had been hauled over hedges and ditches for two miles to get near the hard-pressed schooner *Elizabeth Kilner*, which was being forced towards the Covehithe shore by a south-easterly gale. Seeing the lifeboat positioned conveniently under his lee on the beach, the master immediately made a beeline for the waiting helpers, who rescued him and his crew by rocket line.

As well as the vessels stationed at Southwold and Benacre, Sole Bay's sailing-and-pulling lifeboats comprised the *John Keble* and its two successors at Dunwich, a boat at Sizewell and six others based over the years at Thorpe Ness. Between the opening of the first station at Sizewell in 1826 and the closing of Southwold No.1 station in 1942, after the motor-sailing lifeboat *Mary Scott* was requisitioned to rescue British soldiers from wartime Dunkirk beaches in 1940 and never returned, these Sole Bay lifeboats saved more than 450 lives. Of course, other lifeboats stationed outside the bay also performed valuable service in its waters, coming from Kessingland, Pakefield and Lowestoft in the north and Aldeburgh in the south.

The Southwold station re-opened in 1963 with the commissioning of Inshore Rescue Boat *D36*, a 16ft (4.9m) inflatable, powered by a 40hp outboard engine that could skim it across Sole Bay at 20 knots, 23mph or 37kph. During the decades that followed, the Inshore Rescue Boats were re-classified as Inshore Lifeboats to reflect

John Keble, the first of three Dunwich lifeboats, was built in 1873 by Forrestt at Limehouse in London for £259. A self-righting, pulling boat with ten oars, she measured 30ft x 7ft 8in (9.14m x 2.34m) and was on station until 1887, when she was replaced by the 34ft *Anne Ferguson*. (Dunwich Museum/ Alan Hale)

their increased size and capabilities. The present lifeboat *Leslie Tranmer* is powered by twin 70hp outboard engines which can drive it across the waves at 32 knots (57.4kph). In their first thirty-five years of service, years in which the number of sea-going vessels crossing Sole Bay had reduced from a steady stream to the occasional meagre trickle, by January 1999 the Inshore Rescue Boats and Lifeboats had nevertheless been launched on 627 occasions, an average of eighteen launches a year, saving or assisting 212 people from no fewer than 116 merchant and fishing vessels, 419 pleasure craft, forty-four distressed bathers or marooned anglers as well as aiding forty-eight other casualties, including an aquatic dog and a drowsy adventurer who was being wafted towards Holland on an airbed.

He was lucky. Six other incautious would-be mariners pulled from the sea were no longer living. They included two drowned off Walberswick one February morning in 1972 when a strong south-easterly was busily building breakers on the bar. A party of five men in a motorised dinghy were seen to push away from the riverbank

Soon afterwards the dinghy disappeared in heavy seas at the harbour mouth. Minutes later IRB *191* was crashing through the breakers, searching for the men who were reportedly clinging to the upturned hull. '10/W Cloud. Rain squalls. Poor vis. Wind SE 5/6….Low Water,' reads the service report by crew members Patrick Pile and Martin Helmer, who found the dinghy wallowing a quarter-mile off Walberswick beach with no one aboard. With Pile at the controls and Helmer in the bows, the lifeboat began to scour the area, eventually finding three of the men unconscious in the water. After pulling them into the lifeboat the crew continued the search. Soon Helmer spotted a fourth man, but while he was attempting to lift him aboard, the boat was swamped by a breaking sea

From 1910–19, the 42ft *James Leath* was stationed at Pakefield, close to the northern limb of the Newcome sand. Between 1855 and their closure in 1922, the Pakefield stations saved 273 lives (David Gooch)

which caused the unconscious body to sink. Plunging his head and shoulders underwater, Helmer wrestled the man to the surface and rolled him inboard.

The lifeboat headed for the beach. Here, assisted by fishermen Dinks Cooper and Fred Eades, the crew dragged the four apparently lifeless bodies through the surf and began to pump water from their lungs. After what must have seemed an eternity, three re-commenced breathing and went on to make a full recovery in hospital. Unfortunately, the fourth did not recover, and, in spite of an extensive helicopter search, two days after the accident the body of the fifth had still not been found.

'For this Service,' says a hand-written footnote to the report, 'Mr. P. Pile and Mr. M. Helmer received the Bronze Medal of the Royal National Lifeboat Institution and Mr. D. Cooper and Mr. F. Eades received the thanks of the Institute on Vellum.'

Distanced from *Harriett II* by more than a hundred years of ever-improving technology, today's lifeboat crews have to meet the same savage sea conditions that were encountered by Cragie and Herrington. Lifeboatman Jonathan Adnams recalls that the standard-issue suits of the 1960s were no more watertight than ancient oilies, so driving into a gale-driven North Sea wave must have still seemed like throwing oneself head first under a toppling tombstone.

Adnams performed a softer dockside jump into the Southwold lifeboat service in 1972 at the age of sixteen, urged on by a short-handed coxswain who was understandably impatient to be off, and went on to serve for twenty-seven years as Crew and Senior Helm. One of his missions was in the Atlantic 21 class *Solebay* when it was called out by the firing of two green star-shells in January 1981 to assist the fishing boat *Concord*, an ex-Liverpool class converted lifeboat which had radioed for help from a position a mile east of the harbour entrance. Crewed by Nick Westwood, Steve Taylor and Jonathan Adnams, Coxswain Roger Trigg steered *Solebay* out of the

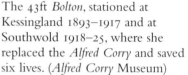

The 43ft *Bolton*, stationed at Kessingland 1893–1917 and at Southwold 1918–25, where she replaced the *Alfred Corry* and saved six lives. (*Alfred Corry* Museum)

harbour into a south-easterly gale on a gloomy midwinter afternoon that was being darkened even more by oncoming curtains of sleet. The lifeboat was accompanied by *Concord*'s owner Tony Chambers, at the wheel of *Broadside*, a 36ft (11m) Norwegian dory. The *Solebay* found *Concord* anchored among breaking waves, its skipper Michael Martin crouched over an engine that was irretrievably dead. Trigg nudged the lifeboat up to *Broadside*, enabling Adnams to scramble aboard. With the *Solebay* stationed astern, *Broadside* slowly manoeuvred towards the piers, by which time it was an hour till low water and the Blyth was still gushing out at high spate. So long as they were in deep water, the towing operation went well. For three quarters of a mile the boats made steady progress, with *Concord* yawing amidst steep but not yet critically dangerous seas coming from astern and the towline alternately slacking and tautening as she slewed off the breaking crests. However, as the waves felt the effects of the shallowing seabed and the outrushing current from the river, they peaked ever higher, converting every wave into a roaring cataract.

'Go and see to the towline!' shouted Chambers, so Adnams went out from the wheelhouse and made towards the bitts at the stern. No sooner had he reached the after end of the well than *Broadside* surged towards the shallowest part of the bar, whereupon 8 unstoppable tons of *Concord* fell off a roaring white tumult and the towline twanged taut and snapped: Adnams recalled:

Mary Scott was at Southwold from 1925–40. Like her predecessors, she was built to the Norfolk & Suffolk design favoured by the Southwold lifeboatmen. Her most notable peacetime service took place in November 1927 when she assisted the Dutch steamer *Georgia*, aground on the Haisboro Sand, thirty-five miles distant. This service earned Coxswain Frank Upcraft an RNLI Bronze Medal. (*Alfred Corry* Museum)

'The first two coils of it whizzed through the air and hit the wheelhouse but the third coil caught me across the forehead and knocked me out. The next thing I remember is Tony shouting, "She's going on the beach! She's going on the beach and we're going in after her!". I got to my feet and saw that Michael and *Concord* were being carried on to the North Hale [Maggs's 'Sand Hail']. Tony got *Broadside* in as close as he could – about 200m or 300m off the beach … By this time it was blowing like shit, sleeting shit, and I thought, "*Concord's* gone! She's gone ashore!" … But then I saw Roger going in among the breakers with the lifeboat … and then *Broadside* took a bloody great wave over the wheelhouse and all our electrics went out … We were beam on to the waves and rolling like hell and I remember hooking my arms and legs over a rail and thinking, "I'm going to let go when the boat rolls ninety degrees!" but though we rolled and rolled we always came back.

'From what I could see it looked like *Concord* was on the beach but somehow Roger manoeuvred among the breakers and got a line aboard her and towed her clear so that eventually we got *Broadside* back alongside and re-secured the towline.'

Sea conditions still being so dangerous on the bar, the battered trio headed north towards a larger lifeboat from Lowestoft that was motoring towards them, eventually handing over the tow to the larger boat and arriving at Lowestoft three

Mary Scott towing the yacht *Damaris*, 1932. (Pimple Thompson)

Mary Scott assists a cruiser/racer to enter harbour against the last of the ebb.

Atlantic 21 class Inshore Rescue Boat *Solebay*, with Coxswain Roger Trigg standing at centre. (Jeff Morris)

and a half hours after launching. For his courageous handling of *Solebay*, Coxswain Roger Trigg was awarded the Bronze Medal of the RNLI.

Nine years later Jonathan Adnams was himself at the helm of another Atlantic 21, sent out in July 1990 to rescue the Belgian yacht *Haura*. Crew member Marcus Gladwell tells the story:

I was sitting in my bay window, thinking, you know, 'There's going to be so many people in trouble today,' an' so I just got out my pager because … er … I get this feeling – and I've had it to within about two minutes on numerous occasions – and I say to people: 'I've got to get my shoes on because I'm going to get a lifeboat shout!' … and people are absolutely amazed but, you know, you can look at the changing combination of conditions and you just think 'WAARGH … someone's going to be caught out in this for sure!'

So I was sitting there, looking out the window, when my pager goes off and I run out into the street, stop a car that was going past and got them to take me to the lifeboat station – the old one that was up by the *Harbour Inn* – and Jonathan Adnams was the helm and Alan Scoggins was the other crew member and we were told that a yacht in distress had been sighted and they asked us to go as close as possible to Benacre Ness and perform a search, but looking at the conditions we thought, 'Well, we're just looking for bodies, really,' because the conditions were such that … you could see no more than a quarter of a mile, what with the wind-driven spume and the fracto-stratus cloud and the rain … It was a bit like those squalls you get in the tropics but it wasn't really heavy rain, it was just a tremendous amount of wind … Anyway, it turned out that the helicopter found the yacht on Newcome Sand, and they said, 'Oh, it's sinking, 'cos there's quite a lot of water goin' over the top of it,' … and so we got from Benacre Ness to the outside of Newcome Sand and then we saw it, about halfway up the sandbank …

Jonathan did a brilliant job of bringing the boat alongside, and … being sort of reasonably agile, and being, y'know, quite happy to have a go at diving from one thing to another, I made a dive for it, caught a hold of the guardrail and swung myself aboard, … and then, erm, I don't know whether you've heard the expression 'Your blood runs cold in your veins'? … You have? Well, it scared me, 'cos I suppose I'd gone into shock! *Well*, to jump from a perfectly good lifeboat on to a boat that you think is sinking … and you're thinking: *'I'm getting on to a boat that's going down!'* … well, it's *so* … Shit a brick! … so *unnatural* …!

The scene when I got below was shocking as well because the reason the boat had got into all these difficulties was that the mainsheet block had carried away and hit the skipper and opened his head up, so there's blood and water going round and round like a washing machine and the guy's wife had gone into shock and she was gripped up – because your perspective goes right down to nothing – and we couldn't get her hands off the wheel and she couldn't speak … so then we called the Coastguard and told them the boat wasn't imminently sinking – it was a well-found steel boat, about 35ft [10.8m] – and … by that time Bert Coleman from the Lowestoft lifeboat had got on board …

Southwold lifeboat crews, 1998.

The Inshore Lifeboat *Quiver* was named after her two nineteenth-century predecessors, all expressly designed for working the coastal shoals. Stationed at Southwold 1985-98, this more recent *Quiver* saved seventy lives. (Paul Russell)

In 2008, Sole Bay is served by the 34-knot *Leslie Tranmer*. (Nicholas Leach)

Spirit of Lowestoft, out on a Sunday morning exercise in 2000. (Nicholas Leach)

and between us we managed to get the main[sail] down and, huh … huh, then Lowestoft passed a tow to us and I was steering the yacht out to sea and up the Stanford …

'Making for Lowestoft?'

Yes … but with [the wind] being SSE, even without any sails up we overtook the lifeboat to the full extent of the tow-rope … Yes, we just surfed straight past it on a big, big breaker! Then Jonathan and Alan in the Southwold boat went into another big wave and went past the vertical and the Lowestoft guys who saw it said 'WAARFFH! SHE'S GOIN' TER FLIP!'

'Gracious!'

But it came back down again the right way up.

On an October day in 2006 that bathed us in warmer autumn weather than any of my neighbours could remember, I waved to Billy Stannard's *Nonsuch* that was fishing off Gun Hill and sailed *Pippin* as far northward as Easton cliffs before turning about and reaching back towards Walberswick Bight on the last of the flood.

Hove-to, shirt sleeves rolled up, I lay back on a cushion and drank coffee. In the bright sunshine and light south-easterly wind Sole Bay was looking its autumnal best. What with sixteen new groynes in place and children on their half-term holiday swimming from the neatly sculpted beach, the Sunrise Coast was looking beautiful, as well as being quite robustly prepared, I thought, to meet the winter storms.

Nine days later a very high tide joined forces with an abnormally high swell to excavate several hundred tons of sand from the beach and fling it on to the newly repaired promenade. The man-made dune protecting the Dingle marshes between Walberswick and Dunwich was extensively breached and the valley of the Hundred River was inundated so deeply that the force of the outrushing water near Benacre sluice swept a man off his feet and carried him out to sea on the ebbing tide.

Minutes later the coastguard control centre at Yarmouth had called out three lifeboats to comb the waters between Lowestoft and Southwold in search of him: the private boat from Caister, the 47ft *Spirit of Lowestoft* and the smaller but marginally nimbler *Leslie Tranmer* from its station in Southwold harbour.

Crewed by Alan Scoggins, Cath Fox and Simon Callaghan, the Southwold boat searched close inshore, weaving among 4m breakers less than 200m from the beach. Sadly, after five hours of extensive searching, the lifeboat crew returned to harbour to report that the missing man had not been found.

6

WHY THE WRECKS?

In October 1789 an averagely amorous but uncommonly literate passenger to Hull named Edward Anderson picked his way through the warren of stinking alleys that debouched on to the Thames and boarded the sailing vessel *Friendship*, along with eight or nine unescorted women and several children.

Why the *Friendship* never got to her destination and what happened to all aboard her is related in 300 lines of rhyming couplets that were composed by Anderson and sold for just one penny. Though some way short of being a masterpiece, his *Description of the October Gale, 1789, when One Hundred sail of Shipping were cast away Near Yarmouth Roads, And more than One Thousand Men were drowned, with Observations and Reflections* is nevertheless worth every farthing, even if his reflections might make your toes curl.

Friendship's troubles began during the hours of darkness, whilst anchored in Yarmouth roads among 300 others, which proved to be more than a few too many. The evening had begun pleasantly, with vessels riding easily on calm and moonlit waters, music and laughter ascending through open skylights to mingle with the shriller cries from boys sculling alongside, holding up fresh herring. Below decks, some of the women made merry with their fellow passengers by singing saucy songs, while their less tuneful but equally sportive companions spread their skirts in the nearby nooks and crannies to play card games that went on till midnight.

'That's a flat back, Eddie boy!'

'Pair riall, says I.'

'Good on yer, me darlin', but how's this? Fifteen two an' a run of four for six!'

'Merkett, you devil you … an' give us a kiss …!'

Anderson sank on to his couch in the early hours, musing on the carnal delights in store for the day ahead. Before he had the chance to taste them he was roused from his dreams by the wind whistling in the rigging and the bosun whistling up the crew, who rapidly filled the air with ill-tempered requests to look to the bleedin' tops'l and pass a few more fugging gaskets, aping the manner of their captain, who was raging drunk.

The wind pressure on the hull and masts pulled *Friendship's* anchor out of the seabed to send her careering downwind towards her nearest neighbour. Though

SS *Hawk*, wrecked 1862. (Pimple Thompson)

the crew promptly let go a second anchor, the captain speedily frustrated their endeavours by following his order to veer out more cable with an over-hasty cry of 'Check her!', thereby causing the cable to break. This mishap allowed *Friendship* to impale herself on a passing bowsprit which demolished the cabin skylight as well as shattering the gaff and boom attached to the mainmast. Seeing the *Friendship* was unable to get clear, the other captain tried to slack away his own cable, a thoroughly seamanlike procedure during which he had the misfortune to catch his flapping coat between the cable and the windlass, which promptly wrenched off his legs.

The bowsprit snapped, *Friendship* broke free and the anchor bit and held, bringing her bows more safely into the wind again. The respite was short-lived. Soon the crippled vessel and her wailing cargo were plunged into two and a half pages of maritime mayhem in which the *Friendship* ran down three more ships, one sinking with all hands, another drifting to destruction with five men on its quarterdeck so benumbed with cold they were unable to grasp lines that were thrown to them.

Its captain in a coma and the crew disputing about what to do for the best, someone had to get a grip, so passenger Anderson took command. With the mate conning from the bows and an exceedingly able seaman heaving the lead, he steered ever southwards, keeping in 3 fathoms close to the shore past Gorleston and Corton, driving down the Stanford channel through seas littered with wrecks and drowning men, including those swept from the rigging of a ship on the Holm Sand, the crew of a sloop that had gone ashore on Lowestoft Ness and a third sunk in the South Road.

Her leaks unstoppable and her spars in splinters, *Friendship* lurched across Sole Bay to be driven thirty miles south of Thorpe Ness by wind and tide until Anderson was able to edge the vessel into the lee of a red cliff near Harwich and run her ashore at quarter-ebb on the Pye Sand, where all but one of the

The barque *Nordhavet*, stranded below Gun Hill in 1887 with a cargo of coal. Her fourteen crewmen were rescued by the surf lifeboat *Quiver No.2*. (*Alfred Corry Museum*)

passengers and crew staggered to safety, followed by a heavily hung-over captain, to whom the Almighty measured out a harsher fate:

> And after he escapéd from shipwreck,
> He fell from off a coach and broke his neck.

Like more than a few clapped-out mariners who believe they have been rescued by divine intervention, Anderson vowed to give up wine, women and song and tread the paths of virtue for the rest of his days.

But is his story true? About parts of it, there are doubts. The insistent message of *October Gale* is that shipwrecks are sent by God to punish their sinful crews. Well, perhaps. But, given that the average eighteenth-century coaster carried a crew of four, it is hard to see how the sinking of a hundred ships could drown as many as a thousand seamen; and the wrenching-off of the legs could be an imported Gothic horror. For all that, his mention of the precise height of tide on the Pye Sand, the business of following a 3-fathom line of sounding, and the snapshot of five hypothermic men unable to grasp a lifeline persuade me that the wrecking of the *Friendship* happened in the way that Anderson said it did. Shorn of its horrors and homilies, *October Gale* would have been admissible evidence in any of the enquiries into the causes of shipwreck which took place in the century that followed.

Although a Parliamentary Select Committee in 1836 and a Royal Commission in '74 neglected to bring the Almighty into their proceedings, they listened to the same sort of evidence about the behaviour of ships and crews in gale-force winds that they could have gleaned from Anderson's poem or the manuscript of the yet unpublished *Southwold Diary, Vol. II*, where Maggs lists nineteen Sole Bay wrecks that are buried among the statistics for the disastrous years 1855–57, including the barque *Cape Horn* and five large brigs cast ashore in the November gale of '55.

The Surveyor-General to the Board of Trade also observed that although 40 per cent of the 368 casualties in 1856 had been wrecked by the same magnitude

The *Idun*, wrecked in January 1912 during a heavy east-south-easterly gale. She had left Antwerp bound for Cadiz but had been driven many miles off course by stormy weather that had probably sprung the mainmast. A steam trawler was endeavouring to tow her to safety when the line broke and she was cast ashore under Kilcock Cliff. Parts of the framework remained visible until the 1960s. (*Alfred Corry* Museum)

Barque *Idun*, photographed from Long Island Cliff. The captain and his nine-man crew were rescued via a breeches buoy and bundled into the *Red Lion* inn. (*Alfred Corry* Museum)

The crew of *Idun* outside the coastguard station on St James' Green. One man had fallen from the breeches buoy and was rescued from the sea by two coastguard officers and a civilian. (Pimple Thompson)

High winds were
not the only cause
of strandings. The
skipper of this punt
lost his bearings
in fog. (Pimple
Thompson)

of stormy weather that Anderson and Maggs had chronicled, a further 46 per cent
had gone down in winds no heavier than a strong breeze. As to the whys of the
sinkings, fifty-four vessels sank or were abandoned because they had been sent out
in an unseaworthy state, twenty-one were wrecked through failing to use the lead
and the remaining seventy-eight went to the bottom because their captains and
pilots mistook lights, were incautious, negligent or drunk. In other words, almost
half of all marine accidents were being caused by avoidable human errors.

It was A Disgraceful State Of Affairs, said the writers of letters to the newspapers,
and The Government Must Do Something About It At Once.

They went on saying it for years. And, as Nicolette Jones points out in *The
Plimsoll Sensation*, for years the government did nothing. In 1868, twelve years
later, 629 vessels were wrecked in British waters, and a further 1,502 were so badly
damaged that they were obliged to get rid of their cargo. All in all, 1868 was a
disastrous year: 2,131 ships were lost or damaged, no fewer than 763 (36 per cent)
of them by collision, with the loss of more than 800 lives.

An example of the government's slothfulness in taking remedial action is the
length of time it took to stop ships from setting off in an unseaworthy state. Ten
long years after the Surveyor-General wrote his 1856 report, a lesser member of
his profession in Liverpool might have been overheard murmuring to Captain
Lean, master of the sailing vessel *Utopia*, such toothless cautions as, to devise one,
'Really, old chap, I myself can't do anything about it, but I think you might be
minded to tell your johnnies to stop loading just as soon as that mark I've drawn
on the hull is level with the water in the dock. Sailing for Bombay, did you say?
And you'll be crossing Biscay in the jolly old ides of March? Anyway … tootle-
pip and the very best of good luck!'

Captain Lean passed on the warning about the danger of overloading to the
cargo owner, who mentally thumbed his nose at the surveyor and went on
loading until the mark was a good few inches underwater before moving *Utopia*

Barque *Chelmsford* at Astoria, Oregon, after rounding Cape Horn on her maiden voyage from Cardiff in 1893–94. The Southwold seaman William 'Prim' Deal was the only Briton among the thirty crewmen inhabiting the fo'c'sle. (Keith Deal)

Magdapur was a fast cargo liner built by Lithgows at Port Glasgow in 1921 for T.&J. Brocklebank of Liverpool. She originally measured 9,237 tons and was 500ft in length. In 1935, probably to economise on running costs, *Magdapur* was shortened by 37ft, her tonnage reduced to 8,641 and her coal-fired boilers were equipped to burn oil fuel. (National Archive of Scotland)

to another dock to take aboard a further 120 tons of coke. At this point Lean protested, was again ignored, and so he resigned. His replacement, Captain Dickie, who also objected, was cowed into submission by the agent's threat that, if Dickie failed to take the *Utopia* to sea, the agent would see to it that he would never again be employed in any ship out of Liverpool.

Woefully undermanned and under-cared-for, *Utopia* was towed out of the Mersey on 10 March 1867 with 4ft of water in the hold to begin her passage to Bombay. Three days later, worn out by unavailing labour at the pumps, Captain Dickie and his crew took to the longboat. Minutes after they had pulled away from her, *Utopia* sank.

Discussing the sinking, *The Lifeboat* magazine of the RNLI argued for the appointment of independent surveyors who would supervise the painting of a thin white line on the sides of all cargo vessels to show the legally binding limit to which they should be loaded. It seemed like a sensible suggestion but it had the serious flaw of leaving the positioning of the line to the discretion of the shipowner, whose profits depended on cramming as much cargo into his ships as he possibly could. In spite of the comical largeness of the loophole (Jones tells of one ship that actually set out from Cardiff with a load line painted on its funnel), owners of the many vessels that were as overladen as *Utopia* saw the proposal as the thin end of a potentially lethal wedge that would kill their profits. Though the load line proposal won the support of the Association of Chambers of Commerce and the more humane shipowners, others set themselves against it, arguing that it would make British shipping uncompetitive, would be an unwarranted interference by the State to restrict the freedom of the individual, would be a namby-pambying insult to the nation's gallant sailors, etcetera. In other words, they were talking tosh.

The long and often bitter campaign for an enforceable load line fixed by the Board of Trade was headed by the social reformer Samuel Plimsoll, who amassed damning evidence of the evils of overloading and the equally pernicious practice of over-insurance, a scam in which shipowners knowingly sent unseaworthy vessels to their doom so as to claim greatly inflated sums from the insurers. He began campaigning for his load line in 1870, was unsuccessfully sued for libel by his opponents over some derogatory remarks about their coffin ships, and went on to win a partial victory with the passing of the Merchant Shipping Act of 1876; but it was not until 1890, twenty-three years after the *Utopia*'s sinking, that Parliament at last decreed that British cargo ships must carry a load line fixed by the Board of Trade. Twenty months later a triumphant Plimsoll declared to the editor of *The Times* that the enforcement of his load line had saved 434 lives in a year.

It would be pleasing to produce figures that would show how greatly the sailors on the Sunrise Coast benefited from his campaign but unfortunately I can't do anything of the kind. In fact, looking at the shipwreck figures for Sole Bay for the twenty years following the 1876 Act, a cynic might argue that, far from improving the lot of Poor Jack, Plimsoll had made his miserable situation a whole lot worse. During the ten years after the Act, sinkings in Sole Bay went up by 30 per cent, and in the decade 1886–95 they increased by a further 11 per cent. The size of the apparent failure is heightened further by the fact that the 1876 Act applied only to British ships and excluded fishing vessels, pleasure yachts, and coasting vessels under 80 tons, which meant that eleven foreign-registered ships and three locally registered fishing smacks wrecked in Sole Bay between 1876 and the passing of the improved Act of 1890 would not have been counted in Plimsoll's calculations. However, despite these early shortcomings and the savage mauling it received in 1906 from the hands of Lloyd George, the then President of the Board of Trade, the other leading maritime nations gradually adopted the improved standards set out by the British Parliament, although it was not until 1930 that the delegates of thirty nations agreed to an internationally enforceable Plimsoll Line.

Universally revered as 'The Sailor's Friend' who looked after the life of Poor Jack in all the seas of the world, Plimsoll was elected the first President of the National Union of Seamen and was honoured on the Sunrise Coast by having a lifeboat named after him. Launched in 1876 from the north beach at Lowestoft, the *Samuel Plimsoll* was on station there for twenty-nine years and saved 165 lives.

The last moments of the *Magdapur*, the largest vessel to be sunk in Sole Bay. The seventy-four survivors were covered in oil, though she was probably burning coal at the time, having sailed from the coal-bunkering port of Shields only two days previously. A ground-floor room of a house in Dunwich Road, Southwold, was furnished with oak tables and chairs cast ashore from the wreck.

Britannia led the way in laying down the law against owners who overloaded their ships but she was reluctant to legislate against mariners who scuppered themselves with booze. Sobriety continued to be a custom more honoured in the breach than in the observance, with judgment and punishment more often than not left to God. So long as it was thought needful to drink good honest beer instead of foul and stinking water, captains could argue for everyone having a quantity of antiseptic alcohol in their stomachs. Added to which, a tot of the hard stuff had long been seen as a customary reward for doing difficult or unpleasant tasks. The occasional modest libations Eric Newby and his watchmates received for their labours in *Moshulu* in the 1930s were the updated equivalent of the morale-building 'barrel of wine for our men that workt hard' recorded by Edward Barlow in the seventeenth century. But in a good many British ships the level of consumption went far beyond what was necessary for keeping-up the people's health or bolstering their team spirit. Anderson's drunken captain was a familiar figure. Reporting on his voyage of 1593, Sir Richard Hawkins complained that the overmuch drinking of alcohol (in this case, wine) was: 'A foul fault, ... too common among seamen, [that] hath been, and is daily, the destruction of many good enterprises,' including the subsequent foundering of a profit-making endeavour with a cargo of red herrings, undertaken by the master of the *Christopher*, caught out in a Channel gale of 1652 which blew his unattended mainsail to pieces while he was slumped in his cabin doorway with a brandy bottle between his legs.

On the other hand, the failings of the stereotypical drunken sailor need to be set against the sobering navigational marvels he achieved even when his mess-table was awash with liquor. In 1803 Captain Matthew Flinders calculated that his twelve-month supply of rum for the eighty-eight persons aboard HMS *Investigator* amounted to 1,483 imperial gallons (6,472 litres), which meant every man jack under his command would be drinking half a pint (0.28 litres) of spirits a day. And that wasn't all. If a sailor ended up in the sick bay and the surgeon was agreeable, his daily rum ration might be supplemented with one whole pint (0.57 litres) of port wine. Yet Flinders went on

Stranded on the bar. Though the day is windless, a moderate swell is sweeping across the barge's deck. (Southwold Museum)

to chart much of the exceedingly lengthy and intricate coastline of Australia with no memorable complaints about drunken behaviour.

There is nothing in Maggs to suggest any shipwreck in Sole Bay was caused by drunkenness, and the Surveyor-General cited only one of the twenty casualties he investigated in 1857 as having liquor as a possible contributory factor. That's as may be, but their evidence is very partial. The Surveyor-General was debarred from examining the captains of uninsured or foreign vessels, and though Maggs is quick to denounce land sharks, he never points a finger of blame in his diary at seamen who lose their ships. In fact, even when a court of law finds a seaman guilty, Maggs stands up and testifies only to the soundness of his character. To hear a different view the reader would need to listen to one or two old-timers in Southwold who could tell of sinkings that happened very soon after Jack and his master had made their way from a dockside pub not exactly stone cold sober. And – if pressed a little harder – they will perhaps admit that they themselves have, just perhaps once or twice in their lifetimes, gone on watch with the occasional bout of double vision and an Alka Seltzer. It is indirect, circumstantial evidence, but it lends a deal of weight to the author Captain Frederick Marryat RN, who held the firm opinion that drink was responsible for more than half of all shipwrecks.

What is striking about the 1857 report is the weakness of the Board of Trade. In fifteen cases no blame was apportioned nor any penalty exacted. Two casualties escaped investigation because the ships were flying a foreign flag or were uninsured; others got off scot free even when the assessors found that they had been going too fast or were on the wrong side of a channel. 'Hit and run' incidents went unpunished; the master of the SS *James Hartley* was allowed to keep his Certificate of Competence even though his vessel had run down the brig *Messenger* and he had been admonished for not going back to search for six drowning members of its crew; and the engineer in the SS *Parana*, who unintentionally killed six people by screwing down the safety valve on a boiler that later exploded, was told only that he had shown 'a great want of judgement'. Boards of Trade came and went and its officials were eventually given sharper teeth, but in the 1930s the engineer in a Lowestoft drifter was still blithely shutting down his safety valves so as to achieve the higher speed that would get his herrings to market ahead of the competition.

The most common failing cited in the report is Neglect of the Lead, but in case the reader should think that heaving a 7lb lump of lead was some kind of sadistical Victorian cure-all for chronic navigational hiccups, I would invite him to journey round the extensive but unwelcoming bosom of East Anglia in the *Elizabeth & Ann* of Boston under the command of Captain Maryatt (not Marryat the author), who wound his way through the tortuous channels of the Wash in November 1841, on passage to some such place as London's Covent Garden with a cargo of potatoes.

Maryatt was a cool-headed opportunist who didn't give a toss for omens or traditions that went against his thinking. He would have set out from Boston on Friday the Thirteenth, not at all worried by the fact that this particular Friday was also twelve months to the day since he had been shipwrecked in a similar vessel called *Ant*. The *Ant* had been a Humber keel, around 68ft (21m) in length and drawing 6ft (1.8m) of water, driven by a huge squaresail and a topsail carried on a single mast, well suited to East Coast rivers and estuaries but not the best sort of boat for passaging the North Sea. If, as seems likely, his *Elizabeth & Ann* too was a keel, her broad, flat bottom would have allowed her to lie very comfortably when discharging cargo on to beaches, but she would more easily have slithered sideways in a seaway.

Captain Maryatt would have wended through twenty-five miles of channels on an ebbing tide, guided for the most part by buoys but relying increasingly on soundings called out by his leadsman to pick his way through the unmarked gatways. Once clear of Blakeney Sands, about seven miles north-east of Wells he would start to feel the first of the flood tide that would carry him into deeper water where he could lay aside his lead for a while and know better where he was by eyeing the relative positions of Cromer and Happisburgh or by taking compass bearings of their respective lights.

Around the time at which Happisburgh was sliding smoothly past his beam, the favourable breeze that had encouraged his departure slowly backed southwards until it was blowing from ahead. There are no means of knowing what thoughts ran through the captain's mind when the wind changed direction but one would have been whether to go forward towards London or to turn back and shelter at Blakeney.

Two hundred tons of perishable potatoes pressing heavier on his mind than the weight of a force five wind, Captain Maryatt tied a reef in his sail and pressed on.

Like Cudlip guessing the movements of the *Fairy*, we may confidently suppose that Maryatt would have been carried clear of the Newarp light vessel by the flood tide and would then have stood out to sea on the starboard tack so as to keep a safe distance off the shoals of the Sunrise Coast. He would have been strengthened in this resolve by painful memories of the wrecking of *Ant* and HMS *Fairy*, when a favourable offshore breeze had turned into the disastrous on-shore gale only twelve months previously.

It is also possible to imagine the feats of heavy-weather seamanship performed aboard the *Elizabeth & Ann* during the next five days when the wind built up to a moderate gale that sank an unnamed schooner in Sole Bay and drove the *Buckingham* on to the Barnard before backing ESE on the fourth day and increasing to a whole gale which wrecked the *Catliff* and *Hope* at Minsmere, the *Mary & Jo Marsden* at Covehithe, and – as if to ensure that the sinful subscribers to Anderson's penny dreadful had understood his message – was again increased on the fifth day by the heavenly clerk of the weather to what must have been a force ten gale which destroyed the unfortunate *Catharine* elsewhere in Sole Bay before suddenly blowing itself out and enveloping the scene in fog.

How Maryatt and his men survived conditions in which so many other larger and more plentifully manned vessels were wrecked will never be known, but survive they did, as too did the *Elizabeth & Ann*.

Maggs records that Maryatt and his ship came on to the beach north of the lifeboat house at Southwold on 19 November, the last day of the gale, beaching on the identical length of sandy shingle where he had been wrecked in the *Ant*, twelve months before. '6 same Evening Calm! & Fog!' exclaimed the diarist, adding *Elizabeth & Ann* was 'got off & repaired' and 700 sackfuls of her potatoes were still wholesome enough six days later to be auctioned. I have the feeling that if the full facts were known, Captain Maryatt and his crew would have received a pat or two on their backs from the insurers for keeping well clear of dangers to leeward and for their exemplary use of the lead.

Yet, thirty-four years after the 1857 report citing eleven instances of want of caution and twenty-one failures to use the lead, ships were still sailing to their doom in only moderate winds because they had approached the land too closely or there had been nobody taking soundings. One of them may have been the ketch *Kate & Elizabeth* of Portsmouth, bound for a northern port with a cargo of ore, that was wrecked on the Barnard in May 1891 when the wind was only 20 knots, force five.

To understand how such accidents could happen we must imagine it is one of the three days in May when the visibility averages two miles or less, and a vessel on passage to, say, Middlesbrough is abeam of the lighthouse on Orford Ness, faintly visible one and a half miles distant through a fine drizzle. The tide is just beginning to ebb northwards and the wind is only moderate but it's north-easterly, blowing on the captain's nose.

If he is determined to press on, he now has two choices: either he can head east for three hours until he finds the 20-fathom contour and then turn north and

The white-roofed building in the foreground housed the Kilcock Cliff Co. in the early years of the twentieth century, by which time the North Channel pilots in the company had been moved to Harwich. (Robert Malster)

Celebrating the 1952 coronation of Elizabeth II aboard the schooner yacht *Wildflower*. (Pimple Thompson)

stem the next flood tide in the belief that he will safely clear the Cross Sand and Newarp Flats off Yarmouth, or he can do a series of zig-zags close inshore, keeping the charted landmarks in sight, in the expectation of sighting the buoys marking the dangers in Sole Bay in good time to avoid them.

The off-shore strategy has the merit of keeping him clear of danger for the ensuing nine hours but it brings the later problem of finding the Newarp light vessel from an imprecisely known position in poor visibility. If he's lucky and has a sextant aboard, perhaps the afternoon sun will come out and he'll be able to fix his position when he's nearing the Newarp. Otherwise, the best he can hope for is that he will be able to sight the lightship at two miles and shape his course accordingly; at worst, he won't see it at all, in which case he will be obliged to rely on the product of a few arithmetical scribbles done when he's bent over the chart and all the while keeping an ear open for the calls of his leadsman.

The inshore passage has the advantage of keeping the mariner in sight of land. Unlike his offshore counterpart, he will be able to take bearings of landmarks and put a cross on his chart at any moment and know it is marking his true position as opposed to an estimated one. This may seem much the more prudent course but it carries its share of risks, not the least of which is his having to venture so close to the shore that he becomes embayed.

Let us suppose the master has chosen to make the inshore passage.

It's a neapish tide, so off Orford Ness during the first hour of ebb the current between the Onion Patch – known then as Nathaniel's Knowl – and Aldeburgh Ridge will be running no more than ½ a knot, which means he has no difficulty in holding a close-hauled course which minutes later brings him in sight of a Martello tower, at which point he downs his helm and goes smartly on to the port tack to skirt a 1½-fathom shoal off Aldeburgh by a quarter of a mile. Ten minutes later he is losing the tower in the drizzle and so he puts about and heads north again, hoping to squeeze between Sizewell Bank and the shore. By this time the tide is running just about a knot and the ketch is moving over the seabed at 7mph. 'Breakers ahead!' cries the lookout in the rigging. Unable to point his bows any more degrees to windward, the master alters course fifty degrees to port and shortly afterwards half-a-dozen Sizewell purlers sidle past him, only 100m astern. Two hundred metres farther on and he is again close hauled on the starboard tack and his masthead lookout is whizzing down the rigging to ready the jib sheets.

With the Sizewell watchbox in transit with Lady Abbey Farm, the master then alters course on to port tack and the wind nudges up to 22 knots, whereupon the mate and the lookout tuck a reef into the mainsail and hand the outer jib. The boat rides a shade easier, enabling the master to snatch a few hasty puffs at his pipe in the lee of his companionway for two minutes during which the watchhouse becomes an indistinct blur while he's peering at the chart and deciding to sail farther from the coast than he'd planned in order to pass well outside the Dunwich bank, where the force five wind against a 1½-knot tide is likely to be kicking up a roughish popple like the Sizewell's.

'Where's that watchbox gorn?'

Mate lifts arm and points.

'Nah, it can't be!'

''tis, Skipper.'

'Tain't!... Anyways, we'll go t'other way! READEE HABOUT!'

There's a thrashing of canvas sails and a clatter of elmwood blocks and soon the ship is heading north again, safely clear of the Dunwich bank and in parallel with a seemingly featureless coast on which watchboxes, windmills and the ruinous remains of All Saints church at Dunwich are slipping past unseen.

'Skipper, wind's veered half point an' it's gettin' thicker ... C'n see nobbut a mile at most ...'

'Now, let's see ...' says the skipper to himself, scratching his nose, '... compass course being East b' North three-quarters North an' its error being two points West means ... sixty minutes at 5-and-a-bit knots, adding on 1-an'-a-bit miles o' tide on her right arse settin' her half a point ter larboard means that ... we should ... be ... just ... lemmy see now ... just about ... erm ... HERE!

'Mate!'

'Skipper?'

Opposite: The stupendous outrigger projecting from the stern of this beach yawl helped spread a vast sail area that could speed it across Sole Bay at up to 16 knots. The vessel could be *Bittern, Baden Powell* or *Victoria.* (Robert Malster)

Left: Southwold Sea Scouts salvage the figurehead of the *Wildflower,* built 1860 at Fairlie on the Clyde and broken up on Blackshore after the great flood of 1953. The ship's bell went to a Scout troop in Bungay, the compass to the longshore boat *Hobo,* the binnacle to *Kerry Louise* and the sails reappeared as the skin of several canoes. (Eric Paisley)

'Where's our Jimmy gorn with the lead?'

'Our Jimmy is getting our dinner just now but ten minutes back he was sounding a quarter less eight.'

'Well, that would've been just about … erm … right. All things considered, Mate, we're two miles sou'east o' Southwold church.'

The mate runs a fingernail round the edge of a silver sixpenny bit in his left-hand trouser pocket and turns it over.

'Skip!' comes a voice from aloft. 'Loom o' land! Two points abaft larboard beam.'

The captain joins the mate at the leeward mizzen shrouds and gives a tremendous sniff.

'Ha! Looks like the drizzle is easing, Mate, so steer East b'North a quarter North an' ease the sheet. An' Jimmy boy!, jus' you leave orf peelin' those tayters an' go forrard lookout. You'll be lookin' for a black buoy wiv a topmark on the port bow …'

Before Jimmy can get to his appointed station the man in the rigging is calling that he can see breakers on the port bow and before the captain can respond to this unwelcome information his vessel is hard aground on the Barnard.

What had happened was that during the few minutes when he had lost his landmarks the ship had been making a larger amount of leeway than he had allowed for and so he had gradually become embayed, with the wind and tide pushing him

farther into the Covehithe Bight and on to the sands on which he joined the eleven other vessels that had already been wrecked on the bank between 1857 and 1891.

In part, the antidote for the shipwreck malady was better training. From 1850 the Board of Trade had run compulsory examinations for foreign-going masters and mates, though not until 1854 was an equivalent examination made available to navigators in the coasting trade. The 1857 report found that 261 wrecked or damaged ships had been commanded by foreign-going masters holding Certificates of Competency and 290 had been in charge of masters with Certificates of Service. Since the greater number of vessels wrecked in Sole Bay were fishermen or coasters, it is only to be expected that the third and largest category, numbering 297 casualties, were coasting vessels whose masters were not required by law to have a Board of Trade ticket.

Although by 1935 masters of the larger coasters were required to pass an examination, most commanders of smaller vessels still had no certificate of any kind. Young Tristan Jones sailed back and forth across the North Sea from London or Hull to Holland and Germany in the spritsail barge *Second Apprentice* until after the outbreak of the Second World War in 1939, yet, during the two years Jones was in her, his uncertificated captain was never seen to consult a chart or open any books other than his ledger, his log and his Holy Bible. And even as late as the 1960s a fair number of officers navigating Sole Bay in coasters of less than 200 tons still had no paperwork to advertise their competence. Billy Stannard sailed as mate in the 56-ton spritsail barge *Marjorie* at the age of sixteen.

'And didn't you have to take any exams?'

'No. There was no paperwork. Merit was what counted, not qualifications. Skippers would tell the owner that so-and-so had the ability to be mate and then

Billy Stannard in his motorised punt *Sylvia* tows the 18ft yacht *Margaretha* over the bar, escorted astern by the Southwold Sailing Club rescue boat *John Svoboda*. This 1962 photo shows a South pier that had been zealously knocked about a bit by His Majesty's sappers in the Second World War to deter an invading enemy. LT 125 *Sylvia* had been re-built in 1946 and is still fishing from Blackshore in 2008. (William Stannard)

Even in moderate winds, conditions at the harbour entrance can be hazardous. The Sailing Club launch *Delphis* pilots a Dutch ketch through tumbling breakers in the 1960s. (*Alfred Corry Museum*)

the owner would come over to you and say "I'd like you to go as mate in the *Marjorie* what's sailing for London with a cargo of grain. Can you be aboard her by the afternoon?"'

Billy's words reflect the same scornful distrust of officialdom and paperwork sturdily expressed in 1894 by Captain Simon Gunn, who boasted he had never lost a ship in all the thirty years he'd been master: 'All I knows I learned m'self ... Book learnin', mister, may be all right to them that needs it, but I takes no stock in it. And I reckon Simon Gunn's as good if not better than the rest.'

Navigation equipment in the *Marjorie* was no different from what Osmond Ferro's fourteenth-century skipper would have been using aboard his cog. 'We had a lead line and a compass but no pilot book,' said Billy. 'We didn't need no pilot book because the skipper knew in his brain that if he were coming up, say, the Swin or the Wallet in fog he could just swing the lead and tell from the colour and stiffness of the mud more or less where he was. The same can be done in Sole Bay. Suppose you're fishing off Southwold with the water tower in line with

Gun Hill and where there's two 9-fathom spots. Now, you know that the inner one is soft mud and the outer one is hard. If you swing your lead and find the bottom is soft, then you know straight away that you're getting into what we call the South End Roughs, where the bottom is foul with boom-defence material and old anchors...'

'So you found your way by lead, log and lookout?'

'Yes, we did ... but the best skippers also had something extra ... skippers like Tommy Farnes from Gravesend, who done his time in West Coast ketches with his dad. I was with him after the war when he was skipper of the *Furmity*, a motor ship that could carry around 440 tons, an' we had a mate with a foreign-going ticket who didn't like being in a ship in which no one else was qualified ... so when we were at Bideford in thick fog this mate said "You're not sailing in this fog, are you?" an' the skipper say "Well, of course we are – we got to go to Teignmouth and load clay." So orf we went, an' after we had dropped the pilot at Bideford bar the skipper say to me, "Go down the engine room and tell the Chief to keep her at ..." I can't remember how many revs it was ... 275 or 300, I think ... "... keep her at those many revs an' don't alter till I say so."

'Well, away we went into the fog, an' next morning it was coming daylight an' the skipper say "Tell the Chief that when I ring *STOP* I mean stop *everything*, the generator and everything. Then I want you to go on the fo'c'sle head and I want you to tell me what you hear."

'Well, this mate looked at him an' he say "You're lost! You haven't got a clue where you are!" An' Tommy – oh, he was such a nice bloke, he never said anything nasty like – said "Well, if that's what you think pr'aps you'd better go down for your breakfast and maybe stay down there for your lunch as well!"

'An' so I went to the fo'c'sle head in the thick fog an' before long I was shouting up to the skipper "I can hear waves breaking on a shingle bank!"

'An' straightaway the skipper calls back, "Right ho then, drop the anchor." An' – d'you know what? – after breakfast the fog lifted and there we were, anchored *just a hundred yards away from the shingle bank off Teignmouth!* Now, how had he managed *that?*'

It was a question that could usefully have been put to Tommy Farnes at Teignmouth as well as to thousands of unnamed other navigators who had found their way through the shoals of the Sunrise Coast in fog, mist, falling snow and rain squalls so heavy that they could barely see their compass. How had they managed *that* without getting themselves wrecked? Four hundred vessels had been lost in Sole Bay, but what about the thousands that had safely reached port ...?

The ringing of a doorbell brought Billy's dog stiffly to its feet. It was time for me to leave.

Outside, a brisk southerly was whirling leaves down the gutters and speckling the flagstones with rain.

'He had what I'd call a sixth sense,' said Billy.

7

'THE PEOPLE' AND
THEIR CAPTAINS

Sailors must be the most familiar to modern eyes of all the working men of the seventeenth
and eighteenth centuries. Their images abound in television, film and historical novels. There
they are, barefoot, bronzed and pigtailed, running up the rigging, performing acrobatics on
the yards, staring from the tops into the blue or stormy yonder on their way to romance and
adventure. There they are, handkerchiefs knotted about their heads, loose breeches flapping,
cutlass in their hands and pistols in their belts, as they storm across the decks of an enemy
ship or drive their captain and officers into the sea in a frenzy of mutiny.

– Peter Earle, *Sailors*

True or not, these modern images of 'the people', as sailors were often called, are
almost always drawn from the Royal Navy or from pirates, rather than from the
many more numerous merchant seamen conducting Britain's fast-growing trade.
At the time of the Battle of Sole Bay in 1672, British shipping amounted to half a
million tons and employed 50,000 men. By the end of the eighteenth century the
tonnage had doubled and the workforce tripled. And only forty years later, when
James Maggs was lifting his gavel on Easton beach to auction his first wreck for £43
to John Magub, 3.5 million tons of British ships were to-ing and fro-ing between
the world's ports, whose inhabitants were becoming increasingly familiar with the
English language coming from the 200,000 sailors who manned them.

Nineteenth-century seamen were mostly boys or unmarried men aged between
sixteen and twenty-five, wearing much the same sorts of working clothes as their
eighteenth-century counterparts described by Earle and not a lot different from
those worn by the sixteenth-century crew of the warship *Mary Rose*, who clad
themselves in woollen stockings, baggy knee-breeches and leather jerkins, topped
off with a woollen hat. Even in the more formally dressed navy of the 1830s,
FitzRoy allowed his officers in *Beagle* – and, by inference, his crew – to wear 'any
kinds of jackets, round hats or caps'. Most Georgian and Victorian seamen were
smaller than modern Britons; fourteen mutinous sailors in 1775 had an average
height of only 4ft 9in (145cm) – (Did the Master-at-Arms chant 'Shortarses have
short fuses!' as he clapped them in irons?) – and nearly seventy years later a muster
list from HMS *Fairy* reveals the majority were between 5ft 5½in (166cm) and 5ft
8in (173cm) tall. Whether they slept in hammocks or bunks, their accommodation

Above: Laden with lead and down by the head? Only the shallowness of the harbour has prevented a sinking. Perhaps the bilge pump failed? 'An avoidable error!' sneer the insurers. (Southwold Museum)

Right: Small likelihood that the owners of this zulu will try to defraud its crew of their earnings because they are probably one and the same. Soon the skipper will douse the lantern and go to his cramped quarters below deck, then smoke will rise from the galley chimney as he pours a wee dram. (Robert Malster)

was cramped, gloomy and fetid. In a wooden merchantman of the 1830s fourteen men breathed, slept, ate, broke wind and cursed the cook in a space no larger than the ten-by-ten living room of a Victorian working-class house. The few who were as much as 5ft 9in (175cm) tall would have been perpetually looking at their feet, while any 6ft 2in Hercules who happened to serve aboard one of the many smaller vessels where the headroom was as little as 4ft 6in (134cm) would have been obliged to move around his living quarters bent double. Later in the century, headroom in steel ships was mercifully greater. In the fo'c'sle of the barque *Elissa*, built in 1877, even a six-footer could straighten his neck and stand upright.

Until modern times, the diet of a foreign-going seaman changed little over the centuries. Daily rations on Frobisher's Arctic expedition sailing across Sole Bay in

1577 were 1lb (450g) of flour or hard biscuit, a double handful of rice and oatmeal and 8.9oz (252g) of peas. He would also have been allotted 1lb (450g) of salt beef or pork, or ½lb (226g) of cheese or buttered stockfish (dried haddock or cod), washed down by one whole gallon (4.5 litres) of beer. Ten generations later a Victorian descendant serving in *Marmora* of South Shields in 1865 was getting half the amount of flour but instead of the hard biscuit he would have been entitled to 1lb of bread. His meat ration was the same as before and ditto with the stockfish. The only significant difference lay in the nature of his liquid intake. Those whose Elizabethan ancestors had only been there for the thirty gallons of beer per month were now having to be there for 1½lb (680g) of coffee and ¼lb (113g) of tea per month instead. Forward to the late 1930s and we find Eric Newby in the barque *Moshulu* existing on the same unvarying diet of bread, salt beef and salt pork ('sometimes floating in a thick heroic kind of pea soup as solid as porridge'), supplemented by the legendary stockfish, which 'resembled clubs used by cannibals for dispatching their victims'. Reappearing on the *Moshulu's* menu is the hard biscuit, but the butter has been supplanted by margarine (invented by a Frenchman in 1869), and the hitherto milkless coffee and tea could now be stiffened with a weekly ration of condensed and heavily (addicts would say deliciously) sweetened milk, always consumed in fewer days than the intended seven, unlike the potatoes – surprisingly absent from the 1865 menu – which were dished up by the bucketful.

Faced with the cut-throat competition from steam-powered merchantmen, some unscrupulous sailing-ship owners were suspected of issuing secret orders compelling their captains to turn a blind eye to the regulations and reduce their voyage expenses to a dangerous minimum. It was all very well for the Board of Trade in London to decree that every man should receive so many ounces of meat or butter, but when his vessel was becalmed in the Doldrums and the nearest British consul was 2,000 miles distant, many a shipmaster might reason that since the difference between profit and loss of his voyage could amount to as little as two guineas a day, it was better to starve his crew than to incur the wrath of his tight-fisted employer. And if painting a load line on one's funnel was too obvious a way of cocking a snook in the direction of London, another Welsh captain might still imitate the dodge practised by his fellow-countryman in the barque *County of Pembroke*, who saved his employer just a few pennies per day by doling out charred biscuit crumbs to his crew while pretending it was coffee.

Crewed by nineteen men and three apprentices, the youngest of whom was fifteen-year-old James Bisset, the *County of Pembroke* left Liverpool in October 1898 on a 12,000-mile passage to Melbourne. Signs of the shipowner's criminal meanness were not long in coming: the official Board of Trade bread ration was straight away doled out in the unwelcome form of five iron-hard biscuits, each with forty-two holes punched into one side to ensure it baked as hard as possible. Ten days out from England all the fresh meat and vegetables had been finished, so for the remainder of the voyage the crew were fed salted or tinned meat, buttressed by weevilly biscuits, rendered palatable by smashing them into small fragments, adding watery meat scraps and baking the resultant pottage to make cracker hash, or with jam and fat to make a pudding known as dandy funk.

Though this diet was a far cry from the *cordon bleu* fare Bisset was to eat when he later commanded the Cunard liner *Queen Elizabeth*, it was common enough shipboard food at that time for young James to tolerate without more than the occasional grumble. In spite of the unwholesome rations, the crew worked the vessel with a will, maintaining a respectable average speed of 130 miles a day during the three-month voyage to Melbourne.

Commanded by the same captain, two years later the *County of Pembroke* again set out from Liverpool bound for New Zealand on a second starvation voyage that was to drive the crew to open revolt. After discharging the outward cargo at Wellington the men were sent overside with scrapers in bitterly cold weather at Dunedin to remove a rich growth of barnacles and weed that had accumulated because the penny-pinching owners had neglected to dry-dock the vessel in two and a half years. Following a passage in ballast from Dunedin to Newcastle in Australia, the *County of Pembroke* shipped a coal cargo for a 7,000-mile voyage to Callao in Peru, where the captain topped up the vessel's water tanks but purchased little in the way of provisions. From Callao she cleared for the Chincha Islands, 110 miles distant, where the crew were obliged to swathe their faces in rags against clouds of choking dust to shovel a cargo of dried bird-droppings into the holds while their Scrooge of a captain again disdained to take aboard adequate food supplies for the rigours of the long passage home.

On Christmas day 1902, approaching Cape Horn in icy weather, the shivering crew were told the porridge oats were finished and that their breakfasts would henceforth comprise only coffee and the hateful biscuits. Worse hardships were to follow. Off Cape Horn they discovered the 'coffee' was the boiled débris of smashed biscuits that had been baked, charred and powdered. Days later their salted meat ration was halved, and the meagre store of butter, jam, molasses, sugar and dried fruits was consumed by the time the vessel reached the latitude of the Falkland Islands, so it was farewell to the dandy funk. Then the 'coffee', tea and cocoa ran out, which left them only water and lime juice to drink. Taken aboard at Callao four months previously, the water turned out to be tainted, causing many to fall to the deck with stomach cramps after drinking it. An attempt to ward off typhoid fever and dysentery by adding permanganate of potash to the water was abandoned because the crew pronounced it undrinkable, and so for the remainder of the voyage all water had to be boiled.

Desperate, emaciated, plagued with boils, the starving men laboured through the calms and squalls of the tropics, lured by promises from the captain to put into the Azores, only to be told when they were some way north of the equator that their ship was now so far westward of the islands it would be quicker to end their miseries by steering a direct course for Falmouth, more than 2,000 miles distant. This

The drifter *Harvest Gleaner*, sunk in 1940 by German planes less than one mile from Southwold lighthouse, typifies the fishing vessels operating from Lowestoft and Yarmouth during the years between the two world wars The slim funnel was known as a Woodbine, after a popular brand of cigarette. (Macolm R.White)

information drove them to mutiny, with the crew refusing any duties except steering the vessel and trimming the yards, while their captain and officers armed themselves with revolvers and kept to the poop, bawling orders from a safe distance.

After a week of eating nothing but weevilly biscuits that had been fried in slush, they sighted a steamer which offered them a small quantity of life-saving provisions. Their endeavours to ferry the stores from the steamer were almost brought to nothing by the dilapidated state of the ship's boats. The first disintegrated before launching because it had been repeatedly painted on to its chocks, while the second was so leaky that it almost foundered, and a precious bagful of sugar was only saved from dissolution by ferrying it on top of the coxwain's head.

The *County of Pembroke* sighted Falmouth on 17 March 1902, 157 days out from Callao, after a round voyage that had lasted almost sixteen months. Knowing that news of his crew's hardships would have preceded his arrival, the wily captain anchored in Falmouth bay, where he greased the palm of a tugboat master to ferry out the ingredients for a series of gargantuan meals that went on for two days. Though re-filling the crew's stomachs stifled the damning complaints they had intended to voice to the local marine superintendent, news of the starving seamen in the *County of Pembroke* provoked outrage from the seamen's benevolent societies and Parliamentary outbursts from Lloyd George which resulted in the stiffening of the Board of Trade regulations and brought in an improved scale of rations known to seamen as the Lloyd George scale.

Bisset was discharged from the *Pembroke* in 1902 with the rating of able seaman at the wage of £3 10s a month to continue a seafaring career that would take him to the top of his profession and earn him a knighthood. A more typical nineteenth-century sailor would spend an average of seven years at sea, earning in the merchant service between 45 and 60s a month when and if he was rated able

Drifter shooting its
fleet of nets in the
early evening.
(M.J. Burns)

seaman, although he might receive a very much higher wage if the voyage was
through especially dangerous waters; nineteenth-century Liverpool shipowners
offered a three-fold wage increase for West Indian voyages during the hurricane
season.

Where did they come from, these British seamen? Many serving in naval ships
would have been born and brought up in the West Country, while those in the
North Sea trade were more likely to have come from London, Essex, Norfolk or
Suffolk, except for the crews of colliers, the most numerous Home Trade vessels to
be wrecked in Sole Bay, who came from Northumberland, Durham and Yorkshire.
For much of the eighteenth and nineteenth centuries collier crews were paid by
the voyage rather than by the month. In 1800, striking seamen on Tyneside were
demanding eleven guineas for the voyage to the Thames and back, which was
reckoned to take four or five weeks, although there were of course many exceptions,
some of which could be put down to the help or hindrance of the weather, while
others like the abortive voyage of *Lord Haddo* were most certainly not.

The *Lord Haddo* left the Tyne on 24 January 1887, laden with coal and coke for
Cartagena, manned by a crew who had been given a month's wages in advance,
irrespective of the length of the voyage. Three days out from the Tyne and signally
unstressed by bad weather, the captain found the hold was flooding so rapidly
he had to run his ship ashore on Covehithe beach to prevent her sinking. A
subsequent examination found the water had come in through twelve auger holes
which had been drilled from inside the hull, most probably by crew members
who had been enticed to scuttle the ship by a bosun who had hinted they could
do themselves a financial favour by making the voyage as short as possible.

Of course, the wind and weather were always the principal dictators of the
length of sailing ship passages. The collier brig *Hilda* in 1862 made the 600-mile
round trip from the Tyne to London and back in only seven days, which included
time discharging 399 tons of coal and loading 70 tons of ballast for the homeward
run. Languishing at the lower end of the speed tables was the brig *Royal Union*.

Attempting the same fast passage nine years earlier, it had been driven hither and thither so greatly by gales that six weeks after leaving the Tyne it was reported to be sheltering in Sweden, still 450 miles from home.

Outnumbering even the colliers were the fishing vessels: longshore punts from the Sole Bay beaches, trawlers and drifters from Yarmouth and Lowestoft, crewed by men and boys from local towns and villages, their numbers swollen in the herring season by a great fleet – 700-strong in the late nineteenth century – of Scots in their zulus and fifies. Fishermen were paid on a 'shares' system, receiving a proportion of the vessel's earnings after all expenses had been met. Though simple in principle, the system in practice was a maze of arithmetical jiggles that baffled common understanding. Vulnerable to the stresses of the weather, the vagaries of the fish and the fraudulent practices of unscrupulous employers, it was by no means unusual for a fisherman to find at the end of a voyage that his take-home pay was non-existent.

Until banknotes became common currency, a youthful first-tripper might be gulled by the sticky-bag trick practised in Lowestoft. At pay-off time the golden sovereigns due to him would be laid out on a table for a few seconds to fix his rapt attention. Before he had time to count them, the coins would then be scooped into a money bag that had a liberally greased interior before being poured out again onto the table. Any coins that stayed stuck in the bag were retained by the ship's owner or his duplicitous clerk. By the 1920s the slightly more numerate and worldly fisherman had to be fleeced in a more sophisticated manner. Before coming to the table he might discover each of the twenty-four shares in his boat was worth £4 3s 4d for every £100 the boat earned and would frame his pay-off expectations accordingly. However, when he actually got to the table the clerk might say,

'In fact, me old joskins, the real figure is … ah … £4 2s 6d *per centum*, an' so you being a net-stower is therefore entitled to three-quarters share plus half a quarter share of … let me see … 'ortymumble pounds ought six, less diddledee pennies deducted for the capstan, doddledoo pennies for the little boat an' …'

'Coo! We jus' landed ninety-one cran! What's coming to me, then?'

'Well, er … nothing.'

'*Norffing?*'

'Fact is, Jack, you're in debt to Ther Company. Yerss … prices at rock bottom …expenses mortally high … an' just look at these deductions! … Seven bob a week to your dear mother, ettyceterrer and so on …' says the clerk, sucking his teeth.

'Ter heck! What's to be done?'

'Don't 'ee worry thyself, Jack! I know th' art a good 'un. I'll put in a word on thy behalf up atop, so they'll not be sending the bailies after thee! An' come on, Jackie boy, don't look so down! … P'raps there'll be a better haul next time round!'

Whether poor Jack was a fisherman or a sailor, if he served in a British ship off the Sunrise Coast in wartime he faced additional dangers in the shape of 70-gun Dutch ships-of-the-line in the seventeenth century, French privateers in the eighteenth and early nineteenth centuries and mine-laying German submarines and aircraft in the two world wars, during the latter of which more than 34 per cent of Britain's 145,000 merchant seamen lost their lives – a far higher proportion than in any of the nation's armed services. Until the late 1850s, seamen in foreign-going merchant ships also had to run the gauntlet set up by the recruiting gangs of the Admiralty's Impressment Service. Returning from the Mediterranean in 1776, the *Favourite* was boarded in the Downs and all her British-born seamen taken for naval service, leaving only her master, two Danes and a Swede to get her to port, 'whereby they were obliged to work night and day', a deplorable state of affairs which came to a head with one of the Danes slugging the gin and the master slugging the Dane. During the Napoleonic Wars which ended in 1815 and the Crimean War of 1853–6, many a vessel returning from the Indies or the Americas was stripped of its crew in sight of their homeland. Describing an incident of 1810, William Richardson invites his readers to picture:

> … a poor sailor arrived from a long voyage, exulting in the pleasure of soon being among his dearest friends and relations. Behold him just entering the door, when a press gang seizes him like a felon, drags him away and puts him in the tender's hold, and from thence he is sent aboard a man-of-war … without seeing either his wife, friends or relations; if he complains he is likely to be seized up and flogged with a cat, much more severe than the negro driver's whip, and if he deserts he is flogged round the fleet nearly to death. Surely they had better shoot a man at once; it would be greater lenity.

However, the Impress Service was not in theory permitted to take sailors from fishing boats or colliers because they were exempted from the press, as too were the many foreigners serving in British merchant ships. Impressment was not abolished until 1859 and the floggings went on into the 1860s.

Privateers – privately owned ships licensed by their governments to capture enemy merchantmen in wartime – flourished between the sixteenth and eighteenth centuries, when they were persistent threats to shipping in the southern North Sea and the English Channel. The French privateers, 'Dunkirkers', used to put out at dusk, and by midnight would be raising havoc among British ships in mid-Channel and beyond, capturing near Dungeness in 1798 the *Vine* of Sunderland, attacking in 1799 the *Shafto* at anchor off the Sunrise Coast, and in 1804 the collier *Scipio* off Cromer. The Frenchmen were as wily as they were bold; while her crew of Geordies were aloft reefing topsails in March 1805, the *Providence* of South Shields was boarded and captured near Sole Bay by *les matelots* in a Dunkirker that was masquerading as a fishing boat. Though their numbers were greatly reduced by the Royal Navy during the Napoleonic Wars, privateering was not officially abolished by international agreement until 1856.

Unlike privateers, pirates operated outside the law and were regarded universally as a scourge of mankind. Before 1700 the seamen of Devon were notorious for

Above: 'Away we haul!' Silver darlings coming aboard by the light of the moon in a rising wind. The tight mizzen sail and the lowered foremast will keep the vessel heading into the waves. (M. J. Burns)

Right: With so many wrecks on the seabed, fishing nets need constant repair. (*Alfred Corry* Museum)

their piracies in the English Channel, while the North Sea was the stomping ground for pirates from Kent, Berwick and Fife. In foreign waters they continued to be a malevolent threat during Maggs's lifetime – a tablet in Southwold church to the memory of David May testifies that he had been murdered by pirates in the Bay of Florida as lately as 1819. Although their activities round the British coasts had supposedly been put an end to by 1720, four years later the Scotsman John Gow led a party of mutineers in the *George Galley*, murdered its captain, took charge of the ship and went on a number of piratical sallies before he was out-foxed and captured in the Orkneys. However, there is no evidence in Maggs that any shipwreck in Sole Bay was caused by Gow or any other pirate. John Gow and his crew could not have been the last of the lawless for the last execution in England for piracy did not take place until 1840.

Short or tall, foreign-going or home trade, smacksmen or bargemen, whether serving in a warship or a merchantman, however much or little take-home pay they ended up with, one thing that all sailors have in common throughout history is the ingrained knowledge that the ship always has first call on their time and energy. Sleeping or waking, the cry 'On deck!' has to be instantly obeyed and the ship's needs attended to for whatever length of time it takes. Beset by a rapid succession of gale-force *pamperos* and calms, the eight men and boys of the starboard watch in the four-masted barque *Moshulu* were 'on deck' or aloft for eleven consecutive hours, twice taking in and re-setting twenty-eight sails – one of which weighed 1½ tons – and twice putting the vessel on to new courses – work that taxed the strength of all its twenty-eight hands, including the cook, to the limit.

The incident happened in 1939 in the South Atlantic but, apart from the unusually rapid sequence of gale and calm, the same could happen in Sole Bay aboard a sailing vessel of any size in any century. Writing in the 1920s, the Northumbrian Walter Runciman recalls North Sea collier brigs:

> … passing here plunging bows under, and their sails blown away when they were driving along with a heavy gale; at intervals furious squalls from the west sometimes blew the sails out through the bolt ropes and sent the ribbons flying over the feather-white sea. I have seen them jumping half out of the water and plunging bows under when carrying a press of canvas, … struggling to make a harbour of refuge …

Among the brigs seeking refuge on a January day in 1895 was the *James & Eleanor* of North Shields, which carried six sailors and a master. Like the captain of *Moshulu*, he would have intended to work his crew 'watch-and-watch' (four hours on duty and four hours off), during the 300-mile passage from the north-eastern coal staithes to the Thames. Man proposes but God of course deals differently, with the result that abreast the Sunrise Coast the collier ran into a force nine south-easterly, the same strength of wind that sorely tried *Moshulu*. Unlike *Moshulu*, though, *James & Eleanor* had no sea room. Long before the gale had reached its full strength, the 'watch-and-watch' routine would have been abandoned, both watches would have been on deck, reefing the principal square sails (called 'courses') and later reducing the topsails as the wind blew harder and the master tried to claw away from the coast to gain some precious room. Far from performing acrobatics on the yards or staring from the tops into a dismally stormy yonder, the sailors would have been screwing their eyes tight against blinding snow squalls and any acrobatic prowess would have been so impaired by their stiff and sodden clothing that they would have moved, and probably felt, like refrigerated zombies. On returning to the deck, they would then have laboured for hours at hauling braces and lines, trying to force their hard-pressed vessel on to a different course that might edge her away from the dangers of the Sunrise Coast.

The complexity of such manoeuvres is described in the second edition of Darcy Lever's *The Young Sea Officer's Sheet Anchor*, published 1819:

> Let it be supposed [begins Lever], that the Main Topsail is handed … and the Fore Topmast Staysail hauled down and stowed away in the Netting. The Ship will then be under Courses: it will be necessary to bring the Yard Tackles aft, for Preventer Braces and Preventer Sheets may be also reeved. – Bentinck Shrouds should be

Torn sails and broken crosstrees. Barge *Decima* after a December gale in 1907. A century later she is still sailing as a charter barge on the Thames. (Southwold Museum)

always rigged preparatory to an expected Gale, and indeed they are of such general use, that it would be well in certain Latitudes to have them constantly set up.

At this point in the manual:

See Appendix, Fig. 1, where the necessity of carrying Bentinck Shrouds no longer exists, the Futtock Shrouds acting as such, by being taken to the lower Masts [Mr Lever's italics], it may be supposed that the parents of any not-so-bright Young Sea Officer swotting for the Victorian equivalent of a GCSE in Nautical Studies would be prising the sheet anchor from his fingers and exchanging it for a winding sheet.

Being now on the larboard Tack: [goes on Darcy Lever, engaging a higher gear] if it be thought expedient to get her on the starboard one, it is done by waring; for which purpose the Main Clew Garnets are well manned: when every thing is ready, the Mizen Topsail and Cross Jack yards are squared, the Main Tack and Bowline eased off, and the *weather* Clew-garnet hauled up, for the reason before-mentioned in starting the weather Sheets of the Topsail: the main Sheet is then eased off, the lee Clew-garnet hauled up, and the Buntlines and Leechlines: the Main and Main Topsail Yards are squared, and the Helm put a-weather.

Whether or not they had weathered their Lever, the seven crew of the *James & Eleanor* were unable to 'ware' ship and gain safety before it was driven onto the shoal off Easton cliff in the early hours of 13 January 1895 by a heavy east-south-easterly gale. Here, in the thin light of dawn, the stricken vessel was spotted by a man who was on his way home from duck shooting. By 7.30 a.m. maroons had been fired to muster the Southwold lifeboat crew and soon the *Alfred Corry* was under way, sailing through heavy quartering seas towards the shoal, one and a half miles distant. The lifeboat closed the wreck half an hour after launching and anchored to windward, intending to veer down and rescue the crewmen from its rigging. Weakened by incessant pounding on the hull, the brig's foremast toppled over the side before the manouevre could be completed, plunging the seven men into a seething maelstrom of splintered masts and woodwork, tangled cordage and icy water. The coxswain then ordered the anchor to be slipped, and the sixteen oarsmen in the *Corry* rowed into the raffle, hooked a grapnel on to the wreckage and began a second rescue bid in which two men were successfully pulled into the lifeboat. The crew had found a third and were attempting to break his hold on the wreckage when the grapnel gave way and the lifeboat was driven broadside onto the beach. Three men of the shore party immediately plunged into the surf and rescued two more, but the captain and two others came ashore dead. By nine o'clock, the hull of the *James & Eleanor* was nothing but matchwood.

The three men who had swum out through the surf were awarded silver medals, and the coxswain of the *Corry* was awarded a second service clasp to the medal he had won for his courageous service in *Harriett II* at the wreck of the *Lucinde* thirty-six years previously.

Even in the best of times in the better ships, a sailor's life was by turns a mix of the demanding, the disgusting, the interesting and the tedious; at other times and in the worst ships it was a watery hell. Runciman recalls:

> … one of these old hookers, which in stormy weather shivered and shook as though she were falling to pieces … The oiled tent-covers that were stretched from head to foot of our canvas hammocks could not prevent some of the water getting on to the pillow, blankets and 'donkey breakfast'. It availed nothing to growl about having to take what sleep we could on wet bedding, or about having to pump or sink. We had to go through with it. Nor was it affection that led me to take service in this money-making swill, but hard necessity.

Driven by a liking for adventure rather than necessity, Eric Newby worked as a sailor for only eight months in 1938–9 but his account of his brief service in *Moshulu* paints a convincing picture of life at sea that had changed little over the centuries. Unlike Runciman's 'old hookers', *Moshulu* was exceptionally strong and seaworthy but the work and its hardships were the same as they always had been: hauling endless lengths of wet cordage at all hours; steering the ship; tedious periods on lookout; dreary, disagreeable hours scrubbing decks or washing greasy dishes without benefit of soap or even, in rough weather, hot water; cleaning holds and lavatories, and – when the weather allowed it – chipping rust, caulking, scraping and painting. Below decks and off watch, conditions were far from pleasant: during

The barque *Princess Augusta*, wrecked near the North pier in 1838 with 308 tons of Russian hemp and linseed from St Petersburg. Benjamin Palmer salvaged its cargo and James Maggs sold the wreck to John Magub & Co. for £150. (National Maritime Museum)

heavy weather the crew's living space in the fo'c'sle was knee-deep in water and their bedding was soaked; in drier times it was crawling with lice.

At sea, the men worked in two teams, each in charge of a mate. Over a two-day period a man in a medium-to-large home-trade or foreign-going vessel would be 'on watch' twenty-four hours in forty-eight, steering the ship or on lookout, doing jobs relating to the navigation of the ship and its safety, which – if it was as rickety as the *Briton* in the 1760s – could include pumping the bilges every fifteen minutes for the month-and-a-half voyage from England to Jamaica. When not on these duties, during daylight hours he would be employed on routine maintenance such as repairing torn sails, re-splicing damaged rigging, overhauling blocks, greasing, oiling and painting, but always ready at the mate's call to brace the yards or adjust sheets and lines in response to any change in the wind. In heavy weather or when it was necessary to put the vessel on to a different course, he would be assisted by the men of the off-duty watch, summoned from their exhausted slumbers by indelicate trillings on the mate's whistle.

In East Indiamen and naval ships, which carried much larger crews than the average merchantman, there would usually be three watches and an average of eight hours' watch-keeping per day, supplemented by more hours of daytime work in which 'the people' would be urged on by officers whose duty was to keep the men working even

'…a ruminating beast, an insatiable, indefatigable lip.' (Wells Photos)

when no work needed doing. The smaller home-trade vessels carried many fewer sailors per ton, especially if they were barges, which often plied the coast in charge of only two men and a boy, making speedy passages without sleep or a formal watchkeeping rota. In the 1930s, the unladen barge *Northdown* once passaged from Yarmouth to Harwich, a distance of fifty-one miles, at an average speed of 10.2 knots.

The work pattern in fishing boats was different again. During the East Anglian herring fishery between October and December, for instance, a smacksman's life was geared to the changes of the moon, when the herring swarms were at their thickest. An afternoon departure from the Sunrise Coast would be followed by a few hours of sailing to a likely-looking spot, the early evening would be filled with the task of 'shooting' the fleets of nets up to three miles in length, and then there would perhaps be four hours below decks for a meal and a snatched sleep, followed at dawn by hauling the nets and shaking out the herring, a task which could take up to eighteen hours.

In port, whether alongside a wharf, anchored off a harbour or intentionally high and dry on a beach, shiftwork was replaced by ten or more hours of day work, unloading cargo into horse-drawn carts or – if they happened to be discharging at Blackshore quay between 1914 and 1929 – the wagons of the Southwold Railway. If no dockside labour had been hired, which was usually the case, the crew would have to re-rig the ship's spars as derricks and haul out the cargo themselves, heaving out maggoty cow-hides and bales of wool from the farms, baskets of herring from the sea, crates of finished goods from the industrial workshops, bagging loose cargoes such as salt or grain and shovelling lime or coal into skips.

Whether employed in coastal or foreign trading, ships would often be forced to spend long periods of idleness in port, waiting either to discharge their outward loads or for the arrival of a return cargo, delays which could drag on for several weeks or even months. Newby records a fast, seventy-eight-day passage by the barque *Pommern* from Belfast to South Australia in 1938 that was followed by ninety-nine days in harbour, and after an eighty-two-day passage *Moshulu* was sixty-four days anchored near Port Victoria, half the time waiting for the ship's agent to secure a cargo of grain or in heaving overboard 300 tons of ballast that included the liquefied remains of two dead dogs the Irish stevedores had tossed into the hold as a leaving present.

Wind and weather often delayed departures and arrivals. As many as 3,000 vessels were sheltering from westerly gales in the lee of the Sunrise Coast for days on end in 1838, and if the gales were from an easterly quarter the port of Southwold would be closed for long periods. Maggs recorded that the harbour was unusable on thirteen occasions between 1808–27, blocked not only for the duration of the gale but also for however long it might take to dig a channel through the now impassable sandbar. Five vessels were held up in this way for eleven days in April 1839; a month later sixteen more were denied entry for ten or eleven days, eventually getting over the bar only after 'lighting by Crafts', a time-consuming and costly process.

Shipboard labour was drudgery on a scale rarely seen in the Western world today. Health and Safety regulations were non-existent. A gigantic 400lb (182kg) replacement anchor requisitioned by Lieutenant Cudlip for the 45ft (13.7m) tender *Violet* in 1840 would have required the combined efforts of several men on a windlass to raise it from the riverbed off Harwich. Well into the twentieth century the on-deck machinery installed by the more conservative sailing-ship owners continued to be powered by 'Armstrong's Patent' rather than by steam. Weighing the bower anchor and 75 fathoms (137m) of chain cable shackled to the 1,098-ton *County of Pembroke* before her departure from the Chincha Islands in December 1902 took fifteen half-starved men and boys more than two hours. Today at Southwold you may observe a solitary, middle-aged, overweight weekend yachtsman on the foredeck of a vessel of similar size to the *Violet* lifting an equally effective anchor weighing no more than 66lb (30kg) just by pressing a button.

Even in port, the calls on a seaman's time and labour were limitless. Anchored off California in 1836, two men from the American vessel *Alert*, given the job of loading stinking hides into an open boat, were three days away from their ship in constant heavy rain and without hot food or sleep; four more were out all night in drenching rain and in the morning rowed their boat *thirty miles* back to the same ship, arriving so exhausted that they were unable to climb the gangway. It was not only the ship's boats that were rowed; when the wind fell away to nothing when the sailing barge *Second Apprentice* was off Spurn Head on an August day in the 1930s, her three-man crew spent twenty-four hours rowing their 95ft vessel up the River Humber to Goole, a distance of forty nautical miles.

The chief architect of a sailor's happiness or misery was not the clerk of the weather who sent him the calms and gales, the shipbuilder who cooped him so closely or the owner who diddled him so deftly, but the captain. Time and again sailors in similar ships on similar voyages were telling greatly different tales about their commanders, although – human nature being what it is – grumbles about 'him up a-top' always outnumbered the implied compliments. Peter Earle's researches into the period 1650–1775 support the judgment that the captains of 'the silent majority of ships' managed their crews in the manner advocated in 1732 by Captain Phillips, who believed it was 'the greatest prudence, as well as interest, of a commander ... to gain his men's good-will and affections by being humane to them', a philosophy practised a century later by FitzRoy of the *Beagle*, who allowed his crew three-quarters of an hour for breakfast, one-and-a-half hours for dinner and three-quarters of an hour for supper when in harbour, and half an hour for breakfast, one hour for dinner and half an hour for supper when at sea.

At the bottom of the popularity league were captains such as Robert Corbet RN, court martialled in 1809 for cruelties which included exceptionally severe floggings that were concluded by poulticing the victim's wounds with salt pickle, and, in the merchant service, Captain James Lowry, who was hanged in 1752 for murder of one of his seamen. More than a century later, allegations of murder against Captain William Burwood Baldry of Southwold brought James Maggs to the Old Bailey in October 1861 to testify to the defendant's previous good character. Baldry, master and part owner of the *Shantung*, was found guilty on the reduced charge of manslaughter and sentenced to nine months' hard labour for repeatedly beating a seaman who was sick with dysentery.

Like Nelson, the most successful commanders led from the front, up there with the people, sharing the pain. Captain Sjögren of *Moshulu*, shoulder to shoulder with his helmsmen, struggling to prevent their ship from being dismasted in a storm, and FitzRoy diving overboard with his carpenters to inspect *Beagle's* keel after a grounding are examples of a practical shipmaster's credo that was passed down through his officers to inspire mutual respect and loyalty that over-rode any divisions of social class. A lieutenant and his five-man crew on a month-long survey of the South American coast in a 9-ton boat which had only 2ft 6in (76cm) headroom in its cabin, worked, ate, slept, smoked and joked together in a way of living that was worlds apart from that which prevailed in the shops, farms and factories of Victorian England.

Ships cannot be run by committees but when faced with serious dangers or hardships commanders have sometimes chosen to, or have been compelled to, act like democrats. Under the Laws of Oléron, a medieval shipmaster was bound to ask his crew if the weather was suitable for departure and to abide by the majority verdict, and prudent captains would consult – or would claim to have consulted – their crews at critical moments. Even the brutal autocrat William Dampier, beset by danger in the Indian Ocean, 'called all our men to consult about our safety, and desired every man freely to give his real opinion and advice what to do in this dangerous juncture'. The same course was adopted in 1776 by the master of the *Thomas & Betsey*, who shrewdly got his crew to gaze upon, and itemise, their much-depleted store of provisions as a way of getting their agreement to reducing their rations.

Though presumably hale and hearty at the start of their voyages, during their average seven years at sea no fewer than 17½ per cent of 'the people' would die, and many of those who hadn't would be discharged with diseases ranging from saltwater boils to syphilis, or with work-related injuries such as a severed limb or a ventral hernia, while those who had made over-long passages on ill-provisioned hulks would probably have been afflicted with scurvy. A few may even have seen a shipmate fall prey to a calenture, a disease peculiar to sailors within the tropics, which drove its demented victims to leap into the sea, babbling of green fields.

Not all of the babbling would have been done in English. An estimated one in every three of the seamen in nineteenth-century British merchant ships came from the nearby coasts of Germany, Holland and Scandinavia, as well as from more distant Mediterranean lands, America, Africa and Asia. The twelve seamen in *County of Pembroke* comprised five Welshmen who commonly conversed in their native language, two Liverpool Irishmen, two Germans, one Norwegian, one Greek and one Maltese, and eight of the twelve foredeck hands on the infamous starvation voyage of 1901–2 '... were of various nationalities – as usual'.

Looking back on their time at sea, what did sailors make of it? Walter Runciman ran away to sea at the age of twelve and was twenty-five years a common sailor, a mate and master in sail and steam before founding a shipping business and becoming a controlling shareholder of the famous Anchor Line. Many of his shipmates would have echoed his verdict that it was 'hard necessity' that drew them to a sailor's life rather than 'affection'. Yet, in spite of his robust disclaimer, Runciman responded to the call of the sea so strongly throughout his business life ashore that he spent much of his leisure time sailing a boat. And Tristan Jones, born aboard a ship off the island of Tristan da Cuhna, sunk three times before his eighteenth birthday, blown up in 1952 off Aden, discharged from the Royal Navy with a spinal injury that left him paralysed, nevertheless went on to sail 400,000 miles in a motley of small vessels, in at least one of which he would not have swapped homes with the king of England. Both Philip Gawdy in 1591 and Eric Newby in 1938 went to sea in a spirit of adventure rather than necessity. Newby's seafaring career lasted only eight months and Gawdy's only five, but for both it was a time which they looked back on with great pleasure. Newby later wrote that he would not have exchanged the experience for the highest honour in the land, and Gawdy wrote:

> I lyke the sea and the sea lyfe and the company at sea, as well as ever I lyved withal. The place is good and healthfull to a willing mynde ... And though there be stormes endured at sea, yet the end is honorable and sweete and pleasing to any that taketh that course.

8

CHRONOLOGY OF SOLE BAY SHIPWRECKS

In the table that follows, the column-heading 'Master' should be understood to mean the person in command of a vessel, be he titled Captain, Commander, Skipper or otherwise. 'Crew' occasionally means the full complement of the vessel, including supernumeraries or passengers.

Dates: some early dates are dates of reporting, not wrecking.

Worst years: 1859 (13), 1782 (12), 1852 (11) 1916 (11), and 1836 (10).

Apparently wreck-free years between 1827–95: 1837, 1846–7, 1863–4 and 1890. (But perhaps some wreck data has been lost or mis-recorded?)

Principal sources

DH	David Higgins
EC	Ernest R. Cooper
GB	George Bumstead
GH	Gillian Hutchinson
HH	Henry C. Hunter
IJ	*Ipswich Journal*
JM	Jeff Morris
LB	*The Lifeboat* magazine or Southwold lifeboat station
LN	Richard & Bridget Larn, and Alan Jones (www.shipwrecks.uk.com)
M1	*The Southwold Diary of James Maggs, Vol. I*
M2	Ditto, *Vol. II*
NC	Nicholas Comfort
PS	*Port and Shipping of Southwold* (James Maggs)
RL	Rachel Lawrence
RM	Robert Malster
RP	Rowland Parker
RW	Receiver of Wreck
SB	Stuart Bacon
SC	Southwold Sailing Club
TC	Tom Cunliffe
V	Various
WS	William Stannard

Year	Day	Location	Vessel	Type	Master	Home Port	Crew	Other information	Source
c.850	?	Off Dunwich	–	Dugout	–	Covehithe area	–	5m long. Trawled up off Dunwich	SB
c.1000	?	1.4M NExE of Covehithe	–	–	–	–	–	Oak side-rudder, as used by medieval vessels. On view in Southwold Museum in Victoria Street. No matching wreck yet found	GH
c.1000	?	Easton Beach	–	–	–	–	–	Second side-rudder, from different vessel than former rudder. On view in Southwold Museum in Victoria St. Again, no matching wreck yet found	GH
"	?	Buss Creek, Southwold	–	Longboat	–	Southwold	–	11.5m long, clinker build, with steering oar	SB
1299	?	Southwold	–	–	–	–	–	Ships of the Earl of Gloucester attacked and sunk. Dunwich men blamed	RL
1367	?	Dunwich Beach	–	–	–	(Prussia)	–	Cargo of flax, bowstaves and barrels of wax belonging to Osmond Ferro	RP
1588?	?	Dunwich Bank	–	–	–	–	–	16th-century cannon recovered, possibly from Armada galleon	SB
1669	?	Barnard Sand	–	–	–	–	–	Woman and coach cast ashore at Covehithe	LN
	Dec-04	Dunwich	–	Packet	–	Harwich	–	Unidentified vessel	LN
1672	May-28	Battle of Sole Bay between Anglo–French Fleet of 128 ships under the Duke of York, & Dutch fleet of 106 ships under Admiral de Ruyter. French took little part. Casualties: 4,750 killed and 800 wounded							V
"	"	Near Red Sand	*Royal James*	1st Rate ship	Richard Haddock	Portsmouth	800	1,416 tons. Flagship of Earl of Sandwich (106 guns). Set afire by *Vrede*. 700 lost	V
"	"	Sole Bay	*Ann & Judith*	Warship	Joseph Harris	–	–	Armed with 6 cannon	V
" (cont'd)	"	Sole Bay	*Fountain*	Warship	Robert Stout	–	–	8 cannon	V

Year	Day	Location	Vessel	Master	Type	Home Port	Crew	Other information	Source
1672 (cont'd)	May-28	Sole Bay	Thomas & George	Theophilus Scott	Warship	–	–	6 cannon	V
"	"	Sole Bay	Alice & Francis	Ezekiel Yennis	Fireship	–	–	6 cannon	V
"	"	Sole Bay	Bantum	Henry Pattison	Fireship	–	–	–	V
"	"	Sole Bay	Katherine	Thomas Andrews	Fireship	–	–	180 tons. Armed with 6 cannon	V
"	"	Red Sand	Vrede	Van der Rijn	Fireship	(Holland)	–	Grappled with the enemy Royal James and presumably sank with her	V
"	"	Sole Bay	Josua	–	Warship	(Holland)	–	54 guns. Sunk by broadside from 72-gun Edgar	V
"	"	Sole Bay	–	–	Warship	(Holland)	–	Sunk while making repairs	V
"	"	Sole Bay	–	–	2 fireships	(Holland)	–	Sunk by fire from stern-chaser cannon of HMS Royal Prince, commanded by Duke of York	V
1742	Jan-15	Sizewell Bank	Otter	Gordon	Sloop	–	–	Harwich-Bremen. Captain and 36 drowned; 18 saved	IJ
1743	Feb-24	Near Southwold	Elizabeth	Ratcliffe	–	Newcastle	–	On passage Newcastle-Dunkirk. All lost	LN
1749	Sep-15	Off Southwold	Unity	Long	–	–	–	On passage Hull-London. All lost	LN
1753	Jan-02	Off Southwold	Delight	Hunter	–	–	–	Rotterdam-London	LN
1757	Jan-28	Near Southwold	Maiters	Hillery	–	–	–	London-Hull	LN
1763	?	Off Southwold	Barley	–	–	–	–	1844: Divers salvaging lead	M1
1770	Dec-18	Between Yarmouth & Dunwich						Between Yarmouth & Thorpe Ness SW gale suddenly veers NW, wrecking 30 vessels on Lowestoft banks and driving ashore 30 more at	EC
1774	Dec-02	Southwold Beach	Dingley	Harrison	–	–	–	Stockholm-London. Crew perished	LN
1789	Oct-31							Between Southwold and Yarmouth, 40 ships, 80 smacks & 70 boats wrecked by violent NE gale	EC
1793	Dec-27	Near Southwold	Dorothea & Margareta	Heugh	–	–	–	London-Bergen. Part cargo salved	LN
1794	?	Easton Cliff	Philip & Ann	–	–	Hull	16	Crew perished	M1

Year	Day	Location	Vessel	Type	Master	Home Port	Crew	Other information	Source
1798	Oct-10	Ashore 'opp. Land'	**Bottle Sloop**	Sloop	Pit[?]	-	-	Crew saved	M1
1801	Aug-25	Benacre Ness	*Olive*	-	Blomfield	Ipswich	-	Cargo coal	LN
"	Nov-13	Southwold Beach	*Elizabeth*	-	Simmons	-	-	Kings Lynn-London. Cargo salved	LN
1802	-	World's first commercial steamship *Charlotte Dundas* enters service							V
"	Jan-20	On 'Sand Hail'	-	Shallop	Clay	-	-	Crew saved by pilot boat *Dove*. A shallop was a small, two-masted sloop	M1
"	"	'Opposite Sand Pit'	*Fire Ship*	Brig	-	-	-	Crew saved	M1
"	Jan-29	Southwold Beach	*Henry*	-	Baldwin	-	-	On passage Cley-London	LN
"	Dec-26	Ashore Southwold	*Sailor's Friend*	Pilot boat	J. Bokenham	Southwold	-	Upset coming ashore. Four men drowned. Sea Fencibles at funeral	M1
"	Dec-27	Off Southwold	*Fredrick*	-	-	London	-	Crew perished	M1
1804	Jul-13	Off Southwold	*Aliancen*	-	Kesner	Stockholm	-	About 200 tons burthen. Cargo iron & deals. Stockholm-Dublin	LN
"	Sep-21	Barnard Sand	*Wanderer*	-	Franklin	-	-	Narva-London	LN
"	Dec-24	Near Southwold	*Neta Hendrika*	-	Margue	-	-	On passage from Embden	LN
1805	Jan-19	Near Southwold	*Union*	-	Spicer	-	-	Southwold-London with corn	LN
1806	May-29	South of Gun Hill	*Zeland*	Galliot	-	(Holland)	-	A small, single-masted coastal trader with bluff bows and leeboards	M1
"	Jun-09	Southwold Bar	*Galley of Burletta*	Sloop of War	-	(Prussia?)	7	4 crew and Prussian emissary lost. Corpse robbed of gold watch & 50gns	M1
1807	Feb-18	Off Southwold	*Traveller*	-	-	-	-	Crew lost	M1
1808-27	-	'Harbour blocked up 13 times and reopened at the expence [sic] of £310 8s 0d.'							M1
1808 (cont'd)	Dec-19	Ashore Southwold	*Neptune*	Sloop	-	Whitby	-	London-Southwold with passengers. All saved	M1

Year	Day	Location	Vessel	Type	Master	Home Port	Crew	Other information	Source
1808 (concl.)	Dec-23	Ashore Southwold	Twilight	–	Ed Twaddell	Newcastle	–	General cargo. Crew saved	M1
1809	Dec-15	Ashore near Southwold	Union	–	Carter	–	–	Sunderland-Weymouth with coal	LN
1810	?	Southwold Beach	Providence	–	Malachi Block	Southwold	3	27 tons. Built 1795. Queenborough. Coal cargo	PS
"	Oct-17	Burnett [Barnard?]	Flora	Brig	–	Weymouth	–	Coal cargo. Crew saved	LN
"	Nov-10	Benacre Ness	Sally	–	Harvey	Colchester	–	Crew saved	LN
"	"	Southwold Beach	Henry	–	Potter	–	–	Deal-Northern port. Crew saved	LN
1811	May-10	Near Southwold	Nelson	–	Crow	–	–	On passage from Sunderland with coal	LN
"	Jun-10	Southwold Beach	Friendship	–	Shaw	–	–	London-Sunderland	LN
1812	Sep-16	Gun Hill, Southwold	Thomas	–	–	–	–	Abandoned offshore. Cargo: timber & deals	M1
"	Sep-29	Off Southwold	Trafalgar	–	Harrison	North Shields	–	Shields-London with coal. Crew saved	LN
"	Nov-16	Near Southwold	Friends	–	Knight	–	–	(Remarkably, four vessels named *Friends* were wrecked in Sole Bay)	LN
1813	Dec-02	Near Southwold	Hull Packet	–	Andrews	Wisbech	–	London-Kings Lynn	LN
1814	Apr-03	Off Southwold	–	Pilot Yawl	–	–	–	Rammed and sunk, possibly intentionally, by yawl *Jubilee*	M2
"	Oct-25	Near Southwold	Vrow Jetze	–	De Jong	Groningen	–	SSE gale. On passage Groningen-London	LN
"	"	Near Southwold	Friends	–	Potter	Selby	–	Cargo of stone. SSE gale	LN
"	Dec-07	Barnard Sand	Perseverance	–	Mallett	London	–	Rouen-Hull with wheat	LN
1817	Aug-01	Southwold Bar	Conqueror	Brig	Peter Palmer	Southwold	6	Built Yarmouth. 132 tons. Coal cargo	PS
1818	Jan-27	Southwold Bar	Maria Ross	–	Clark	Sunderland	–	Carrying coal	LN
"	Sept	Off Southwold	Lapwing	–	–	Southwold	–	–	LN
1819	Jul-15	'The first time a Steam Vessel passed this Town – she was from the Northward bound for London.'							M1

Year	Day	Location	Vessel	Type	Master	Home Port	Crew	Other information	Source
1820	Mar-02	Ashore Southwold	–	Sloop	–	–	–	Carrying grindstones	MI
1821	Jul-23	Sole Bay	–	Fishing boat	–	Walb'wick	2	Upset by sudden squall. 2 drowned. One body later buried in Easton Cliffs	MI
1823	Jan-11	Newcome Sand	–	Brig	–	–	–	Bound London with general cargo. Assisted by *Seaman's Assistant* but foundered	TC
"	Jan-11	Sole Bay	*Seaman's Assistant*	Pilot Yawl	William Butcher	Lowestoft	7	Pilot & crew lost. Owned by J. Denny, prop. of *Herring Fishery* pub in Lowestoft	MI
"	Mar-02	Easton Cliff	*Friends*	–	–	–	–	General cargo. Crew took to boat and drowned; Captain saved	MI
1824	?	Barnard Sand	*Dorset*	–	–	Dover	–	Cargo of spirits	MI
1827	Jan-26	Btwn Easton & Lowestoft	–	14 vessels	–	–	–	'Tremendous gale. Not a soul lost.'	MI
"	Mar-07	Ashore Southwold	*Fame*	Sloop	–	–	–	Cargo: potatoes. Crew saved	MI
"	Dec-17	Sizewell Bank	*Vine*	–	–	S. Shields	–	Run down by *Brothers* of South Shields. Crew saved	LN
1828	Jan-01	Ashore Southwold	*Liberty*	–	–	North Shields	–	No one aboard	MI
"	Jan-16	Ashore Thorpe Ness	*Reaper*	Brig	Stratford	Sunderland	–	Pillau–London. Only one crew saved	JM
"	May-24	Barnard Sand	*North Star*	–	–	North Shields	–	Crew perished. Bottom came ashore Feb 1829; sold for £51	MI
"	Aug-09	Southwold Beach	*Thomas & Betsy*	–	Samuel Sayer	Southwold	4	53 tons. Prize vessel, captured 1813	PS
1829	May-27	Southwold	*Suffolk*	Steam packet	–	–	–	Put into harbour on fire. (Earliest recorded entry of steamer into Southwold)	MI
" (cont'd)	Sep-20	Ashore Southwold	*Ceres*	–	James Warren	London	–	Cargo: tallow and isinglass. Towed ashore. No one aboard	MI

Year	Day	Location	Vessel	Type	Master	Home Port	Crew	Other information	Source
1829 (cont'd)	Sep-20	Off Southwold		3 vessels	–	–	–	Lost with all hands	EC
"	Nov-24	Sole Bay	–	3 vessels	–	–	–	Heavy E'ly gale with snow. Many men lost	M1
"	"	Ashore Walberswick	–	–	–	–	–	Unnamed vessel. '1 man perished'	M2
"	"	Ashore South of Dunwich	–	2 vessels	–	–	–	Crews saved	M1
1830	Jan-15	Btwn Thorpe & Dunwich	–	2 vessels	–	–	–	Stern frames washed ashore	LN
"	Jan-20	Sizewell Beach	*Thomas*	–	Clegg	–	–	On passage Poole-Hull. Only one crew saved	LN
"	Aug-13	Off Sizewell	*Hector*	–	Wilson	–	2	Danzig-London. 'Tremendous thunderstorm'. Crew lost	LN
"	Dec-20	Barnard Shoal	*Hawk*	–	Capes	–	–	London to Leeds (via the Aire and Calder canal). NNW-NW gale	LN
1831	?	Southwold	*Samuel*	Pilot Cutter	William Easy	Southwold	6	Built 1796, Yarmouth. Broken up in its 36th year	DH
"	Jan-27	Barnard Sand	*Cumberland*	–	Sinclair	Newcastle	–	London-N'castle. Crew saved by Trinity pilots from Southwold	M1
"	Dec-20	Thorpe Ness	*Three Friends*	–		Stockton	–	Stockton-London. Collided with another vessel. Crew saved	LN
1832	Mar-06	Barnard Sand	*Richard*	Thames Barge	–	London	3	Cargo: wood. One crew lost	LN
"	Jul-09	Off Easton	–	Fishing boat	–	–	3	Upset by squall while trawling. All lost	M1
1833	Feb-20	Thorpe Ness	*Pallion*	–	Johnson	–	–	Sunderland-London with coal. Crew saved	LN
" (cont'd)	Apr-01	Sizewell Bank	*Caldecot Castle*	–	Sanders	–	–	Newcastle-London with coal. Crew saved	LN

Year	Day	Location	Vessel	Type	Master	Home Port	Crew	Other information	Source
1833 (cont'd)	Apr-09	Ashore Southwold	-	Brig	-	(Denmark)	-	Wreck with no one aboard towed ashore & sold. Cargo: timber and deals	M1
1834	?	Southwold	*Alert*	-	Edward Palmer	Southwold	10	16 tons. Built 1821, Southwold. 'Broke up.'	PS
"	Jan-30	Barnard Sand	*Providence*	-	Watson	Scarboro'	-	Anchor warp parted during violent gale	LN
"	Oct-17	Off Southwold	*Enterprise*	-	Kay	-	-	On passage to Bordeaux. Sank in 10 fathoms. Crew saved	LN
"	Oct-25	Barnard Sand	*Ditto*	Snow	F. Luce	Liverpool	-	-	LN
1835	Jan-22	Barnard Sand	*Aurora*	-	-	Shields	-	A captured prize vessel	LN
"	Dec-19	Between Kessingland and Corton 23 vessels and 49 people lost in ENE gale							M1
1836	Feb-03	Barnard Sand	-	5 colliers	-	-	-	Heavy ENE gale. All crews lost	M1
"	Feb-04	Barnard Sand	-	Brig	-	-	-	Abandoned by crew; all lost	LN
"	"	Barnard Sand	*Speedwell*	Brig	-	South Shields	-	One survivor rescued by Lowestoft LB *Frances Ann* & landed at Kessingland	RM
"	"	Barnard Sand	*David Ricardo*	Brig	Spurgeon	Great Yarmouth	7	165 tons. Crew saved by LB *Frances Ann*	LN
"	Feb-18	27 vessels driven ashore between Kessingland and Lowestoft. All crews saved							M1
"	Mar-01	New York Cliff	*Anne*	-	Darling	Newcastle	-	Cargo: beans & wheat. Crew saved	M1
"	Mar-22	Off Dunwich	*Fly*	-	Barnes Hill	-	3	17 tons. Built 1823, Yarmouth South Town.	PS
1838	Jan-08	Newcome Sand	*Peace*	Pilot Yawl	-	Southwold	15	Wreckage, including hats, washed ashore at Pakefield on 9 Jan. All crew lost	M1
"	Jan-10	Barnard Sand	*Sir Walter Scott*	Smack	Dick	Leith	-	ENE gale. Lost rudder on passage to London. Two passengers.	LN
"	Feb-26	Covehithe	*Ariel*	-	Watson	Stockton	-	199 tons. Lost on Cross Sand; wreck came ashore at Covehithe; sold for £165	M1
" (cont'd)	Apr-16	Barnard Sand	*Diamond*	Brig	-	-	-	-	M1

Year	Day	Location	Vessel	Type	Master	Home Port	Crew	Other information	Source
1838 (cont'd)	Oct-28	North of N pier	Princess Augusta	Barque	Fidgett	London	-	308 tons. Cargo: hemp and linseed from St Petersburg. Crew saved. Wreck sold £150	M1
"	Nov-19	2,500 to 3,000 vessels under sail between Yarmouth & Lowestoft during five hours of a single day; so close and uninterrupted that the sea could not be discerned beyond them'. (Yarmouth Mercury)							DH
c. 1839	?	Southwold	The Screw	Gig	-	Southwold	-	Built Vauxhall, London. Owned by Long Island Cliff Co. Broken up	DH
1839	?	N of N Pier	Thos Betsey	-	-	Southwold	-	About 40 tons. (Pictured in painting by Henry Davy, 1839)	-
"	?	Southwold	Pilot	Gig	-	Southwold	-	Owned by Long Island Cliff Co. Broken up	DH
"	Jan-06	Easton	Young Susannah	Sloop	Jo King	London	-	Cargo: potatoes. Crew saved. Wreck sold for £30	M1
"	Feb-11	Offshore	Barbara	Heavy Brig	Grimson	North Shields	-	Run down by brig Derwent of Newcastle. Crew saved	M1
"	May-19	Easton	Eliza	-	-	London	-	Found abandoned and towed ashore by pilot cutter John & Mary	M1
"	Jun-08	3M ESE of Southwold	-	Steam tug	Thompson	Yarmouth	-	Boiler burst; crew saved. [First instance of steamer wreck in Sole Bay]	M1
"	Jul-27	Southwold Bar	British Queen	Brig	-	Newcastle	-	51 tons. Cargo coals. Wreck sold four days later for £11	M1
"	Oct-30	2M South of piers	Enterprize	Fishing boat	Stephen Capps	Lowestoft	13	9 drowned; 4 saved	M1
1840	Jan-27	N of Dunwich	Request	Brig	Baines	Newcastle	10	Cargo: coal. Six crew lost, but 4 saved from foretop by Manby's Life Gun	M1
"	May-20	Off Dunwich	-	Fishing boat	Clarke	-	-	Squall upset boat while trawling	M1
"	Nov-13	Maggs records tremendous ESE gales (but Ipswich Journal reports gales starting at SSW)							M1
" (cont'd)	"	Kilcock Cliff	Ant	Humber Keel	Maryatt	Boston	-	Crew and part cargo of wheat saved. Wreck sold 16 Nov for £22	M1

Year	Day	Location	Vessel	Type	Master	Home Port	Crew	Other information	Source
1840 (cont'd)	Nov-13	Btwn Easton & Southwold	HMS *Fairy*	Brig sloop	William Hewett	—	63	233 tons. 90ft long. Surveying N Sea since 1831. Crew lost. Wreck not found	M1
"	"	Off Southwold	—	Collier	—	Newcastle	—	—	IJ
"	"	Barnard Sand	—	Brig	—	—	—	Crew perished	M1
"	Nov-22	Near Barnard	—	Brig	—	—	—	Unusual tide & heavy gale. Crew lost	M1
1841	Jan?	Easton	*Elton*	Brig	—	Stockton	—	Wreck auctioned 5 Feb	M1
"	Jan-24	Off Southwold	*Star*	Schooner	Stevens	Perth	—	Blown south on passage from Yarmouth to Sunderland and foundered	LN
"	Aug	First Southwold lifeboat *Solebay* enters service. Norfolk and Suffolk type, 40ft long, with dipping lug mizzen and twelve oars. (Referred to by Maggs as the *Conservative*)							LB
"	Nov-14	Barnard Sand	*Buckingham*	—	Nossiter	Dartmouth	—	SE gale. Crew lost. Cargo: tallow. Wreck ashore Sizewell 17th, sold 18th	M1
"	"	Sole Bay	—	Schooner	—	—	—	Crew lost	M1
"	Nov-18	Minsmere	*Catliff*	—	—	—	—	ESE gale increased	M1
"	"	Ashore Minsmere	*Hope*	—	Marshall	Goole	—	Cargo: coal. Maggs sells hull and materials on 25 Nov	M1
"	"	Covehithe	*Mary & Jo Marsden*	—	Crooke	Goole	—	Crew saved. Cargo of oats sold by Maggs 24 Nov	M1
"	Nov-19	Sole Bay	*Catharine*	—	Usher	Goole	—	Gale increased further, but by 6 p.m. calm, with fog. Crew saved by Sizewell LB	M1
"	"	N of Lifeboat House	*Elizabeth & Ann*	*Humber keel?*	Maryatt	Boston	—	Cargo: potatoes. Crew saved	M1
1842	Sep-08	Walberswick	*John & Elizabeth*	Fishing smack	Robert English	Walb'wick	—	Built 1781, Gillingham. 9 tons. Crew saved	M1
1843	Jan-13	*Esther* of South Shields strands on Gunfleet Sand in Thames Estuary. Her eight crew voyage thirteen hours through gale in an open boat to land safely at Southwold								M1
" (cont'd)	Apr-03	'A fleet of fro[m] 7 to 8 hundred sail of vessels appeared between the two Nesses!!'								M1

Year	Day	Location	Vessel	Type	Master	Home Port	Crew	Other information	Source
1843 (cont'd)	Oct 28/9	South Pier	*Nancy*	–	–	Ipswich	–	SE gale. In running for the harbour, vessel went ashore at back of South pier	M1
"	Oct-29	Barnard Sand	–	3 vessels	–	–	–	All crews perished except one man	M1
"	Nov-03	Walberswick	*Sally*	–	Welham	Ipswich	–	Goole-Ipswich with coal. Driven ashore in gale. Master drowned	M2
1844	Oct-24	Southwold Beach	*Jubilee*	Pilot boat	Edward Palmer	Southwold	–	Wrecked on launching into onshore wind and sea. Skipper lost	M1
"	Nov-05	Back of South pier	*Lord Nelson*	Smack	E. N .Cook	Ipswich	–	Cargo of cement. Hull sold for £10	M1
"	Dec-09	Barnard Sand	*Fortuna*	–	Emsley	S. Shields	–	Crew saved	M1
1845	Feb-08	Barnard Sand	*Emerald*	–	Harrison	Belfast	–	London to Aberdeen with cargo of guano. Crew saved	M1
"	Apr-18	'The Burrows [?]'	*Industry*	–	Jo Laws	–	–	'Struck upon the "Burrows" in a fog and went down.'	M1
"	Jul-01	Off Southwold	–	Fishing boat	Robert English	–	3	SW gale. R. English saved by *Solebay* & fishing boat but two sons drowned	M1
1848	Jan-05	Off Barnard Sand	*James & Mary*	Barge	More	Rochester	3	Reported by Hutchins, Master of another barge. 3 lost	M2
"	Mar-21	Sizewell Bank	*Cleofrid*	Brig	James Simm	Newcastle	9	Crew rescued by lifeboat *Solebay*	M2
"	Dec-04	Barnard Sand	*Ury*	Schooner	–	Sunderland	5	Cargo of coals. 3 drowned, but two others saved by *Solebay*	M2
1849	Oct-13	Ashore Southwold	*Opzeemans Hoop*	Skute	Klaus Leenderd	Katwyk	8	Capsized off Yarmouth on 12th. Six drowned	M2
1850	Jan-26	Off Southwold	*Anna Maria*	–	–	–	–	Run down by barque. Only 1 man saved	M2
1851 (cont'd)	Mar?	Walberswick	*Jeanne d'Arc*	–	Francois Wacgone	Boulogne	6	On passage Blyth-Boulogne. Wreck sold 2 April 1851	M2

Year	Day	Location	Vessel	Type	Master	Home Port	Crew	Other information	Source
1851 (cont'd)	Mar-20	Off Sizewell Bank	Naiad	Brig	David Myers	Hartlepool	–	Run down by *Vesper* of North Shields. Mate killed by falling mast	M2
"	Sep-03	Scroby Sand	Sarah	–	–	Whitehaven	–	Towed ashore derelict nr Gun Hill by Kilcock Cliff men. Wreck sold £22	M2
"	Oct	Blythburgh	New Prosperous	Barge	J. Snell (Owner)	Southwold	–	At 61 tons, 'the largest vessel ever... to have gone further [up the Blyth] than New Quay'	
1852	Jan-07	Southwold Bar	Spring	Schooner	R. Chapman	Hull	4	Middlesbrough-Southwold with coal. *Wind SSW*, force 9. Crew saved	M2
"	Jan-08	Thorpe Ness	John	Snow	John Burton	Newcastle	10	261 tons. Newcastle-London with coal and 4 passengers. All saved by Joshua Chard	M2
"	Jan-10	Barnard Sand	Bransberg	Brig	Clark	–	9	London-Newcastle in ballast. Wind SSW	LN
"	Jan-11	Sizewell Bank	London	Brig	Moorsom	Whitby	–	186 tons. Hartlepool-Rochester with coal. Wind S, force 9. One man lost	LN
"	''	Ashore Southwold	William Cook	Schooner	William Cook	Gt Y'mouth	7	93 tons. Hartlepool-Ramsgate with coal. Wind SSE,10. Five saved	M2
"	Jan-26	Thorpe Ness	Frederick	Brig	Raine	Sunderland	5	Sunderland-Boulogne with coal. Wind S, force 8	LN
"	''	Sizewell Bank	Victory	Schooner	Brooks	Maldon	–	Sunderland-Maldon with coal. *Wind SSW*, force 8, with heavy rain	LN
"	''	Sizewell Bank	–	Brig	–	–	–	Vessel not identified. Two rescued by Joshua Chard of Thorpe Ness	EC
"	Oct-03	Off Southwold	Esk	Brig	–	Whitby	9	267 tons. Hartlepool-London with coal	LB
" (cont'd)	Oct-08								LB

New lifeboat *Harriett* replaces *Solebay*. Self-righting, 38ft long, with two lugsails and twelve oars.

Year	Day	Location	Vessel	Type	Master	Home Port	Crew	Other information	Source
1852 (cont'd)	Dec-19	Sizewell Bank	–	Brig	–	–	–	Captain picked up near Southwold	HH
"	Dec-19	Sizewell Bank	Ann & Mary	Brig	Thomas Collins	Sunderland	8	Seaham–London w coal. SSW gale.7 saved by Thorpe Ness lifeboat & yawl; 1 lost	M2
1853	Aug-26	Sizewell Bank	William & Ann	Sloop	–	Goole	–	Goole–Southampton. Crew saved	LN
"	Oct-18	Barnard Sand	Lucia	Schooner	–	–	5	Foundered. Three crew lost	LN
"	Nov-29	Ashore Southwold	Sheraton Grange	Brig	William Turnbull	Hartlepool	9	263 tons. Cargo: coal. SSW gale. Struck wreck. Crew saved by Harriett	M2
"	Dec-10	Sizewell Bank	Richard White	Snow	R. Gladstone	South Shields	9	259 tons. Wind ENE, 10. Crew saved	LN
1854	Jan-24	Newcome Sand	Hebe	Barque	–	–	–	450 tons. Shields–Lisbon with coal. Struck Newcome in fog. Crew saved	RW
"	Nov-28	Ashore Southwold	Venus	Schooner	–	Lowestoft	–	57 tons.Middlesbrough–Southwold with coal. Struck pier while entering with strong tide	RW
"	Dec-15	Newcome Sand	Isis	Schooner	–	Blakeney	–	London–Blakeney w coal. Missed stays while tacking in force 8 WxN and sank	RW
1855	Oct-28	Off Southwold	Dispatch	–	William Magub	–	–	Crew saved	M2
"	"	Ashore Covehithe	Lucie	Schooner	–	St Malo	–	Crew perished. Maggs sells wreck for £50 on following day (duty 50s)	M2
"	Nov-03	Kilcock Cliff (North Cliff)	Nelson	Brig	–	S. Shields	–	Sold 7 Nov	M2
"	"	Long Island Cliff	Hylton Castle	Brig	–	Sunderland	–	215 tons. Wreck sold 14 Nov. (See chart C11 showing wrecks)	M2
" (cont'd)	"	N of N Pier	Cape Horn	Barque	Wake	Whitby	–	173 tons. Hull and stores sold 7 Nov	M2

Year	Day	Location	Vessel	Type	Master	Home Port	Crew	Other information	Source
1855 (cont'd)	Nov-03	N of N Pier	*Ocean*	Brig	–	Whitby	–	Maggs sells wreck and stores six days later	M2
"	"	Close by N Pier	*Emma*	Brig	Glen	Sunderland	–	232 tons. Sold 'for getting off' 14 November but becomes a wreck	M2
"	"	Minsmere	*Pilgrim*	Brig	George Howe	Sunderland	–	163 tons. Wreck and stores sold 13 November	M2
"	Dec-31	A second *Harriett* replaces lifeboat of same name. *Harriett II* is Norfolk & Suffolk type, not self-righting, 40ft long, with 12 oars							LB
1856	Feb-06	Southwold Bar	*Glenmoriston*	-	–	–	–	Crew saved. Maggs sells stores 18 Feb & wreck 20 Feb	M2
"	Apr	Barnard Sand	*Odin*	Brig	George Gardner	–	–	–	M2
"	Early May?	Walberswick beach	*William IV*	-	Edward Stanley	–	–	Wreck sold 12 May at Walberswick. Figurehead in Sailors' Reading Room	M2
"	Nov-03	Sole Bay shores	–	5 vessels	–	–	–	'Gale…Crews saved,' writes Maggs, adding no further details	M2
"	Dec-06	Off Southwold	–	Boat	–	Southwold	–	Heavy snowfall. Collided with brig. All drowned	M2
1857	Jan-07	Off Minsmere	*Cheverell*	Bark	Thomas Caygill	Whitby	–	318 tons. Crew saved. A week later, Maggs sells wreck and stores	M2
1858	Feb-27	Lifeboat *Harriett II* capsizes while returning from exercise; 3 passengers drowned, including curate of Wangford							EC
"	Aug-29	Off Southwold	*Teazer*	Pilot Yawl	–		13	Collided with pilot yawl *Cricketer* while boarding steamer. Crew saved	M2
"	Dec-30	Barnard Sand	*Henry's*	Snow	Newman	Sunderland	10	310 tons. Cargo: bones. One man lost	LN
c. 1859	?	Southwold	*Mayflower*	Gig	–	Southwold	–	35ft long. Built 1838 by Jas. Critten for Kilcock Cliff Co. Broken up	DH
1859 (cont'd)	Feb?	Off Minsmere	*Jubilee*	Brigantine	–	Guernsey	–	100 tons. Wreck to auction on 4 March	M2

Year	Day	Location	Vessel	Type	Master	Home Port	Crew	Other information	Source
1859 (cont'd)	Apr-02	Sizewell Bank	*Velocity*	Brig	–	Sunderland	8	SSW gale and heavy seas. Thorpe Ness lifeboat rescues crew	JM
"	Aug?	Easton Bavents	*Patriot*	Schooner	B. Skipsey	Sunderland	–	95 tons. Crew saved. Wreck auctioned 1 Sep	M2
"	Sep-17	Minsmere Haven	*Lucinde*	Large Brig	H.R. Boctheher	Memel	10	To Rochester with sleepers. *Harriett II* saves 9. Maggs sells wreck 11 Nov	M2
"	Oct-28	Ashore Southwold Hbr	*Neptune*	–	–	Whitby		–	M2
"	Oct-30	Nr Southwold LB House	*Ann Emma*	–	–	Shields	–	Maggs sells hull and stores	M2
"	Nov-01	Covehithe	*Royalist*	–	–	S. Shields	–	Maggs sells hull and stores	M2
"	"	Covehithe	*Silva*	–	–	Shields	–	–	M2
"	"	Covehithe	*Salira*	–	–	Sunderland	–	Crew saved by rocket apparatus	RM
"	Dec-01?	Dunwich	*Raven*	–	–	–	–	–	M2
"	Dec-03	Sizewell Bank	*Countess*	Brigantine	–	Ipswich	–	–	JM
"	Dec-10	Sizewell Bank	*Henry Morton*	Snow	Robertson	Sunderland	–	–	LN
"	Dec-13	Thorpe Ness	*Sybil*	Brigantine	J. Jones	Caernarvon	–	Built 1856, Prince Edward Island, Canada	LN
1860	Jan-24	Sizewell Bank	*Pallas*	Snow	Rock	Newcastle	8	233 tons. Cargo: coal. Wind force 9. 5 crew lost. (Date possibly erroneous)	LN
"	Jan-26	Off Southwold	*John & Isabella*	–	–	Shields	–	Crew saved	M2
"	Feb-10	Easton	*Ralph Barnel*	Fishing Smack	Ross	London	–	Crew saved	M2
"	May-03	Thorpe Rocks	*Vanguard*	Brig	–	Whitby	–	Joshua Chard of Thorpe Ness rescues 7 in own lifeboat	HH
1861 (cont'd)	Feb-12	Sizewell Bank	*Content*	Snow	J. Howes	Sunderland	5	233 tons. Cargo: coal. Struck sunken wreck. Crew saved	LN

Year	Day	Location	Vessel	Type	Master	Home Port	Crew	Other information	Source
1861 (concl.)	Dec?	Ashore Minsmere	Content	-	-	Sunderland	5	Wreck auctioned 18 Dec. (Perhaps a replacement vessel for 12 Feb loss?)	M2
1862	?	Sizewell Beach	Dora	Brig	-	Exeter	-	Aground Sizewell Bank in gale. Probably wrecked on beach	EC
"	Jan-28	Sizewell Bank	Princess Alice	Schooner	Leggett	Ipswich	-	Cargo: coal. Harriett II saves five men and a dog	M2
"	Oct-20	Off Thorpe Ness	Henry Everest	Thames Barge	-	Rochester	4	-	LN
"	Early Nov?	Ashore Southwold	Fanny	Steam Yacht	J. McDonald	Newcastle	-	Built Glasgow 1861. 25 tons. Wreck for auction 7 Nov	M2
1862	Mid Nov?	Dunwich	Harry King	-	-	-	-	Wreck sold 17 Nov	M2
"	Nov-20	Ashore Southwold	Hawk	Screw Steamer	-	London	-	800 tons. Wreck sold for £40	M2
1865	Oct-26	Newcome Sand	Centaur	Schooner	-	Newcastle	7	Newcastle–Topsham with coal. Wind S, 9. Two lost	LN
1866	Jan-13	'South of landing place'	Billy	Brig	-	Whitby	6	119 tons, w coal cargo. Wind SSW, 10. Rescue attempt by Harriett but all lost	M2
"	July	Off Dunwich	-	Boat	-	-	2	Capsized. Both lost	M2
"	Aug-16	Off Easton	-	Fishing boat	-	Southwold	1	Upset by sudden gust. Drowned	M2
"	Aug-23	Self-righting Surf Lifeboat Quiver enters service							LB
"	Dec-12	Barnard Sand	William & Mary	Lugger	-	-	11	-	LN
1867	Jan?	2 miles off Southwold	-	Fishing boat	-	Southwold	4	Capsized by gust. Only one person rescued	M2
"	Dec-03	Barnard Sand	Iddo	Snow	J. Small	-	7	Cargo: coal. Five crew lost. Wind NE, force 9	LN
"	"	Barnard Sand	Queen Victoria	Brig	-	-	8	Cargo: coal. Seven crew lost. Wind NNE, force 9	LN
1868	Jan-24	Thorpe Ness Point	Comorn	Brigantine	J. Martin	-	5	Cargo: coal. All lost	LN
"	Dec-24	Off Southwold	-	-	Fishing boat	-	2	One saved; one lost	M2

Year	Day	Location	Vessel	Type	Master	Home Port	Crew	Other information	Source
c. 1869	?	Southwold	*Swiftsure*	Beach yawl	-	Southwold	-	49ft long. Blt 1847 for Kilcock Cliff Co. 1855: cut *Reliance* in two. Broken up	DH
1869	Jan-02	Sizewell Bank	*Belle*	Brig	G. Featherstone	Whitby	10	250 tons. Sunderland-Ostend with coal. Wind SSW, 9. One crew lost	LN
"	Jan-15	Sizewell Bank	*Lord Coke*	-	Muttett	Middlesbro'	4	Cargo of bricks. Crew rescued by *Harriett II*	M2
"	Jan-24	'just below Southwold'	-	Fishing boat	-	Southwold	3	Foster Bokenham & two others drowned	M2
"	April	Lifeboat *Harriett II* renamed *London Coal Exchange* in recognizance of £700 gift from London coal merchants							EC
"	Dec?	Walberswick	*Elsinore*	-	Elsinore	-	-	600 tons. Auction 30 Dec 1869	M2
c. 1870	?	Sole Bay	*Reliance*	Pilot yawl	-	-	-	Built 1846 to replace *Jubilee*. 1855: cut in two by *Swiftsure*. Part later salvaged & repaired. Broken up c.1870	M1
1871	Jan-25	Barnard Sand	*John & Susannah*	Dandy	-	Lowestoft	3	Lowestoft-London with fish. Wind E, force 7. All crew lost	LN
"	Feb-10	Barnard Sand	*Franckfort*	Snow	-	Shields	8	Sunderland-London with coal. Wind E, force 10. All crew lost	LN
"	"	Dunwich Bank	*Two H. H.*	Sloop	-	Goole	3	Maldon-Goole with wheat. Wind SSE, 9. Crew lost	LN
"	Dec-07	Ashore Southwold	*Friends*	Billy-boy	Mapplebeck	Goole	-	London-Southwold w 30 tons cattle cake. Lost anchors in E'ly gale. Crew saved	M2
1872	Oct-16	Covehithe Point	*Eiderstedt*	Paddle steamer	Clausen	Tonning	-	London-Tonning with coal. Originally built to run blockade in US Civil War	M2
"	Nov-30	Barnard Sand	*Celeste Maria*	Schooner	J.M.L.Verez	Ile Diaz	-	Grimsby-Dieppe with 150 tons of coal. Crew saved. Wreck sold for £32	M2
1873 (cont'd)	?	Southwold	*John Bull*	Beach yawl	-	Southwold	-	Built by Jas. Critten, 1849 for Long Island Cliff Co. 55ft long, with 3 masts. Broken up	DH

Year	Day	Location	Vessel	Type	Master	Home Port	Crew	Other information	Source
1873 (cont'd)	Jan-19	Off Minsmere	Belle Isle	Brig	–	Shoreham	8	Crew saved by surf lifeboat Quiver	EC
"	Jan?	Ashore Dunwich	Mary Russell	–	–	Dundee	–	200 tons. Maggs auctions wreck and part of oat cargo 3 Feb at Dunwich	M2
1874	?	Southwold	Friendship	Beach yawl	–	Southwold	–	Known as Job. Built 1851. 64ft long, so perhaps largest Southwold beachboat. Broken up.	DH
"	Apr-15	Sizewell Bank	Alma	Barque	–	Tonsberg	10	Crew & pilot saved by Coal Exchange & Thorpe Ness LB. Wreck sold May 1	M2
"	"	Barnard Sand	Pandora	Schooner	–	Portsmouth	5	Crew saved by Coal Exchange	EC
1875	Aug-11	2M ENE of Southwold	Jane Innes	Brigantine	–	Scarboro'	5	138 tons. Newcastle-Boulogne with coal. Impaled on own anchor and sank	LN
1876	Oct	Sizewell Gap	Peter	Brig	–	Copenh'gn	8	Memel-London. Wind ESE, force 7. One crew lost	LN
1877	Jul-27	4M E of Southwold	Sauce Polly	Fishing Lugger	H. Hurr	Lowestoft	–	Run down by steamship	LN
"	Dec-12	Benacre	Barkley	Schooner	J. Vince	Ipswich	5	109 tons. Sunderland-Ipswich with coal. Wind SSW, force 5	LN
1878	Jan-25	Barnard Sand	Reindeer	Brig	W. Myers	Scarboro'	6	200 tons. Seaham-London with coal. One crew lost	LN
"	Feb-28	Barnard Sand	Valadamir	Brig	Muller	(Russia)	8	Rochester-Grimsby in ballast. Wind ExS, force 9	LN
"	Jul-13	5M off Southwold	Admiral	Dandy	W. Mullett	Great Yarmouth	5	Sprang leak. Wind NW, force 6. Crew saved	LN
"	Nov-10	Thorpe Ness	Margaret	Schooner	T. Wales	London	5	100 tons. Goole-London, carrying stone. SSW gale. Crew saved by LB Ipswich	LN
"	Dec-31	Southwold Beach	Cowan	Brig	J. Dennier	S. Shields	8	214 tons. Rouen-South Shields with chalk. Wind SWxW, force 4	LN

Year	Day	Location	Vessel	Type	Master	Home Port	Crew	Other information	Source
c. 1879	?	Southwold	Nil Desperandum	Beach yawl	–	Southwold	–	Known as Nelly. 45ft long. Built by Jas. Critten. Broken up	DH
1879	Jan-13	Barnard Sand	Cleopas	Barque	W. McDougall	North Shields	10	359 tons. Liverpool-Tyne with salt. Wind SW, force 5	LN
"	Apl 27	4M off Southwold	Eliza B	Brig	H. Goldfinch	Faversham	7	178 tons. Built New Brunswick. Run down by steamer	LN
1880s	?	Sizewell Sluice	Woodland Lass	–	–	Southwold	–	120 tons. Built Ltoft 1851. Owner: Ed Chapman. Last trader to Blythburgh	EC
1881	Jan-18	Centre Cliff, Southwold	Martina Maria	Barque	W. Folster	North Shields	12	567 tons. Tyne-Monaco. Nine crew lost. Wind ESE force 9	EC
"		Dunwich	Olive Branch	Dandy	G. Crisp	Great Yarmouth	6	Wind ESE, 9, Dandies had a large mizzen sail sheeted to a bumkin	LN
"		Sizewell Beach	Leader	Cutter	W. Gibson	W'dbridge	8	Wind ESE, force 11	LN
"	Jan-18	Sizewell	Palestine	Barque	R. Mossman	Hartlepool	9	520 tons. Dover-Hartlepool. Wind ESE, force 10	LN
"	Jan-19	Minsmere Cliffs	Rosette Patrone	Barque	L. Bisso	Genoa	15	North Shields-Genoa. Wind ENE, force 7. All crew lost	LN
"	Oct-14	Thorpe Ness	Mary's	Brig	T. Hewson	Whitby	8	Newcastle-Sheerness with coal. Wind WxS, force 11	LN
1882	Oct-27	Twenty vessels are driven ashore between Yarmouth and Southwold							EC
"	Dec	Surf Lifeboat Quiver is replaced by non-self-righting lifeboat Quiver No.2							LB
1883	Nov-06	Off Thorpe Ness	Thankful	Snow	W. Watson	North Shields	7	209 tons. Newcastle-Cowes with coal. Wind WSW, force 8	LN
1884	Dec-22	Near Covehithe Ness	Isabellas	Brigantine	G.H. Mills	North Shields	6	133 tons. London-Middlesbrough with wood. Wind NE, force 7	LN
"	Dec-23	Sizewell Gap	Florence	Schooner	J. Grindell	Lowestoft	4	Sunderland-London with empty bottles. Wind NNE, force 7	LN
1885 (cont'd)	Oct-26	Near Covehithe CG station	Edith Marie	Schooner	J. Ford	Hull	4	London-Hull with linseed oil. Wind SW, force 6	LN

Year	Day	Location	Vessel	Type	Master	Home Port	Crew	Other information	Source
1885 (concl.)	Oct-26	Off Thorpe Ness	*Topaz*	Thames Barge	W. Ling	London	3	London–Yarmouth with rice. Wind SW, force 9. Crew lost	LN
1886	Nov-03	Thorpe Rocks	*Lady Ernestine*	Schooner	W. Wroath	Fowey	6	Newcastle–Plymouth with coal. Wind SW, force 7	LN
"	Dec-27	Off Sizewell Buildings	*Day Star*	Schooner	–	Ipswich	4	Wind S, 9. 3 crew saved by LBs *Coal Exchange* & *John Keble*. Cook lost	EC
"	"	Thorpe Ness	*Trixie V*	Brig	G. Morley	Folkestone	7	201 tons. Cargo: coal. Wind ESE, 8.	EC
"	"	Sizewell Gap	*Magnet*	Brig	A. Storm	Dundee	7	237 tons. Shields–London with coal. Wind SE, force 8. Six crew lost	LN
1887	Jan-27	Thorpe Ness	*Nancy*	Smack	J. Bushell	Ramsgate	4	Fishing. Wind SW, force 3	LN
"	May-02	Ashore Gun Hill	*Nordhavet*	Barque	H.A. Holversen	Porsgrund	14	610 tons. Coal cargo. Wind NNE, force 4. Crew saved by *Quiver No.2*	EC
"	Dec-13	Dunwich	*Rebecca*	Brigantine	A. May	Plymouth	7	Rotterdam–Newcastle with barrel hoops and sand. Wind SSW, force 7	LN
1888	Mar-14	Sizewell Bank	*Hoppett*	Barque	O.C. Larsen	Laurvig	12	Laurvig–London with wood. Wind SE, force 10	LN
"	Mar-16	Benacre	*Active*	Sloop	J. Wilkinson	Goole	2	Lowestoft–Burnham with railway sleepers. Wind ENE, force 6	LN
"	Nov-03	Sizewell Bank	*Flora*	Barque	A.F. Skekstrom	Aland	14	Dunkirk–Stettin with phosphate. Wind E,7. Leaking, beached.Crew saved by Dunwich LB	JM
"	"	Near Thorpe Ness	*Sirius*	Steamship	–	Ghent	15	Ghent–London with stone. Cargo shifted. Wind E, 8. Crew & cat saved by Aldeburgh lifeboat	JM
"	Nov-08	Sizewell Bank	*Prudentia*	Barque	Hvillardsen	Christiania (Oslo)	10	Cargo: boards for Bristol. Crew saved by Aldeburgh LB *George Hounsfield*	JM

Year	Day	Location	Vessel	Type	Master	Home Port	Crew	Other information	Source
1889	?	Southwold	Bittern (I)	Beach yawl	–	Southwold	–	Blt 1860. 49ft long. Bought by Kilcock Cliff Co. from Old Co. of L'toft. Broken up	DH
"	Feb-04	Off Southwold	Johns	Schooner	R. Goodworth	Goole	4	Goole-Gravesend with coal. Wind ENE, force 8	LN
"	Feb-10	Sizewell Bank	Clarissa	Brig	J. Ball	Shoreham	7	Sunderland-Southampton with coal. Wind SE, force 5	LN
1891	Feb-02	5M N of Southwold	Arndilly	Steamship	J. Mutch	Aberdeen	21	1,522 tons. Smyrna-Hull with barley and lead ingots. Run down by SS Ormerod	LN
"	May-18	Barnard Sand	Kate & Elizabeth	Ketch	G.B. Green	Portsmouth	5	Southamton-Hartlepool with ore. Wind NE, force 5	LN
"	Oct-13	Dunwich Bay	Agatha	Snow	T.W. Bell	Kings Lynn	4	187 tons. Wind S, force 9. Broke adrift from moorings as temporary wreck marker	LN
"	Nov-11	Thorpe Ness	Winnifred	Barque	L.A. Larsen	Laurvig	17	Sweden-London. Crew saved by Aldeburgh lifeboat. Wind SW, 10	JM
"	Nov-11	Thorpe Ness	Richard L Wood	Ketch	H. Sweeting	Goole	3	London-Yarmouth with oil and cake. Wind SSE, 9	LN
1892	Feb-15	Covehithe	Elizabeth Kilner	Schooner	C. Pearson	London	5	88 tons. London-Invergordon with meal. Wind SE, force 9. Crew saved by Coastguard	EC
"	Oct-14	Thorpe Ness	Australia	Ketch	C. Haynes	Grimsby	5	Fishing. Wind ENE, force 10	LN
1893	Jan-17	Sizewell Beach	Caroline	Dandy	G.J. Linder	Lowestoft	5	Cargo: fish. Wind ESE, force 4	LN
"	Easter Day	Lifeboat Alfred Corry enters service at Southwold with eighteen crew							EC
"	Oct-11	Sizewell Bank	Saint Louis	Brig	Larcheveque	St Valery-en-Caux	6	Newcastle-Courselles with coal. Wind SSW, force 6	LN
"	Nov-02	Thorpe Ness	Amcott	Steamship	R. Henman	Hartlepool	–	998 tons. Tyne-Belfast with coal. Stranded	LN
1894	Jul-13	4M ExN of Southwold	Harmeka	Ketch	H. Heyen	(Germany)	4	Cargo: sand. Wind NNW, force 8	LN
" (cont'd)	Oct-24	Off Dunwich	Nina	Barque	J.P. Jorgensen	Christiania	–	Cargo: firewood. SxE, 8. Run down by steamer. Alf Corry & Dunwich LB assist	EC

Year	Day	Location	Vessel	Type	Master	Home Port	Crew	Other information	Source
1894 (concl.)	Dec-02	7.5M off Southwold	*Kenmore*	Steamship	G. Taylor	Dundee	15	Cargo: coal & coke. Run down by SS *Cymbeline* in calm seas	LN
1895	Jan-13	B'twn Southwold & Easton	*James & Eleanor*	Brig	R. Beedle	North Shields	7	Cargo: coal. Wind SSE, force 10. 4 saved by *Alfred Corry* but 3 others lost	EC
1897	Apr-09	4M SSE of Southwold	*Donnachadh*	Lugger	D.R. Watson	Southwold	1	Wind SSW, force 4. Run down by SS *Vildosala*	LN
"	May-29	5M SE of Southwold	*Isabella Wilson*	Schooner	W. Clarke	Littleh'mpt'n	7	Cargo: coal. Wind SxW, force 4. Run down by SS *York*. Two crew lost	LN
"	Sep-07	Norfolk & Suffolk-type lifeboat *Rescue* enters service at Southwold, replacing *Quiver No.2*. 32ft long, with twelve oars								EC
"	Nov-08	Sizewell Bank	*Sly Boots*	Brigantine	G. Bennett	Brixham	6	Cargo: coal. Wind SSE , force 4	LN
1898	Aug-07	Between S'well & Aldeburgh	*Francesco Crispi*	Steamship	D. Guifre	Messina	22	2,068 tons. Cargo: coal. Wind ENE, 5. Crew saved, plus monkey and pet ram	JM
"	Dec-04	5M SE of Southwold	*Clifton*	Steamship	W. Gibson	Newcastle	9	252 tons. Cargo: coal. Foundered in SW wind, force 6	LN
1899	Jul-11	5M ENE of Southwold	*Daisy*	Ketch	W. Warner	Hull	4	Cargo: coal. Wind SExS, force 2. Run down by SS *Britannia*	LN
"	Dec-03	Sizewell Bank	*Speedwell*	Ketch	W. Olley	Colchester	5	Cargo: coal. Caught fire and sank. Wind WNW, force 2	LN
"	Dec-28	Covehithe	*Economy*	Brigantine	W. Reason	Harwich	4	Cargo: coal.Wind SE, force 8. Crew saved by *Alfred Corry*	EC
1900		Closure of Thorpe Ness Lifeboat Station							JM
1902	Feb-27	Off Minsmere CG station	*Loveid*	Barque	S.B. Halborsen	Portsgrund	10	Cargo: ice.Wind ESE, 2. Run down by passing steamer. Crew saved by LB *Bolton*	JM
1903		Closure of Dunwich lifeboat station – ' there not being sufficient men at Dunwich to work her'.							EC
1904	Aug-08	4M SSE of Southwold	*Victor*	Ketch	L. Allary	(Belgium)	5	Fishing. Foundered in SE wind, force 3	LN

Year	Day	Location	Vessel	Type	Master	Home Port	Crew	Other information	Source
1905	Nov-27	Covehithe Point	*Joseph et Yvonne*	Smack	J. Bauche	Dunkirk	5	Wind WSW, 8. Crew saved by *Alfred Corry* & Covehithe Rocket Brigade	EC
1906	Jun-23	8M SE of Lowestoft	*Rosaline-Fidaline*	Smack	F. Goetghebeur	Ostend	4	Run down by steamship. Crew saved (1 of whom had been saved here in 1905)	EC
1907	Jan-14	3M E of Southwold	*Ivanhoe*	Ketch	C. Willgoss	Lowestoft	5	Fishing. Wind SW, force 3. Run down by SS *Tanfield*. Crew lost	LN
"	Feb-10	Off Southwold	*Sofia*	Brigantine	J.H. Harper	London	6	Cargo: stone. Wind W, force 5. Run down by SS *Holmside*. Crew lost	LN
"	Feb-11	Barnard Sand	*Herald*	Ketch	T. Foster	Ramsgate	3	Fishing. Wind SxW, force 5. (Yet another steamship collision?)	LN
1912	Jan-17	Off St James' Green	*Idun*	Barque	Kornelius Christensen	Christians'd	9	Antwerp–Cadiz, but far off course. Wind SE 8, with snow. Crew saved by breeches buoy	EC
"	"	Near Sizewell	*Voorwaarts*	Schooner	Laan	(Holland)	–	*Alfred Corry* rescues crew. Vessel later repaired and refloated	WS
"	Jul-01	Ashore Dunwich	*Olive*	Smack	–	Ramsgate	–	Crew saved	EC
1914	May-13	Off Southwold	*Turret Hill*	Steamship	Hultgren	Newcastle	13	691 tons. Goole-Poole with coal. Capsized and sank. Two crew saved	LN
1914–18	First World War: German submarines and aircraft attack British, French and neutral vessels and bombard Southwold town								V
1915	Jun-23	Barnard Sand	*Tunisiana*	Steamship	A. Wallace	London	–	4,220 tons. Montreal-Hull with wheat. Torpedoed by German submarine *UB-16*	LN
"	Jul-28	Near Sizewell Bank	*Mangara*	Steamship	H.M. Beattie	Glasgow	18	1,821 tons. Bilbao-Hartlepool with iron ore. Torpedoed by *UB-16*. Eleven drown	LN
" (cont'd)	Aug-28	Off Thorpe Ness	*Dane*	Steam Trawler	–	Grimsby	8	265 tons. Serving as minesweeper with Royal Navy. Eight naval crew lost	LN

Year	Day	Location	Vessel	Type	Master	Home Port	Crew	Other information	Source
1915 (cont'd)	Nov-06	4M E of Southwold	Alastair	Steamship	T.G. Auld	Aberdeen	10	366 tons. Cargo: ore. Sunk by German mine. Seven crew lost	LN
"	Nov-11	6M SE of Southwold	Rhineland	Steamship	W.E. Steel	Liverpool	21	Middlesbrough–Nantes with steel bars and rods. Struck mine. 20 crew lost	LN
"	Dec-08	3M ENE of Thorpe Ness	Ignis	Steamship	–	London	20	2,042 tons. Tyne–London with coal. Mined by submarine UC-7	LN
"	Dec-10	3.8M E of Thorpe Ness	Ingstad	Steamship	K. Dant	Bergen	–	780 tons. Tyne–Nantes with coal. Struck mine laid by UC-1	LN
1916	Feb-23	Ashore Sizewell	Carmenta	Brigantine	W. Joiner	Faversham	6	Severe ENE gale. Alfred Corry attempts rescue but crew saved by rocket line	LN
"	Feb-25	7M SSE of Southwold	Southford	Steamship	J. McCarty	Glasgow	16	Tyne–Boulogne with coke. Struck German mine. Four crew lost	LN
"	May-02	3M E of Southwold	Rochester City	Steamship	A. Hardy	Sunderland	17	1,239 tons. Tyne–Rochester with coal. Struck mine. One crew lost	LN
"	May-26	6M South East by South of Southwold	El Argentino	Steamship	H. Goodrick	Liverpool	64	6,809 tons. In ballast. Struck mine laid by submarine UG-1, itself sunk 1917	LN
"	Jun-04	5M SSE of Southwold	Eagre	Steamship	–	London	4	90 tons. Cargo: wheat. Sank in heavy weather	LN
"	Jul-30	7M ESE of Barnard	Claudia	Steamship	C. Jordan	Stockton	21	Cargo: iron ore and general. Struck mine. Three crew lost	LN
"	Sep-01	2.25M SE of Benacre	Dronning Maud	Steamship	E. Ringer	Christiania	–	1,102 tons. Cargo: cement. Struck mine laid by submarine UC-1	LN
"	Sep-02	Off Southwold	Farmatyr	Steamship	C. Christiansen	Copenh'gen	–	1,426 tons. Shields–Rouen with coal. Struck German mine	LN
" (cont'd)	Sep-03	5.3M E of Dunwich Bank	Mascotte	Steamship	W.A. Miller	Leith	21	1,097 tons. General cargo, Rotterdam–Leith. Mined by sub UC-6. One crew lost	LN

Year	Day	Location	Vessel	Type	Master	Home Port	Crew	Other information	Source
1916 (cont'd)	Oct-28	c.8M South West by South of Holm Buoy	*Sparta*	Steamship	Finlayson	London	12	480 tons. Cargo: coke. Mined. Four crew lost	LN
"	Nov-09	4M ENE of Southwold	*Sunniside*	Steamship	R. Strickland	London	13	Hull-Rotterdam with general cargo. Struck mine. Four crew lost	LN
1917	Jan-07	Near Sole Bay coast	–	Minesweeper	–	(British)	–	'Blown up', probably by German mine. Some lives lost.	GB
"	Feb-20	About 0.5M off Southwold	–	–	–	(British?)	–	Sunk by enemy action. 'Only 2 masts visible'	GB
"	Mar-11	Off Southwold	*Kwasind*	Steamship	F. Shapter	Quebec	23	2,211 tons. Bilbao-Hartlepool with iron ore. Twelve crew lost	LN
"	May-01	Off Southwold	*Gena*	Steamship	W.R. Peguiro	Whitby	26	2,784 tons. Cargo: coal. Sunk by seaplane torpedo	LN
"	Aug-11	Off Southwold	*Jay*	Steam Trawler	–	–	–	Serving as RN warship. Sunk by German submarine	LN
"	Aug-20	6.2M ExN of Sizewell	*Eldernian*	Steamship	H. Roberts	Cardiff	31	3,588 tons. Middlesbrough-Dieppe with steel. Torpedoed. 14 crew lost	LN
1918	Sep 29/30	Dunwich beach	*Pomona*	Minesweeper	–	–	10	Nine crew rescued by Lowestoft lifeboat *Kentwell*. Skipper drowned	HH
"	Sep-30	Off Dunwich Sluice	*Sea King*	Tug	–	London	3	26 tons. London-Hull. Foundered	LN
1919	Nov-01	*Alfred Corry* is replaced by *Bolton*, former Kessingland lifeboat							LB
1920	Apr-19	Closure of Southwold No.2 station; *Rescue* withdrawn							LB
1922	Jan-12	0.5M NE of Benacre	*Tidal*	Steam & sail	–	–	–	On passage Seaham-Weymouth with coal	LN
1925	Jun-20	*Bolton* replaced by motor-sailing lifeboat *Mary Scott*, 46ft 6in long, with petrol engine and lugger rig							LB
1926	?	Southwold	*Bittern* (II)	Beach yawl	–	Southwold	–	49ft long. Built Yarmouth 1890 by Jas. Beeching. Broken up	DH
1927	Jun-19	Ashore Sizewell	*G L Munro*	Ketch	–	Yarmouth	–	Crew saved by rocket apparatus	JM

Year	Day	Location	Vessel	Type	Master	Home Port	Crew	Other information	Source
1930?	–	Easton Bavents	–	Steamship	–	–	–	–	WS
1938	Nov-23	Near Sizewell Bank	*Astrid*	Barge	–	Rochester	2	Crew rescued by Aldeburgh lifeboat *Abdy Beauclerk*	JM
1939-45		Second World War: German submarines and aircraft again attack British, Allied and neutral vessels and bomb Southwold town							V
1939-45	–	Off Thorpe Ness	–	2 mine-sweepers	–	–	–	House-in-Clouds in transit w tall hse, in 11 fathoms. Reported by 'old fishermen'	WS
1939	Sep-10	3.2M ExN of Thorpe Ness	*Magdapur*	Steamship	Dixon	Liverpool	80	Mined. 74 saved by Aldeburgh LB *Abdy Beauclerk* and nearby steamers	JM
"	Sep-24	4M NE of Aldeburgh	*Phryne*	Steamship	–	Caen	24	Sunk by enemy action. Crew saved by lifeboat	JM
1940	Jun-01	Manned by RN crew, *Mary Scott* rescues 150 British soldiers from Dunkirk beach, becomes disabled and is later found abandoned at Dover							V
"	Oct-28	0.75M NE of Southwold LH	*Harvest Gleaner*	Drifter	–	–	–	96 tons. Armed, with RN crew. Four lost. Sunk by air attack	LN
1942	Dec	Closure of Southwold No.1 station							LB
1943	Jan-14	11M NExN of Thorpe Ness	*Wyetown*	Steamship	–	Leith	–	624 tons. Hull-Ipswich with phosphate	LN
1945	Mar-13	7.5M ENE of Southwold	*Taber Park*	Steamship	–	Montreal	28	2,878 tons. Tyne-London with coal. Sunk by mine or midget sub. All lost	LN
"	Spring?	Wal'wick hse in line w. old piles	–	Submarine	–	(Germany)	–	292ft long. Said to carry escaping Nazis, who scuttled sub & shot crew	WS
1946?	–	Sole Bay	Picket boat of HMS *Solebay*	–	–	–	–	Crew rescued	WS
1950s?	–	Sole Bay	*White Lady*	Sailing Yacht	–	–	–	About 18ft, with lead ballast. Put out to view Royal Yacht. Capsized. 2 drown	WS
1953	Jan-31	Blackshore	*Wildflower*	Schooner Yacht	–	Wexford	–	Blt Clyde 1860. Wrecked Blackshore by Great Flood. Figurehead in Sailing Club	SC

Year	Day	Location	Vessel	Type	Master	Home Port	Crew	Other information	Source
Mid-1950s	-	Off Southwold Pier	-	Tugboat	-	-	-	c. 25ft with clinker hull. On fire. Crew rescued by Southwold Sailing Club launch *John Svoboda*	WS
1959	Oct-28	N of Southwold Harbour	*Raffler*	c. 48ft MV	-	-	-	Cargo: pipes for Sizewell Power Station. Collided with The Knuckle	WS
Early 1960s	-	Blackshore (Broken up)	*Martin Luther*	Thames Barge	-	Rochester	-	83ft long. Said to have sailed into Southwold 1939 with German Jews fleeing Nazis	WS
1963	July	Re-opening of lifeboat service at Southwold with arrival of 'D'-class Inshore Rescue Boat (IRB) *D36*							LB
1966	Aug-15	Southwold bar	*Calypso*	Yacht	P.G. Tadman	Scarboro'	-	3 tons. Wind NNE, 5. Crew rescued by T. Cross & P. Pile in IRB *D36*	LB
1972	Feb-06	Off Walberswick	-	Motor dinghy	J. Hamilton	-	-	Wind SE, 6. IRB *191* rescues three men, but two others drown	LB
"	Nov-30	8M off Southwold	*Burtonia*	Motor Vessel	Ash	Goole	-	498 tons. Cargo: lead & concentrates. Sinks in gale; 4 lost. Aldeburgh LB attends	LN
1973	Jun-04	Just N of Southwold Harbour	*Solebay*	Motor FV	-	-	-	Wind SE, 3. Engine failed. Stranded on beach and became total loss	LB
"	July	Atlantic 21 Class Lifeboat *Solebay* enters service at Southwold							LB
1977	Jul-08	Near Sizewell Bank	*Eva Witte*	Motor Vessel	-	Bremen	-	419 tons. Berwick-Whistable. Collided in fog with tanker *Tamames*. Crew saved	LN
1979	Aug-04	Off Sizewell	*Cresta*	Cabin cruiser	-	-	3	Crew saved by Aldeburgh lifeboat *Charles Dibdin*	JM
1985	-	*Quiver*, a second Atlantic 21 Class boat, replaces *Solebay*							LB
1998	Oct-31	*Quiver* is replaced by Inshore Life Boat (ILB) *Leslie Tranmer*, Atlantic 75 Class							LB

APPENDIX 1

THE STORM THAT SANK THE *FAIRY*

The great storm of November 1840 was an atmospheric cocktail with a phenomenal punch. Meteorologist Alan Watts suspects that it grew out of a time-worn hurricane that had sucked-in gouts of rejuvenating cold air as it moved eastward across the Atlantic towards northern Europe. Like many other low-pressure systems, it tracked across the middle of England towards the North Sea. What made it abnormal was its small but vigorously fizzing centre moving so very, very slowly that the cocktail had time to acquire a number of lethal extras before pouring itself onto the Sunrise Coast.

The gale was unusually severe but its character may not have been unique. Although there is insufficient data from the 1840 gale to draw any firm conclusions, Watts's analysis of the notorious Fastnet Storm of 1979 provides clues to understanding the gale that destroyed *Fairy*.

The 1979 storm sank five vessels and drowned fifteen crew in an area of sea between Cornwall and Ireland extending over 150 miles. The 1840 storm sank twelve vessels and drowned at least eighty crew in a thirty-mile stretch between Orford Ness and Yarmouth. In both, boats only a few miles apart fared very differently: *Violet* survived the gale at Harwich where the wind was SW, whereas only thirty-five miles to the north *Fairy* was battling against an ESE gale that sank her. Similar contrasts occurred among vessels in the Fastnet fleet.

Though the two storms were widely separate in their locations, Watts believes they may have been closely related in character.

Contrary to the general assumption that wind directions within the various sectors of *any* storm are more-or-less consistent, in his analysis Watts discovered other, deeper lows embedded within the Fastnet storm that generated force 10–12 winds blowing down narrow corridors between areas of wind coming from widely different directions at significantly different speeds. These conflicting winds created immense, 40ft (12m) waves that fell upon the yachts from all sides simultaneously. The opposing wave-trains resulted in chaotic conditions in which Beaufort's sail-handling agenda was irrelevant and effective boat-handling almost impossible. Some yachts were rolled 360°; others pitch-poled head-over-heels.

A memorial plaque to *Fairy*'s crew was placed in the church of St Nicholas in Harwich by the officers and men of HMS *Shearwater*, appointed in 1841 to complete the North Sea survey. From the wording on the plaque it seems that no bodies were recovered, which is strange. Whether chronicled by Maggs or the RNLI, shipwrecks are usually followed by the finding of bodies. In the days after the Sole Bay storm, the southern North Sea would have been criss-crossed by hundreds of vessels and fished by hundreds more. Yet it seems that none of *Fairy*'s sixty-three crew was ever found.

APPENDIX 2

BEAUFORT'S WONDERFUL WIND SCALE

Francis Beaufort's enduring legacy was his system for measuring the wind. Simple to use and easy to remember, it has stood the test of time for more than two centuries, surviving in the face of competition from modern electronic instruments. As Lyall Watson has pointed out, Beaufort's scale is eminently practical, marvellously elegant and astonishingly profound. Each of the twelve points on his scale marks a decisive step in the behaviour of the ship and its handling. The increase from force 1 to force 2 enabled a frigate in pursuit of an enemy to advance from barely having steerage way to a significantly challenging stance in which it was making perceptible speed through the water towards its quarry. The upward move from force 3 to 4 was marked by the vessel under full sail heeling decisively to the wind and registering 5 or 6 knots by her log line. The next step to force 5 marked the moment when the commander had to think about shortening sail, and forces 7, 8 and 9 were clearly linked with his need to put specific extra reefs in the topsails.

Linking the wind speed to critical stages in the vessel's behaviour and the necessary responses from its crew was a brilliant concept. Set against our present computerized methods, Beaufort's 'hands-on' approach gives his system the edge. The most user-friendly anemometer does nothing more than inform the mariner how fast air is moving at a particular height above the waves at a particular moment – which is all very interesting, but what the sailor really wants to know is the total effect of the wind on his ship and what he should do about his sails. Beaufort's system tells him precisely that.

Even more marvellously, Beaufort's numbers correlate exactly with the increase in the power of the wind. At any given speed above force 1 *the wind pressure increases as the exact cube of its Beaufort number.* In other words, if the wind rises to force 3 the pressure increases by 3 x 3 x 3 = 27 times above what it was at force 1. At force 7 it will be 7 x 7 x 7 = 343 times greater, and at force 10 it will be exerting 1,000 times as much pressure even though it is blowing only twenty-five times faster. Watson goes on to say that this isn't just a mathematical curiosity. Whether the naval architect, the bridge-builder or the sailmaker is calculating the wind pressure in pounds per square inch or kilograms per square metre, and whether it's blowing on to a begonia or a battleship, there is always a direct relation between the actual wind force and its Beaufort number. That, I think, is amazing.

ADMIRAL BEAUFORT'S WIND SCALE (DEVISED 1806)

Beaufort number	Wind speed in knots	Wave height in feet	Standard name	Effect on 19th-century frigate in chase	Deep sea criteria
0	<1	–	Calm	–	Flat calm, mirror smooth
1	1–3	1/4	Light air	Just gives steerage way	Small wavelets with no crests
2	4–6	1/2	Light breeze	Speed 1–2 knots	Small wavelets. Crests glassy but do not break
3	7–10	2	Gentle breeze	Speed 3–4 knots	Large wavelets. Crests begin to break
4	11–16	3 1/2	Moderate breeze	Speed 5–6 knots	Small waves, becoming longer. Crests break frequently
5	17–21	6	Fresh breeze	Can just carry all sails	Moderate waves with longer, breaking crests
6	22–27	9 1/2	Strong breeze	Can just carry whole topsail	Large waves forming. Crests break more frequently

7	28–33	13 1/2	Moderate gale	Single-reefed topsail	Large waves with streaky foam
8	34–40	18	Fresh gale	Double-reefed topsail	Large waves of increasing length. Crests form spindrift
9	41–47	23	Strong gale	Close-reefed topsail	High waves with dense streaks of foam. Crests roll over
10	48–55	29	Whole gale	Can barely carry reefed lower mainsail	Very high waves and long overhanging crests. Surface of sea white with foam
11	56–63	37	Storm	Reduced to storm staysails	Exceptionally high waves. Sea completely covered with foam
12	>63	—	Hurricane	No canvas can withstand	The air filled with spray. Visibility seriously affected

THE *ALFRED CORRY*

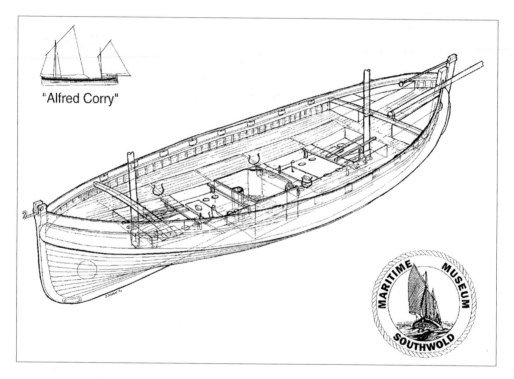

"Alfred Corry"

Plan by David Cragie.

Based on the lines of local clinker beach-yawls and constructed by Beeching of
  Yarmouth in 1893 from Canadian rock elm and mahogany.
Length: 44ft 1in x 12ft beam, plus 2ft 2in buoyant outboard walings (13.44m x 3.66m +
  0.66m).
Weight: 8.3 tons, plus 5 tons of water ballast admitted via eighteen 4in-diameter (102mm)
  tubes.
Improved Norfolk-and-Suffolk type, non-self-righting, capable of carrying 150
  people.
Rigged with dipping lugsail on foremast and standing lug on mizzen.
Designed to be rowed with fourteen oars but equipped with sixteen at the insistence
  of the beachmen who manned her.
Served as Southwold No.1 lifeboat 1893–1918, launched on forty-one service missions
  and saved forty-seven lives.

Above, left: John Cragie, coxswain of the Southwold lifeboat 1893–98. (*Alfred Corry* Museum)

Above, centre: Sam May served as coxswain from 1898 till 1918. (*Alfred Corry* Museum)

Above, right: Charles Jarvis, last cox of the *Alfred Corry*, went on to command *Bolton* and *Mary Scott*. (*Alfred Corry* Museum)

Until 1908 *Alfred Corry* was housed in a shed on the dunes north of the harbour mouth and subsequently stationed on the riverbank near the ferry. She was sold out of service for £40 in 1919 to Lord Albemarle, who re-named her *Alba*, added cabins, converted her to a gaff ketch and sailed her as a yacht. The *Corry* was laid up at West Mersea 1939-45 for the duration of hostilities, after which she had the distinction of being the first British yacht to enter Ostend after the Second World War. Subsequently re-named *Thorfinn*, she was mainly used as a houseboat until abandoned as derlict on the bank of the River Blackwater, where she was purchased in 1976 by the great-grandson of her first coxswain, who restored her to seaworthiness and gave her back her original name. Between 1980 and her eventual retirement from active life in the early 1990s, *Alfred Corry* cruised mainly the South and East Coasts, calling from time to time at Southwold. In 1994 she was returned by road to her original home, where a team of volunteers began work on restoring her original condition as a lifeboat. In 2008, with the restoration nearing completion, the *Alfred Corry* is open to view, housed in an historic lifeboat house at the Southwold harbour entrance, hard by the waters from which she saved so many lives.

LYKING THE SEA LYFE WITHAL ...

William 'Prim' Deal, born in 1872 in Primrose Alley, Southwold, went to sea at fourteen, fishing mackerel in the Irish Sea. Rated an Ordinary Seaman at sixteen in the foreign-going *Erne* and swiftly promoted, he shipped as able seaman in the barques *Orontes, Beechbank, Mount Stewart, Chelmsford, Colony* and *Wexford*, sailing the blue-water routes to the Americas, Australia and the China Sea. 'Life in the windjammers was rough,' he told the BBC in 1938. During his eighteen months in the *Chelmsford* 'the crew had such a lousy time that most of them rolled up'. Whether the rollers-up were discharged sick, dead or deserted, their departures were accelerated by the activities of their incompetent cook. Glad of anything to vary their diet of salt beef and salt pork, one day in the Gulf of California the crew captured some sleeping turtles and were looking forward to eating them for dinner '... but our lubber of a cook boiled the turtles whole – insides as well – and when we started scoffing the mixture we were all as sick as dogs'.

Prim Deal survived the cooking but did not escape the sea unharmed. His narrowest shave was on the Pacific coast of Mexico when the capstan reversed with a violent jerk that flung

The steel windjammer *Mount Stewart*, 1,903 tons, one of the last sailing vessels built for the Australian wool trade. In 1893-94 she passaged from Sydney to the Strait of Dover in the very good time of eighty-five days. Of the six barques that Deal served in, only *Mount Stewart* survived beyond the end of the First World War in 1918. (Keith Deal)

Above: Nobody here can manage a smile, probably
because the white-aproned cook had poisoned his
shipmates by feeding them turtles'entrails. Prim
Deal, standing second right, was eighteen months
aboard the *Chelmsford* in 1894–95, under Captain
W.B. Thomson. *Chelmsford* was subsequently sold to
three further owners, the last of whom re-named her
Inverlogie. Commanded by Captain W.J. Ryder, she
was torpedoed and sunk by a German U-boat on 9
March 1917, fifteen miles south-west of the Smalls
lighthouse, on passage from Barry to Archangel with
coal. (Keith Deal)

Right: Able Seaman Deal, aged twenty-one. (Keith
Deal)

The two VGs at the foot of his discharge certificate tell of Deal's character and ability. Less meritorious seamen would have earned G for 'Good', M for 'Middling' or I for 'Indifferent'. The murderous cook would have paid off with either a D ('Declined') or an NS ('Not Stated'). (Keith Deal)

Dykes Stannard and Prim Deal row ashore King George VI to visit the London Boys' Camp on Southwold common in 1938. The twin-funnelled Royal Yacht *Victoria and Albert* lies anchored two miles off. (Keith Deal)

Above: About to set sail in his eighties.
(Keith Deal)

Left: Prim, on right, in festive attire with
his friend Dykes Stannard, enjoying semi-
retirement on the shores of Sole Bay.
(Keith Deal)

him fifty yards out to sea. Years later, the sailor who rescued him gave Deal an introductory
drill in the London Fire Brigade that prepared him for First World War air attacks by Zeppelins
and Gotha bombers.

The instructor and his pupil had left the sea in good time. Dangerous though fire-fighting
was, if Deal had continued his seafaring career he would probably have been dead before the
war ended, for the *Wexford* foundered in 1913 in the Great Lakes, and both *Chelmsford* and
Colony were sunk in 1917–18 by German U-boats.

Deal was twenty-five years in the fire brigade before going back to sea in his own longshore
boat in Sole Bay. A burly six-footer, he died in Southwold in 1963 at the age of ninety. Like his
fellow townsman James Maggs, he revealed little of his feelings about the sea, the small 'WD'
tattooed on his wrist being about as far as he went in matters of personal statement. 'It was an
exciting life, anyway,' he told his interviewer – and left it at that.

BIBLIOGRAPHY

In writing this brief account of Sole Bay shipwrecks I have not thought it appropriate to burden the text with footnotes or superscript references to sources. Here instead is a list of the publications that have provided much of the factual information for my book.

ADMIRALTY: *North Sea Pilot, Vol. III,* 12th Edn. (Hydrographic Office, 1960) & *Manual of Seamanship, Vol. I* (HMSO, 1937)

ANDERSON, Edward: *Description of the October Gale, 1789* (Workington, *c.*1800)

BACON, Stuart: *A Pre-disturbance Survey of the Wreck Site at Buss Creek* (Suffolk Underwater Studies, Orford, 1992)

BARKER, James P.: *The Log of a Limejuicer* (Huntington Press, USA, 1933)

BISSET, Sir James: *Sail Ho!* (Angus & Robertson, 1958)

BOTTOMLEY, Alan (Ed.): *The Southwold Diary of James Maggs* (2 Vols.) (Suffolk Records Society and The Boydell Press, 1983–4)

BUMSTEAD, George: 'Southwold at War: The Twentieth Century' in *Southwold: Portraits of a Seaside Town* (Eds. Rebecca & Stephen Clegg, Phillimore & Co., 1999)

BUTCHER, David: *The Driftermen* (Tops'l Books, 1979)

CABLE, James: *A Lifeboatman's Days* (John Lovett, Aldeburgh, undated)

CHILDERS, S. (Ed.): *A Mariner of England: An Account of the Career of William Richardson* [1780-1819] (Conway Maritime, 1970)

COMFORT, Nicholas: *The Lost City of Dunwich* (Terence Dalton, 1994)

COOPER, Ernest R.: *Seventy Years' Work of Southwold Lifeboats* (Southwold Press, 1912)

Idem., *A Suffolk Coast Garland* (Heath Cranton, 1928); and *Storm Warriors of the Suffolk Coast* (Heath Cranton, 1937)

CUNLIFFE, Tom (Ed.): *Pilots, Vol 2* (Chatham House, 2002)

DANA, R.H.: *Two Years Before the Mast* (Hutchinson, *c.*1942)

EARLE, Peter: *Sailors: English Merchant Seamen, 1650-1775* (Methuen, 1998)

FAYLE, C.E.: *A Short History of the World's Shipping Industry* (London, 1933)

FINCH, Roger: *Sailing Craft of the British Isles* (Collins, 1976)

FLINDERS, Matthew: *A Voyage to Terra Australis …1801-3* (pub. 1814)

GLASSPOOL, John: *Boats of the Longshoremen* (Nautical Publishing, 1977)

HEWSON, J.B.: *A History of the Practice of Navigation* (Brown, Son & Ferguson, 1983)

HIGGINS, David: *The Beachmen* (Terence Dalton, 1987)

HOPE, Ronald: *A New History of British Shipping* (John Murray, 1990) and *Poor Jack* (Chatham Publishing, 2001)

HUNTER, H.C.: *How England Got Its Merchant Marine, 1066-1776* (Nat. Council of American Shipbuilders, 1935)

HUTCHINSON, Gillian: *Two English Side-Rudders* (Vikingeskibshallen I Roskilde, Denmark, 1995)

JARVIS, Stan: *Smuggling in East Anglia, 1700-1840* (Countryside Books, 1987)

JEAYES, I.H. (Ed.): *Letters of Philip Gawdy* (J. B. Nichols and Sons, 1906)

JONES, Nicolette: *The Plimsoll Sensation* (Little, Brown, 2006)

JONES, Tristan: *A Steady Trade* (Triad Grafton, 1988)

KEMP, Peter (Ed.): *Oxford Companion to Ships and the Sea* (OUP, 1976)

KEYS, D. & SMITH, K.: *Black Diamonds by Sea* (Newcastle on Tyne Libraries & Information Service, 1998)

LARN, Richard & Bridget: *Shipwreck Index of the British Isles, Vol 3: East Coast of England* (Lloyd's Register of Shipping, 1997)

LAWRENCE, Rachel: *Southwold River* (Suffolk Books, 1990) and 'Southwold at War: Disputes in the Middle Ages' in *Southwold: Portraits of a Seaside Town* (Eds. Rebecca & Stephen Clegg, Phillimore & Co., 1999)

LEACH, Nicholas: *Suffolk's Lifeboats* (John Nickalls Publications, 2001)

LLOYD, Christopher: *The British Seaman* (Paladin, 1970)

LLOYD'S: *Lloyd's War Losses: The First World War* (Lloyd's of London Press, 1990)

LUBBOCK, Basil (Ed.): *Barlow's Journal* (Hurst & Blackett, 1934)

MAGGS, James: *Hand Book to the Port and Shipping of Southwold* (Southwold Press, 1842)

MALSTER, Robert: *Saved from the Sea* (Terence Dalton, 1974) and *Lowestoft – East Coast Port* (Terence Dalton, 1987)

MEYERSTEIN, E.H.W. (Ed.): *Adventures by Sea of Edward Coxere* (OUP, 1946)

MORRIS, Jeff: *The Story of the Aldeburgh Lifeboats* (Pub. by author, undated)

MUNN, Geoffrey C.: *Southwold: An Earthly Paradise* (Antique Collectors' Club, 2006)

NEWBY, Eric: *The Last Grain Race* (Pan Books, 1990)

PARKER, Rowland: *Men of Dunwich* (Readers Union, 1981)

RITCHIE, G.S.: *The Admiralty Chart* (Pentland Press, 1995)

ROBERTS, Bob: *Coasting Bargemaster* (Seafarer Books, 2000)

RODGER, N.A.M.: *The Wooden World: An Anatomy of the Georgian Navy* (Fontana, 1990)

RUNCIMAN, Walter: *Collier Brigs and Their Sailors* (T. Fisher Unwin, 1926)

SIMPER, Robert: *East Coast Sail* (Seafarer Books, 1972), *North East Sail* (David & Charles), *East Anglian Coast and Waterways* (East Anglian Magazine, 1985), and *Sunrise Coast* (Creekside Publishing, 2002)

STAMMERS, Michael: *Suffolk Shipping* (Tempus Publishing, 2003)

STANBURY, David (ed.): *A Narrative of the Voyage of the HMS Beagle* (The Folio Society, 1977)

WATERS, David W.: *The Art of Navigation in England in Elizabethan and Early Stuart Times* (Hollis & Carter, 1958)

WATSON, Lyall: *Heaven's Breath* (Hodder & Stoughton, 1984)

WOODMAN, Richard: *The History of the Ship* (Conway Maritime, 1997)

INDEX OF VESSELS

References to Colour Plates are in **bold italic**

Abdy Beauclerk, 81, 174
Abercraig, 84
Active, 29, 53, 168
Admiral, 166
Agatha, 169
Alastair, 172
Alba (see Alfred Corry)
Albion, 53
Alert, 36, 146, 156
Alfred Corry (alias Alba and Thorfinn), 37, 99, 100-104, 108, 143, 169-73, 180-81, **22**
Aliancen, 152
Alice & Francis, 151
Alma, 98, 166
Alpha, 68
Amelia, 46
Amicitia, 60
Amcott, 169
Ann & Judith, 150
Ann & Mary, 161
Ann Emma, 163
Anna Maria, 159
Anne, 156
Anne Ferguson, 106
Ant, 124-25, 157
Ariel, 156
Arndilly, 169
Astrid, 174
Aurora, 156
Australia, 169

Baden Powell, 34, 128
Bantum, 151
Barbara, 157

Barkley, 166
Barley, 151
Beagle, 64-8, 132, 147
Beechbank, 182
Belle, 165
Belle Isle, 62, 166
Berbice, 53, 77
Billy, 164
Bittern (I) (1860-89), 60, 169
Bittern (II) (1890-1926), 32, 60, 93, 97, 128, 173
Bolton, 108, 170, 173, 181
Bottle Sloop, 152
Bransberg, 160
Britannia, 170
British Queen, 157
British Tar, 90
Broadside, 108-9
Brothers, 154
Brother's Friend, 53
Buckingham, 125, 158
Burletta, 152
Burtonia, 175

Caldecot Castle, 155
Calypso, 175
Cape Horn, 21, 117, 161
Carmenta, 172
Caroline, 169
Caster, 92
Catharine, 125, 158
Catliff, 158
Celeste Maria, 165
Ceres, 87, 154
Charles Dibdin, 175
Charlotte Dundas, 152
Chelmsford, 81, 120, 182-83, 185

Cheverell, 162
Christopher, 122
Clarissa, 169
Claudia, 172
Cleofrid, 159
Cleopas, 167
Clifton, 170
Coal Exchange (see Harriett II)
Colony, 182, 185
Commerce, 31, 36
Comorn, 164
Concord, 107-9
Conqueror, 153
Conservative (see Solebay lifeboat)
Content, 76, 163-4
Countess, 163
County of Pembroke, 134-36, 146, 148
Cowan, 166
Cresta, 175
Cricketer, 60, 162
Cumberland, 61, 91, 155
Cymbeline, 70
Cynthia, 60

Daisy, 170
Damaris, 110
Dane, 171
Dart, 95
David Ricardo, 156
Day Star, 168
Decima, 142
Delight, 151
Delphis, 130
Derwent, 157
Diamond, 156
Dingley, 151
Dispatch, 53, 95, 161
Ditto, 156
Donnachadh, 170
Dora, 164
Dorothea & Margareta, 151
Dorset, 154
Dove, 91, 152
Dronning Maud, 172

Eagre, 172
Economy, 170
Edgar, 151
Edith Marie, 167
Eiderstedt, 39, 165
El Argentino, 172
Eldernian, 173

Elissa, 81, 133
Eliza, 157
Elizabeth (1743), 72, 151
Elizabeth (1801), 152
Elizabeth & Ann, 124-25, 158
Eliza B, 167
Elizabeth Kilner, 105, 169
Eliza Frances, 92
Elsinore. 165
Elton, 158
Emerald, 159
Emma, 21, 162
Enterprise, 156
Enterprize, 157
Erne, 182
Esk, 160
Esther, 158
Eva Witte, 175
Excelsior, **18**

Fairy, 20, 64, 66-8, 124-25, 132, 158, 176
Fame, 154
Fanny, 164
Farmatyr, 172
Favourite, 139
Fire Ship, 72, 152
Flora (1810), 153
Flora (1888), 168
Florence, 167
Fly, 156
Folkestone, 89
Fortuna, 159
Frances Ann, 156
Francesco Crispi, 170
Franckfort, 165
Frederick, 160
Fredrick, 152
Friends (1812), 153
Friends (1814), 153
Friends (1823), 154
Friends (1871), 165
Friendship, 115-16, 153
Friendship (beach yawl), alias Job, 166
Furmity, 131

G.L. Munro, 173
Gartness, 85
Gena, 173
George Galley, 140
George Hounsfield, 168
Georgia, 109
Georgiana, 34

Gleaner, 53
Glenmoriston, 162
Greyhound, 53
Groot Hollandia, 80

Halesworth Trader (32 tons), 52
Halesworth Trader (95 tons), 52
Harmeka, 169
Harriett I, 96, 98, 161-62
Harriett II, 96-8, 102-3, 107, 143, 162-65, 168
Harry King, 164
Harvest Gleaner, 136, 174
Harwich, 78
Haura, 111
Hawk (1830), 155
Hawk (1862), 116
Hebe, 161
Hector, 155
Henry (1802), 152
Henry (1810), 153
Henry Everest, 164
Henry Morton, 163
Henry's, 162
Herald, 171
Hilda, 137
Hobo, 128
Holmside, 171
Hope, 128
Hoppett, 168
Hull Packet, 153
Hylton Castle, 21, 161

Iddo, 164
Idun, 80-1, 93, 118, 171
Ignis, 172
Industry, 159
Ingstad, 172
Inverlogie (see Chelmsford)
Investigator, 122
IRB D36, 175
IRB 191, 175
Isabella Wilson, 170
Isabellas, 94, 167
Isis, 161
Ivanhoe, 171

James & Eleanor, 73, 141-43, 170, 18
James & Mary, 159
James Hartley, 123
James Leath, 107
Jane Innes, 166
Jay, 173

Jeanne d'Arc, 159
Job (see beach yawl Friendship)
John (1852), 160
John & Elizabeth, 29, 158
John & Isabella, 163
John & Mary, 157
John & Susannah, 79, 165
John Bull, 90, 165
John Keble, 105-6, 168
Johns, 169
John Svoboda, 130, 175
Joseph et Yvonne, 104, 171
Josua, 80, 151
Jubilee, 36, 60, 90-2, 153, 159, 162, 165

Kate & Elizabeth, 125, 169
Katherine, 151
Kenmore, 170
Kentwell, 173
Kerry Louise, 128
Kirstine Jensen, 87
Kwasind, 173
Kylie, 52

Lady Ernestine, 168
Lady Nelson, 36
Lapwing, 153
Leslie Tranmer, 106, 113-14, 175
Liberty, 30, 36, 154
Lily Bird, 91, 6
London, 160
London Coal Exchange (see Harriett II)
Lord Coke, 165
Lord Haddo, 137
Lord Nelson, 93, 159
Louisa Elizabeth, 53
Loveid, 170
Lucia, 161
Lucie, 161
Lucinde, 103, 143, 163

Magdapur, 14, 81, 120, 122, 174
Magnet, 168
Maiters, 151
Mangara, 171
Margaret, 76, 166
Margarete, 71
Margaretha, 130
Marmora, 134
Marriar (Maria?) Charlotte, 92
Maria Ross, 153
Marjorie, 78, 129, 130, 5

Martin Luther, 43, 75, 86, 175, **10**
Martina Maria, 167, **20**
Mary & Jo Marsden, 125, 158
Mary Rose, 132
Mary Russell, 166
Mary's, 167
Mary Scott, 105, 109-10, 173-74, 181
Mascotte, 172
Mayflower, 90, 162
Messenger, 124
Moshulu, 76, 81, 122, 134, 141, 143, 145, 147
Mount Stewart, 81, 182

Naiad, 160
Nancy, 159
Nelson (1811), 153
Nelson (1855), 161
Neptune (1808), 152
Neptune (1859), 163
Neta Hendrika, 152
New Prosperous, 160
Nil Desperandum (alias Nelly), 167
Nina, 98, 100, 169
Nonsuch, 62, 114
Nordhavet, 80-1, 117, 168, **27**
Northdown, 145
North Star, 154
Nuculana, 66

Ocean, 21, 162
Odin, 162
Olive (1801), 152
Olive (1912), 171
Olivebank, 81
Olive Branch, 79, 167
Opzeemans Hoop, 159
Ordinence, 86
Ormerod, 169
Orontes, 182
Orwell, 27
Otter, 151

Pallas, 163
Palestine, 80, 167
Pallion, 155
Pandora, 166
Parana, 124
Patriot, 163
Peace, 36, 156
Pegasus, 53
Pendennis, 78
Permanent, 29

Perseverance, 53, 95, 153
Peter, 166
Philip & Ann, 151
Phoebe, 105
Phryne, 174
Pilgrim, 157
Pilot, 157
Pippin, 49, 114
Pommern, 145
Pomona, 173
Princess Alice, 98, 164
Princess Augusta, 144, 157
Princess Victoria, 30, 92
Providence (1805 & 1810), 92, 139, 153
Providence (1834), 60, 156
Prudentia, 168

Queen Elizabeth, 135
Queen Victoria, 164
Quiver, 104-5, 112, 164, 175
Quiver No.2, 104-5, 117, 167-8, 170

Raffler, 175
Ralph Barnel, 163
Ranger, 89
Raven, 163
Reaper, 154
Rebecca, 168
Reliance, 93, 97, 103, 165
Request, 157
Rescue, 98, 104, 170, 173
Resolution, 72
Rhineland, 172
Richard, 155
Richard White, 161
Richard L. Wood, 169, **14**
River Trent, 42
Robert & James, 57
Rochester City, 172
Rose & June, 53
Royalist, 163
Royal James, 59, 72, 80, 150
Royal Prince, 151

Sailor's Friend, 152
Saint Louis, 169
Salira, 163
Sally (1810), 153
Sally (1843), 159
Samuel, 91, 155
Sarah, 160
Sauce Polly, 166

Scipio, 139
Screw, The, 157
Sea King, 173
Seaman's Assistant, 154
Second Apprentice, 87, 129, 146
Shafto, 139
Shearwater, 176
Sheraton Grange, 96, 98, 161
Silva, 163
Sirius, 168
Sir Walter Scott, 156
Sly Boots, 170
Sofia, 171
Solebay (destroyer), 174
Solebay (fishing boat), 175
Solebay (lifeboat), 77, 93, 95-6, 98, 102, 107-8, 110, 111, 158-60, 175
Southford, 172
Southwold Belle, 54
Sparta, 173
Speedwell (1836), 156
Speedwell (1899), 170
Spirit of Lowestoft, 113-14
Spring, 52, 83, 160
Star, 53, 76, 158
Suffolk, 12, 154
Sunniside, 173
Swiftsure, 60, 91, 165
Sybil, 163
Sylvia, 130

Taber Park, 174
Tamames, 175
Tanfield, 171
Teazer, 162
Téméraire, 33
Thankful, 167
Thomas (1812), 153
Thomas (1830), 155
Thomas & Betsey (or Betsy), 147, 154
Thorfinn (see Alfred Corry)
Thos Betsey, 157
Three Friends, 155
Three Sisters, 32

Tidal, 173
Topaz, 75, 168
Torpedo boat 119, 84
Trafalgar, 153
Traveller, 152
Trixie V, 168
Tunisiana, 171
Turret Hill, 171
Twilight, 153
Two H.H., 165

UB-16, 171
UC-1, 172
UC-6, 172
UC-7, 172
Union (1805), 152
Union (1809), 153
Unity, 151
Ury, 76, 159
Utopia, 119-20

Valadamir, 166
Vanguard, 163
Velocity, 163
Vesper, 160
Victoria, 32, 53, 72-3, 128
Victoria & Albert, 184
Violet, 66-7, 146, 176
Voorwaartz, 93-4, 171
Vrede, 80, 150-51

Wanderer, 152
Wexford, 182, 185
White Lady, 174
Wildflower, 43, 126, 128, 174, **8**
William IV, 162, **21**
William & Ann, 161
William & Mary, 164
William Cook, 96, 160
Winnifred, 169
Woodland Lass, 52-3

Zeland, 91, 152

If you are interested in purchasing other books published by The History Press,
or in case you have difficulty finding any History Press books in your local bookshop,
you can also place orders directly through our website

www.thehistorypress.co.uk